Praise for The Natural Step

The whole world has dreamt about a solid definition of
sustainability that would allow systematic step-by-step planning.
When the definition arrived, delivered by The Natural Step,
it was remarkable to see how simple it was. Why hadn't
anybody thought about it before?
— Paul Hawken, coauthor of *Natural Capitalism*

When we where introduced to The Natural Step, we realized
we had found our framework.
— Tachi Kiuchi, CEO, Mitsubishi Electric America

The work of Karl-Henrik Robèrt and his colleagues
through The Natural Step process in Sweden is one of the leading
examples in the world today of society-wide learning. Learning
based on systems thinking and continued dialogue is not only
transforming Sweden`s approach to sustainable industrial
development but holds great promise for many of the
most intractable societal issues of our time.
— Dr. Peter Senge, Centre for Organizational Learning, MIT

The Natural Step is already a major player in the movement by
corporations and other organizations to make "sustainability" their
ultimate brand. Now the cancer specialist who started it all has
written its dramatic and deeply meaningful story. This is the story of
a good idea, and how a scientific consensus was built around it.
It's a lucid description of how we — *homo* we hope *sapiens* — can
adjust our minds and our consequent behavior to make the human
adventure work for everyone. And sparkling through, it's a story
of how, by thinking clearly and working hard, one man starting
in a small country can make a huge difference.
— Harlan Cleveland, President Emeritus,
World Academy of Art and Science

With the living cell as the point of departure,
Karl-Henrik Robèrt brilliantly helps us understand the non-negotiable conditions of a sustainable society. He and The Natural Step
offer a scientific, yet very inspiring and operational model for helping us, individuals as well as corporations, in setting a new course.
— Dr. Göran Carstedt, former President of IKEA, North America

Systems Thinking needs to be introduced not only to business,
but the broader society as well to have a potential for a full and
more powerful impact. Learning about Dr.Robèrt's work gives me
real hope that this could happen. He has applied systems
thinking to our ultimate frontier: the Planet Earth.
— Dr. Iva M. Wilson, President, Philips Components, North
America

Dr. Karl-Henrik Robèrt has succeeded in the extraordinarily
difficult task of getting scientists to agree on fundamental systems
conditions for a sustainable society. Now we can all benefit.
The Natural Step concepts allow top management to view
environmental considerations in a systematic way and to integrate
them into corporate strategy for long term prosperity.
— John Naisbitt, Megatrends Ltd, USA

The Natural Step is the leading international movement
encouraging businesses to be sustainability-promoting.
— Philip Sutton, Director, Policy and Strategy,
Green Innovations Inc., Australia

As a guiding star, a compass, for our environmental work,
we have adopted the (Natural Step) four System Conditions for a
sustainable society. Everyone who has attended IKEA's environmental training has learned of the importance of these conditions.
Each of us in our various roles must now seek to put these into
practice, within the framework of IKEA's business idea.
— Anders Moberg, former President, IKEA,
today Vice President, Home Depot

What it's all about really is to utilize the resources that we
have on this planet in the best way. That is part of our vision.
We say that we are turning from the resource over-consuming
society to a resource-saving society, and the environment
discussion is really about taking care of resources in a better way.
Everybody still acts as if these resources will be unlimited,
and that we will always find other sources. But they will hit the
funnel as described by The Natural Step. By focusing on these
items — energy, water and waste — we are creating competitive
advantages. We are also saving the environment.
— Roland Nilsson, CEO, Scandic Hotels

Interface is committed to shifting from linear
industrial processes to cyclical ones. To do this, we use a compass to
guide us, and a set of tools to help us. They are both the result of
The Natural Step. Interface will use four fundamental principles of
sustainability described by The Natural Step as a guide to reduce
its impact and footprint upon the planet. We believe that institutions
that continuously violate these principles will suffer economically.
— Ray Anderson, CEO, Interface

The Natural Step is one of the easier things to get people to buy
into even though they may not be able to remember what the four
System Conditions are. Once they've been exposed to them,
they have an instinctive understanding of what is being talked about.
It's easier to get people to relate to this as opposed to other
management concepts that are designed to motivate people.
This is one that you can internalize quickly.
— Jim Quinn, CEO, Collins Pine Company

The Natural Step provides an elegant framework, a compass,
to guide us on the road ahead and is a powerful tool for all seeking a
new mental model to move their businesses into a sustainable future.
— Maurice Strong, Secretary-General, 1992 UN Earth Summit

It is very refreshing to be able to work with an organization
that truly, genuinely wants to help you.
— Sarah Severn, Director of Corporate Responsibility
Development, Nike

The Natural Step is a clear voice in the commotion.
— Leif Johansson, CEO, Volvo

To work towards sustainability in business is not only
the right thing to do. It is also profitable. In the short term,
non-sustainability has already started to cost more resources
and money than most people realize. And in the long term,
head-over-heels investments in sustainable practices will be more and
more costly, the longer you wait. To strategically earn money from
step-by-step progress towards social and ecological sustainability, you
need feeling, thought and competence. It was love at first sight
when I learnt about The Natural Step and its methods.
— Mats Lederhausen, Executive Vice President,
McDonald's Corporation

the NATURAL STEP story

the NATURAL STEP story

SEEDING A QUIET REVOLUTION

Karl-Henrik Robèrt

NEW SOCIETY PUBLISHERS

Cataloguing in Publication Data:
A catalog record for this publication is available from the National Library of Canada.

Copyright © 2002 by The Natural Step International.
All rights reserved.

Cover design by Diane McIntosh; cover image ©PhotoDisc.

Printed in Canada on acid-free, partially recycled (20 percent post-consumer) paper using soy-based inks by Transcontinental/Best Book Manufacturers.

New Society Publishers acknowledges the support of the Government of Canada through the Book Publishing Industry Development Program

(BPIDP) for our publishing activities, and the assistance of the Province of British Columbia through the British Columbia Arts Council.

BRITISH
COLUMBIA
ARTS COUNCIL
Supported by the Province of British Columbia

Paperback ISBN: 0-86571-453-3

Inquiries regarding requests to reprint all or part of *The Natural Step Story* should be addressed to New Society Publishers at the address below.

To order directly from the publishers, please add $4.50 shipping to the price of the first copy, and $1.00 for each additional copy (plus GST in Canada). Send check or money order to:

New Society Publishers
P.O. Box 189, Gabriola Island, BC V0R 1X0, Canada
1-800-567-6772

New Society Publishers' mission is to publish books that contribute in fundamental ways to building an ecologically sustainable and just society, and to do so with the least possible impact on the environment, in a manner that models this vision. We are committed to doing this not just through education, but through action. We are acting on our commitment to the world's remaining ancient forests by phasing out our paper supply from ancient forests worldwide. This book is one step towards ending global deforestation and climate change. It is printed on acid-free paper that is **100% old growth forest-free (100% post-consumer recycled)**, processed chlorine free, and printed with vegetable based, low VOC inks. For further information, or to browse our full list of books and purchase securely, visit our website at: www.newsociety.com

NEW SOCIETY PUBLISHERS   www.newsociety.com

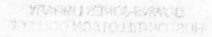

Contents

Foreword

Ray Anderson

ITS BEGINNING CAN BE TRACED to the inventive act of one man. The man was Thomas Newcomen. The invention was the steam driven pump. The year was 1712, and what began was the Industrial Revolution.

The pump solved a big problem, water in the English coal mines, water that needed to be removed if the miners were going to use their time efficiently to mine. So, for the first time ever, nature (stored sunlight, a billion years old) was harnessed and turned on nature to exploit nature through the power of a machine, for the sake of miner productivity – more coal per man-hour. Then more iron per man-hour, and more textiles per man-hour, and on and on. Today the mantra includes more computer chips per man-hour and more gizmos per man-hour. Same system, same goal, more sophisticated products. The chosen route to elusive abundance for all continues to be increasing labor productivity at the expense of nature.

When people were scarce and nature was bountiful, seemingly unlimited, what could be more sensible than to extract and use nature to increase human productivity? And when nature was bountiful, seemingly unlimited, what could be more sensible than to dump the polluted remains of exploited nature back into nature. Never mind how much pollution, never mind how poisonous, nature could handle it.

That is the way the industrial revolution unfolded – taking, making, wasting, and polluting, as Paul Hawken describes in his landmark book, *The Ecology of Commerce* (Harper Business, 1993) in pursuit of increased labor productivity, thus prosperity. There was no plan for the industrial revolution, no grand vision, not even a name, until modern times gave it one retrospectively. It just happened, guided only by Adam Smith's "invisible hand" of the market and a mind-set, flawed in its perception of nature as an unlimited source and a bottomless sink, a mind-set that rendered the invisible hand effectively blind as well as invisible.

Blind to what? Blind to the consequences, what modern economic theory calls, "the externalities" – such societal costs as increasing cancer in children, disappearing forests and wetlands, polluted rivers, streams, aquifers, and oceans, rising global temperatures, exotic disease vectors, disappearing species.

When we in the developed world look around at the skyscrapers and motorways, ocean liners and rocketships, we cannot help but marvel at the civilization that has emerged from the industrial revolution. Labor productivity and nature's abundance have brought us a long way. The prosperity we enjoy stands in stark contrast to the deprivation of 1712. Who could possibly question the efficacy of the industrial age? Well perhaps those bearing the cost of the externalities such as the children with cancer and their parents have a question or two. Perhaps the threatened species, could they only speak, would have a question or two. Perhaps the two-thirds of humanity who have been left out by the modern industrial system have some questions of us who enjoy such abundance through sheer accidents of birth. Perhaps those of us who depend on forest and stream, aquifer and ocean for oxygen, water, and food have a question or two. But, wait. Isn't that all of us?

Asking the right questions brings a certain clarity. We step back and look at this industrial age, and we see vast wealth, concentrated in the developed world and derived at the expense of nature, upon which all – we and perhaps 30 million other species – are utterly dependent. The truly enlightened question then emerges, "How long can this go on?"

How long, indeed? An industrial age, dating from 1712, has existed for only the blink of an eye in geologic or evolutionary time. How much longer can nature sustain such taking, wasting, and polluting as accompanies our making and using? How much externality can we afford? The nature that we have finally recognized as finite, thanks to pictures of the earth from space, has only so much to give and so much capacity to absorb, assimilate, and endure. Therefore, the present system is, by definition, unsustainable.

So, what's a species – intent on being around for a few more millennia and sharing a growing prosperity with an ever larger population – to do? Common sense answers, "Do something different." Maybe it is a time to think differently about productivity. Perhaps we should be seeking resource productivity, as well as labor productivity – the productivity of all resources – and how to create abundance for all using less of nature. As the magnitude of the challenge dawns on us and the urgency to do something different grips us, where is a species to turn for answers and solutions?

Mightn't we, finally, at this already late stage, consider turning to our scientists? Our scientists who seek facts rather than opinions, who deal in objective observations rather than wishes, have been telling us for quite a long time that we simply cannot go on and on and on, practicing the ways and guided by the prevailing mind-set of the last three centuries. Surely, those ways and that mind-set, euphemistically called the industrial age, growing out of Thomas Newcomen's revolution, must give way to a new industrial revolution. Perhaps we should call this one "Rachel Carson's Revolution," in honor of that great woman who in 1962 with her earth-shaking *Silent Spring*, began the process of unveiling the abuses of the modern industrial system, and set the stage for the scientists' admonitions and for the next industrial revolution.

This time, let us hope we can get it right, this business of creating wealth and sharing it with a growing human population, by asking our scientists to describe the benign rather than abusive, the renewable rather than extractive, way forward. How *do* we increase the productivity of all resources and spare Earth from our abuse? We might, in fact, turn to one scientist in particular, who has thought long and hard, on his own and with his peers, about the underlying principles and essential practices of such a new industrial system. That person is Karl-Henrik Robért, author of this book; and the enlightened way forward that he describes is the way of sustainability.

I first met Karl-Henrik while reading Paul Hawken's aforementioned book in 1994. That was my introduction to him and to The Natural Step. I met him in person two years later when he came to my city, Atlanta, to lecture. I have been his disciple ever since. The wit and the charm of the man are exceeded only by the depth of his thoughts and the honesty of his convictions. The reader will meet all those qualities – wit, charm, depth, honesty – in *The Natural Step Story*. More importantly, the reader will find within its pages illumination for the path toward a sustainable civilization.

Ray C. Anderson
Interface Inc.,
November, 2001

Introduction

O N ONE LEVEL it may seem that the preliminary success of The
Natural Step (TNS) in Sweden has become an odyssey of ongoing success. As we continue to serve as a bridge between scientists and
decision makers, our achievements are documented at both ends of this
bridge: scientific studies and doctoral dissertations on the one hand and
concrete case studies on progress in business and politics on the other.

As of 2001, TNS offices exist in nine countries: Sweden, the US,
the UK, Canada, Australia, New Zealand, Japan, Israel, and South
Africa. Each office has a voting member on TNS's international board.
(The ownership of The Natural Step was handed over from Sweden to
this board in Portland, Oregon, US, in April 1999.) Even if I were to
withdraw now, the organization would still be there. All the assets
exist — an organizational structure, tools for strategic decision making, case studies on good examples and role models, and networks of
intelligent managers who apply the TNS framework as a shared mental model — a sort of language for strategic sustainable development.
We have succeeded.

Yet, not one day has passed since the Swedish launch in April 1989
that TNS has not experienced problems and worries. One problem is
financial: it is not easy to find money for an abstract idea that breaks
new intellectual ground. In fact, we still don't know if we are going to
make it, not even from an organizational point of view. But the idea
to study what we can agree on and then to base decisions on such
knowledge is so good that it mustn't fail. We in TNS had better stay
focused and concentrated if we want to continue to make a difference
and support sustainable development.

Some problems are paradoxical. Thirteen years ago, when TNS
started its activities, the perception of business being totally environmentally ignorant was greater than it is today. The environmental
debate was new and fresh and shocking, and business was caught off
guard. Rachel Carson's book *Silent Spring*, and other efforts of that
kind, had successfully created a market demand from business that
didn't show any signs of fading away. The only problem was to know
what to do. We wanted to help structure all the conflicting views in a
way that made sense for decision making — and that made equally
good sense for business. So what TNS offered was compelling.

1

Today, environmental issues are on the business agenda almost every day. A majority of large companies have developed various structures for decision making and communication about environmental matters, and many have started to introduce environmental management systems (EMS). Consequently they think they are on top of the problem. But the administrative tools *per se* are of no value, unless people have a clear idea of where to go. (It's like having a sailboat with a manual and a log but no map and no compass. You can sail around with the boat in perfect shape, but you'll be going in circles.)

The problem is that EMSs mostly live their own lives, un-integrated into the overall business strategies. Though heads of environmental departments generally know more than top management about resources and sustainability trends, they are rarely consulted about investments. Meanwhile, management teams run business more or less as usual. Paradoxically, then, as long as they remain un-integrated, the administrative tools for sustainable development pose a danger to business and to sustainable development. Furthermore they may lull top management teams into feeling a control that they really do not have. Thus, the need for frameworks that can give guidance is as high as ever, but the awareness of being pressured is much lower than it was thirteen years ago.

Some of the obstacles that TNS encounters are about simple resistance. TNS is all about dialog to discover what we need *not* fight about. Yet if you try to change some of the established norms of society and don't encounter resistance — well, it would be good to consider what is fundamentally wrong with the effort. A friendly attitude will not be enough to prevent fights and struggles — and it's not even certain that this would be desirable. The objective of TNS is not to make friends with everyone but to use a friendly and listening attitude as a tool to find more solid platforms for decision making on social and ecological matters.

Mats Lederhausen (the previous CEO of McDonald's in Sweden) embodies what TNS is trying to do. Mats is positive, friendly, supportive, intelligent, structured, and successful. He is a master in applying the TNS framework for strategic decision making, and his successes in Swedish business has made him senior vice president for McDonald's corporation, head of corporate strategy.

At one five-day workshop in the US, Mats faced 600 Americans from business, NGOs, and government. Before he started his speech, he began to take photos of the audience from the stage. It was a surprising thing to do, so people started to laugh — carefully in the beginning. It was even more surprising, since Mats took his time, mumbling as if he were talking to himself. But, through the microphone attached to his tie, everyone could hear what he said:

> Karl-Henrik and I have been cooperating on the barricades for almost ten years, and we are used to slightly smaller assemblies than this in Sweden — the little, remote part of the world that we represent (more laughter could be heard now). We have a lot of success to celebrate. But we have also felt a lot of frustration — for instance, in confrontations with our enemies. And them we don't like at all…. (At this point the audience burst out in laughter that I would label "surprised relief.") We will send them these photos, and we will tell them that now the *Americans* get it.

Mats's introduction encapsulates what TNS is all about: a friendly attitude and a respectful, listening dialog. The world doesn't want more gurus. I even think that we should fear them. For change today, we need cooperation and shared ownership for responsibility and power; to that end we need every person to identify the guru within himself or herself.

This book is about the struggle of The Natural Step and the knowledge that this struggle has brought about. The non-sustainable path of society is not about some natural catastrophe that we need to tackle. It's about human desires and curiosity and wittiness and the decisions that lie behind our non-sustainable development, as well as behind the tensions in the public debate about it. So I think there are things to be learned, not only from the intellectual achievements of TNS but also from the breakthroughs and mistakes of the organization. Therefore, this book will be presented as a story. It is my wish to make the story so entertaining, trustworthy, and relevant that it may recruit more people into the dialog on how to apply systems thinking for strategic planning toward a socially and ecologically sustainable world — a dialog that I hope has only begun.

PART ONE

The Challenge

CHAPTER 1

WHY TNS?

E VER SINCE I WAS A BOY, I have loved being outdoors, preferably in that marginal area between town and open country where human creations coexist with nature. There, nature pleases the senses without burdening them with too many intrusive questions. I grew up in such a place — Hagalund, as depicted by the Swedish landscape painter Olle Ohlsson.

Though never one for brooding, I have felt an anxiety about my beloved outdoors for as long as I can remember. Even as a child, I viewed the expansion of the city limits as an act of vandalism against my personal environment. Woods and coppices were exchanged for ugly industrial houses. The old No. 15 trams were taken out of service and replaced with stinking buses that left their riders nauseated at the end of the journey. The tram depot was paved over and turned into a gigantic parking lot. Gradually my anxieties became more conscious. When would we ever be finished? When would all this construction end? Would people ever say that now, at last, we are done?

My awareness continued to grow as I got older. My wife Rigmor had an unceasing commitment to environmental issues. Partly because of a long-standing interest in botany, she never felt out of place in the forest, and she deepened my engagement in the environment. And when our two boys began to ask existential questions, I started to take in poverty, crime, wars, the greenhouse effect, ozone depletion, and deforestation with an even higher degree of concern and anxiety.

The worrying social and ecological symptoms I was seeing were side effects of an industrialism that influenced my childhood in a negative way but now seemed to run amok in the world at large as well. The problems were spreading on the global scale, but there appeared to be no general, agreed-upon vision in society of what we could have

6

instead. I certainly didn't know of any cultures that had gone backward in development and then lived happily ever after. Development or collapse seemed to be the two merciless cultural alternatives of history.

The Public Debate

During the late 1980s, when my earliest ideas for The Natural Step began, the public debate on environmentalism was confrontational and fragmented — even stupid at times. Every environmental problem was handled one by one as it appeared and only for as long as the mass media found it interesting to pay attention. Then something else moved onto the agenda, but its relationship to the first problem was rarely considered. Are there, for instance, any relevant connections at all between Chernobyl and the spotted owl?

Blame was spread around for every individual problem, creating defense mechanisms and more or less entrenched positions among the participants of the debate. People were pointing fingers: "greens" to business leaders and politicians, industrialists to politicians and greens, and politicians to each other. New Age efforts to implement a new culture by creating a sort of top-down intellectualism (a conscious blend of Jungian psychology, Einstein's science, and some Asian wisdom) were perceived as flaky and failed to transform us. So, at the same time that my children were starting to pose existential questions, frightening clouds were looming on the horizon of the postindustrial era, and society at large seemed devoid of ideas to deal with the situation.

Arguments and sayings that were flying around in the public debate at the time, although generally relevant, were not completely accurate. They had a kind of fuzziness that missed the target and helped confuse the debate. For instance:

"Solutions to environmental problems are almost always at odds with each other, which vastly complicates the whole matter." That was obviously true, the way society dealt with the problems. Because of high efficiency, CFCs (chlorofluorocarbons) reduced the use of energy in freezers. But they degraded the ozone layer. Did it have to be that way? Wouldn't it be possible to confront ecological and economic problems at more fundamental levels in the system? Edward Goldsmith, an English ecologist, had coined the expression "solution multipliers" to describe how measures at the right level in a system could not only solve the problems at hand but even bring benefits that we hadn't even thought about.

"Environmental degradation is far worse in countries outside the industrialized Western world." This seemed obvious when I considered reportage on TV from industrial areas of Eastern Europe, for instance. But waste of one kind or another appears in all processes, and countries like Sweden and the US *per capita* consumed or transformed more resources into products and eventual waste than did less affluent countries. It was true that we could afford to protect our own ground relatively better, but it was also true that we produced more greenhouse gases and CFCs on the global level. Maybe we just pushed the problems ahead of us? Maybe we were actually looking into our own future when we stared in horror at the environmental black spots of, for instance, Russia?

"We should stop honing our margins at home and concentrate on simply giving aid to the poorer nations." Sometimes I felt irritation when I heard this, because it gave me the impression that we in the affluent world (being so close to perfect?) didn't need to change. And once that position was established, maybe the idea to help others would not be that vigorously needed after all. Furthermore, was it really likely that foreign aid in its traditional sense — more or less as penance — could suffice in the long term? How could we believe in the future, unless we could find rational and self-perpetuating ways to cooperate and maintain equity on the international level?

"The West is greedy and selfish, and doesn't care about its children's future." Was greed and selfishness really constitutional in people from the West? Didn't I witness the opposite every day in my cancer ward, when people took care of each other and sacrificed almost everything to help and support each other into the future?

"The destruction goes on, because selfishness and greed pay off." This argument was often heard from the green movement, in anger, and it seemed to hold greed as the prime human motivator. But was it true that greed (if it really were at the heart of the problem) would be likely to pay off? Would it? Even from a self-benefiting point of view? On some level I felt that greed was counterproductive even in the short term. Certainly society at large needed stricter accounting systems and more powerful reward systems for being proactive. But to get those things, we needed to do it right and not start off from an incomplete picture.

The issue of greed as a prime motivator had been explored in a story about two friends in prison — "The Prisoners' Dilemma." The prisoners were isolated and instructed by the guards to tell on each other in order to be released. The first to put the blame on his friend would be released (the payoff), though his friend would get the full punishment. If neither of them said anything, both would get half-time sentences. What would they do? The fact that there was even a story like this was promising: if we were all truly stupid and greedy machines, the two friends would just compete to be first to blame the other, and there would be no dilemma.

Perhaps a more environmentally relevant example would be one about a village whose herds of cattle had outgrown their habitat. If each family reduced the number of its cattle a little, they would be in balance again. But each villager might say, "Why should our family reduce our herd if the others don't?" The answer, of course, was social institutions. You sit down together and come to an agreement. Such institutions don't evolve from some power above but from people's own will to live good lives together. Darwin didn't talk about "survival of the fittest"; he talked about "survival of the fitting," meaning that if a species wanted to be successful in an environment, it must engage in mutual support. Certainly this also often applied on a more individual level: suppose that one of the families took the lead and actually reduced its stock and convinced the others to do the same? Wouldn't that act be rewarded ecologically as well as socially? Wouldn't that particular family have a reason to feel some extra pride?

It was true that people, institutions, and business corporations committed greedy acts, and that in the global economy it was even easier to do so in the absence of social pressure from our neighbors. But from what I had seen in the hospital, the problem was not that greed and selfishness outweighed our good traits. Instead, there must have been some unconscious vicious cycle that made business corporations and firms greedy — a sort of non-personal, cultural greed. I was sure that very few people, if any, were actually happier because of it. That was a hopeful thought, because it generated a possibility that business could be made partners in the search for solutions to the prisoners' dilemma.

"Tackling environmental problems will surely cost a lot of money!" It seemed to me that spending money on environmental measures was like putting lubricants in a car engine — more of an investment than a cost.

"We should feel a moral and economic responsibility for future generations." I had a vague feeling that we were already losing substantial amounts of our quality of life, money, cultural assets, social welfare, and other resources because of the defective long-term planning of our predecessors.

"If we were to really invest in sustainable development, there would be a transition period during which our products would become more expensive, and we would lose competitive edge. Furthermore, the problem is global, so we must act with international agreement." How fast would agreed-upon international decisions lead us in the right direction? First, I felt almost certain that this argument, although it was used to convince politicians to work for international cooperation, was double-edged. On the one hand, individual business corporations might relax their efforts, with negative effects: "Yes, we will do it, but it must be done internationally, so we have to wait for those decisions." On the other hand, there must be ways to earn money from ecologically and socially smart solutions — even in the short term, and even if you were alone with the effort. And wasn't that the greatest need of all: to find smart strategies to combine ecology and economy, without waiting for others? In fact, wouldn't such role models and good examples be drivers and act as prerequisites for successful international agreements?

"To save the environment, we must have economic growth." Growth of what? It seemed okay to me to dream of sustainable growth only if it could be truly value-based from a whole systems perspective, including social and ecological standards. Good stuff should then increase and bad stuff decrease. And after a period of physically increasing the good stuff (easy-to-use photovoltaics and sustainable farms, for instance), we would know how to make the transition to development. "Growth," as I saw it, meant an increase in limited resource use along with an accompanying emission of waste, whereas "development" meant an improvement in the human condition, including health, education, intelligence, wisdom, freedom, and the capacity to love. Physical growth is inherently limited, but development can go on forever — an important distinction. We needed wise national economists more than ever.

Economics

What would an economic system look like that could stimulate our economy in the direction of sustainability? All the systems I knew of existed according to certain conditions that placed physical limits on their potential growth. Physically, growth could exist only during a transitional period as when, for example, you build the frame of a house to fit the size of your lot and income, or when a body grows. Thereafter, growth must be transformed into development — the house frame stops growing, evolves, and eventually turns into a home; the child stops growing and becomes mature.

In integrated systems of high-level performance, continued physical growth becomes counterproductive to development. For this reason, sustainable systems have built-in mechanisms to slow down and eventually arrest growth in a controlled way. If this "smart" mechanism is not present in growing systems, then, as with bacteria multiplying in a laboratory testing dish, the only outcome beyond a certain point of exponential growth is sudden death and extinction (the bacteria don't die from starvation but from their own toxins). This is also true of cancer cells that multiply without developing. Finally the tumor threatens the system on which it feeds (as with the bacteria, the threat to the host generally does not come from competition for nutrients, but from side effects from the growth of the tumor). Was it the same with economic growth? The global spread of greenhouse and ozone-depleting gases seemed to indicate that it was.

Development was another story. It had certainly worked in biological evolution — for around 3.5 billion years! Perhaps it could work in industry, as well. Quality was linked to development, and quality could probably be improved *ad infinitum*. That was certainly true of computer technology. As quality improved, computers became smaller and cheaper. True, the industry had gone through a period of intense growth and dramatically increasing sales because of technological advances. But even that growth had certain limits, because society had need of other industries. After a certain point, if the IT (Information Technology) industry wanted to continue to grow, it would only be able to do so by improving quality and services to people — not by ongoing physical growth. Quality was a good term with a lot of meaning to modern industry — it didn't need promotion to be taken seriously.

Business

Business seemed to be the overall driver of the problems at hand. Businesses polluted, and we polluted when we used their products.

Business corporations were attacked, and they defended themselves, and neither seemed particularly difficult.

Since there was no structured systems perspective in the debate, the octopus technique always worked: anybody could hide in a cloud of fragmented facts. The "green" activists could rightly claim that it was business that produced CFCs. And business could rightly counter by saying that the "greens" bought refrigerators and that most of them didn't know how to produce refrigerators, anyway.

The green movement had been successful in bringing the news of non-sustainability to the public, and business people were now challenged by very aggressive attacks. Greenpeace's efforts to stop over-fishing and its chimney-plugging stunts had grabbed the attention of most people. It had not only influenced business through increasing demands on the market but had also inspired some early signs of tougher legislation. Greenpeace activists were our heroes. At least, they were my heroes (and still are). However, we also needed other measures than attacking each other and point-ing fingers didn't seem promising in the long run.

The problem was that the heart of business was not into sustain-ability yet, in spite of growing demands on the market. And the green movement was not yet particularly good at helping business get over that problem — each effort from business to comply was rejected as "yet another attempt to fool us and earn more money." It wasn't easy, and the process was slow.

Make "Dad" Listen

Industrialism appeared to me as a father, who certainly provided many of his children with toys and money. But he seemed to have lost his youth and vitality, and now he had started to lose his responsibility and even his wits. The only thing that remained was his power — and it seemed to be channeled into a brutal and greedy senility, growing by the hour, threatening the whole world on the social and ecologi-cal level. How could we make "Dad" listen and become proactive rather than reactive?

I found some help from my experience as a cancer doctor and sci-entist at Huddinge Hospital, the largest and most modern university hospital in Sweden. My primary observation was not, as I have seen documented in many books and articles, that I saw a steady increase of pollution-related cancers. I didn't. Instead some other essential observations impressed me that were yet not exploited as assets to the green movement.

One observation came from my microscope and the study of normal and cancerous cells. We cannot discuss politics or ideologies with cells; they are only concerned with the conditions necessary for sustaining and propagating life. They also remind us that we are inescapably a part of nature. There is much less difference between the cell of a human and that of a plant than is commonly understood. And if we compare our cells with those of other animals, we would need to go to the molecular level in order to perceive some differences that do exist and that are mainly linked to the genes — the "blueprints" of the total body. Even on this level, the differences are surprisingly small. Our genes are identical to the genes of chimpanzees to more than 98 percent. Some people find this embarrassing; others regard it as a relief. Regardless, it is true. From a biological standpoint, we are not the masters of nature or even its caretakers. The basic structures and functions of our bodies are nearly identical to those of eagles and seals, all the way down to the molecular level. We are part of nature.

It was clear that if the prerequisites of cells were not met, species would go, and the most advanced ones — the newcomers in evolution that are the most complex and vulnerable — would suffer the greatest losses. If pollution and deterioration of our habitat continued, the endpoint would be a republic of grass, microbes, and insects. It was scientifically valid to say that politicians and presidents were also made up of cells. On that level, we were all the same. Could that be an embryo for consensus?

Another observation came from my patients. An endless stream of parents came to see me, holding their cancer-diseased children by their hands. There was no limit to how wonderful people were on these occasions, and there seemed to be no limit to their preparedness to sacrifice. Yet we sometimes said about ourselves, at least in the public debate, that we don't care about our children if they competed with making another buck in the stock market. That was simply not true!

At times it seems as if we understand more when we think less and become progressively more insane the harder we labor with our precious intellects. People really grow in stature in times of crisis, finding deeper and greater reserves than they ever needed in their bustling daily lives. It is as if they are all speeding through life in high gear but have a number of slower but stronger gears when needed. Was it possible to apply those, not only in times of crisis, but to avoid crises? That was the question.

People were magnificent when they started fighting for a sick child or loved one. Parents even gave emotional support to the hospital personnel to help us sustain the psychological battering of seeing children suffer or die. From a bird's-eye perspective this was wonderful: down there among that vulnerable species, when somebody got pale and started staggering, others gathered and spent enormous resources to make him or her strong again. And business people were certainly no exception to the rule.

Daydreams

I started to daydream. One daydream had me dashing into the broadcast room of the TV news, just screaming out what I knew: I am a scientist and medical doctor, I would say, working with cancer cells and with cancer patients. Each patient is battling a disease that originally evolved from one single cell entering malignant transformation. Society gladly spends millions per sick child, and parents are prepared to do whatever it takes to save their child. But, I would say, now we are devouring our own habitat and allowing the gap between rich and poor to grow. And we are steadily increasing pollutants on a global scale. The public quibbling about economic growth and how much it will cost to save us is neither worthy of our intellectual and emotional standards, nor is it representative of how people generally are. It is a lie, broadcast to the world day in and day out. I saw myself on the daily news, opposing the lie until guards succeeded in pulling me away from the camera.

Another daydream had me simply approaching peer scientists and asking them to join forces with me. We would describe, in consensus, that there was no future in the way we were living our lives. From a scientific systems perspective, we would describe how to get past the daily debate and quibbling over details and find clarifying, structured knowledge that would be relevant for decision making. Our consensus report would be mailed to all Swedish households and schools, so that I could reach people without the embarrassing scene of dashing into TV studios.

The second daydream seemed as impossible as the first. Who could afford to mail a booklet to 4.3 million Swedish households? Nevertheless, this daydream slowly evolved into a plan.

Early Planning

Was it possible that I had discovered a way of making "Dad" listen? Maybe it would be possible to simply structure the enormous problem from a scientific systems perspective and then present the result to his business eyes. "Dad" could even be made part of the process, thereby taking active responsibility and sharing ownership of it. Maybe industrial society could be persuaded to take the same responsibility that I had seen business leaders take for their children at my cancer ward.

Business was the economic engine of modern society. Could this fact — along with the fact that people as wonderful as those in general society populate business corporations — be used as a challenging possibility? Industrialism came in as a vital and promising power not so many years ago. Could we exchange moral blame for a more fruitful attitude? Could we say, "Thank you for a wonderful era of success. Now we are suffering from some serious side effects; could you be as clever again?" Could we approach sustainability through an overall perspective of the marketplace?

How did the picture look from a business eye? Naturally, I didn't know much about that on a detailed level, but I didn't need to if we were working with the broad picture. I saw mankind running into the open end of a funnel of declining life-sustaining resources and increasing demands. The main problem was not (as so many business people seemed to believe) that we were running out of nonrenewable resources such as petroleum. Rather, our life-sustaining resources were suffering negative effects from the waste of nonrenewable resources: we had heavy metals in soils, sulfurous acid rain in lakes, and greenhouse gases in the atmosphere.

The converging walls of the funnel represented the globally declining productivity of renewable resources *per capita* — the resource base that feeds us, gives us clean water, fresh air, and renewable resources and that sustains our spirits with beautiful images. Each unit of production from forests, agricultural land, and fishing waters required more and more resource input. More pesticides and fertilizers for the same harvest and larger fishing boats for the same catch. At the same time, this declining, vital, life-sustaining resource base was being exposed to climate change and increasing concentrations of pollutants. Finally, the population of the world was increasing and projected to reach ten billion people in the next generation, even as the traditions that keep our cultures together were getting weaker and weaker.

Per capita, we were certainly entering deeper and deeper into the funnel. Wasn't it possible — or almost certain — that this would change conditions in the market? So why not disregard international agreements for a while? Why not allow international agreements and legislation to follow from examples given by proactive and smart role models that could undertake at least part of the transition on their own? If people could foresee the principles of a smarter future and a business rationale for approaching it, the rest could be taken step by step.

Systems Thinking

I needed a structured way of thinking. I needed a comprehensive and meaningful description of the whole system — a truly interdisciplinary approach. I felt that the clue was in systems thinking, but what was that, and how could it be applied in this particular context? Since nobody had described what I was going for, it needed to be discovered along with people who, most likely, needed to be smarter than me. So I needed not only a new way of thinking; I also needed a sort of language to attract people into the process. If you combine a simple language with disciplined thinking to create comprehension, people respond. If you include emotional aspects that are mutual among humans, for instance our love for our children, people generally like that, too. Particularly if you do it in a neutral way that doesn't push your personal spiritual beliefs onto others. I decided to look deeper into systems thinking.

CHAPTER 2

SYSTEMS THINKING AND CONSENSUS

I WAS GOING TO REALIZE a dream. I was going to send a consensus report of such logical and irrefutable quality to all Swedish households and schools that its impact would initiate an ongoing learning process and eventually support cultural change. And I was going to use a systems approach to do it. The whole "biosphere/society" system would be described in a way that would not allow misunderstanding. Neither would there be any intellectual escape routes — it would be intellectually tight. Yet, to be helpful, the consensus would be compelling, challenging, easy to understand, and at the same time, relevant for decision making. Was it possible? I thought so. In fact, my belief was almost palpable.

It was obvious from my work experience (cell science on malignant blood disorders) that teams of devoted people could handle remarkably complex systems in a very structured way. In the networks of cancer teams that operated in the arena in which I was active, the frontier of knowledge was systematically moving farther and farther out into a periphery made up of an increasingly complex interrelationship of details — a phenomenon typical of all learning processes.

The Tree As a Metaphor for Complex Systems

I thought that the tree made a relevant metaphor for any complex system. The trunk and branches represent a system's framework of basic principles, and the leaves correspond to its details. Together, trunk, branches, and leaves create a beautiful system. In spite of their transience, the leaves (the sum of all the details) are vital to the continuance of the system. And to a great degree, they embody its beauty and power of attraction. The trunk and branches alone compose a sterile structure; similarly, the leaves alone become a boring pile. Both framework and details are needed to make the system complete.

The metaphor could apply to many systems. In a learning process, for instance, we generally move along the overriding "branches" of principle knowledge to the more and more refined and subtle "twigs and leaves" of details. Apply the metaphor to a game such as chess, and the trunk and branches represent the rules of the game, while the leaves represent the different strategies and moves that are possible from relevant interpretations of the rules. Apply it to business, and the trunk and branches are the fixed and solid structures, while the leaves move and renew themselves each season with trends on the market. In every case, the details make sense because we understand the principles that underlie them.

The Individual As a Genius

When I thought about it, I realized we were all geniuses when it came to understanding and managing complex systems. Things that we considered simple because we generally all learn them with such ease were, in fact, extraordinarily complex. For instance, we had learned our first language by decoding the systematic principles that govern it — all without having a language to think by! We had lain there in the cradle and listened to its sounds (part of the "foliage" of a language system), and then each one of us had managed to discover all its "branches" of grammar and meaning. And we had gone on to apply that knowledge in the creative use of our mother tongue ever since — an achievement that ought to have made one or two neurophysiologists religious! It certainly didn't seem any less impressive to me than cancer science.

Even a deceptively easy action like driving a car was based on exquisitely complex operations. Drivers had to process a constant stream of data, such as evaluations of distances, angles, velocity, the psychology of other motorists, sensory information, sound, and the mechanical state of their cars (detailed "leaves" of information) as they drove. Simultaneously, they had to function according to the basic principles (the "trunks and branches") of two integrated systems: the mechanical system of the car and the traffic system.

The demands of taking in all the information necessary to driving — processing the details that are relevant with reference to the principles and discarding the rest — were so great that as far as information theory went, it should not have been possible to drive without having an accident. Yet once most of us had assimilated and practiced the fundamentals, it seemed easy to us, and we were quite capable of driving home from work while daydreaming about other things.

The fact was that the brain has a capacity for internal communication that does away with long checklists of digital inputs: the details did not have to be inputted one by one. Instead we were capable of absorbing and processing all the details of driving while we were actually doing it. When it came to systems thinking, the brain made the most advanced supercomputer look like a ridiculous toy!

Groups As Managers of Complex Systems

Although individuals seemed ingenious enough to deal with complex systems, groups of people often performed on very primitive levels. Sometimes groups appeared dumber to me than the dumbest participant of the whole group. Although we are sociable creatures, biologically equipped for teamwork, problems often arose when entire organizations — companies, municipalities, or nations — operated as systems. Together, we were devouring our own habitat, and together we successfully disguised the underlying reasons for doing so. We were like monkeys in a dying tree, quibbling about the leaves while the trunk and the branches deteriorated. We sought knowledge but were drowning in information.

What was the reason for the discrepancy between the individual brain and many brains together? The individual brain operates by cooperation among a number of specialized sites — centers for the computing of vision, hearing, logical deduction, personality aspects, and so on. When these centers communicate with each other, the basic principles of the intellectual task guide the process, and the dialog is transparent to the centers via a number of feedback loops and controls. Sometimes you can even hear the inner dialog as it deals with complexity — as when, for instance, you work a jigsaw puzzle. "Hum," you might think (or even say aloud), "where are the edge pieces and the corners? The distinct colors?" You don't just grab randomly selected pieces (the "foliage") and try to push them together. Instead your inner dialog works with larger patterns (the "trunk and branches"), arranging the complexity of the jigsaw according to certain principles common to all jigsaw puzzles — a much smarter strategy.

When we communicate within a group (in a firm for instance), we tend to get sloppy. We may neglect to agree on the overall principles of a successful outcome before we start running with a project, or maybe we just take it for granted that everyone has the same under-standing of its objectives. But how much time do we spend checking, confirming, or correcting our assumptions before we launch projects? Experts take responsibility for their own fields within the "foliage," but rapport between people from various fields on the "trunk and branch" level — such as occurs between the different areas of specific compe-tencies within the human brain — seldom happens automatically. Thus, organizations are often at the mercy of coincidence as well as of the vague dreams and sudden inspirations of their influential leaders.

Smaller groups, however — perhaps departments or divisions with-in larger entities — often exhibit impressive cooperation between employees. Innovative and creative individuals establish communica-tion based on a fixed framework, upon which they soon begin to make technical improvements. The end result can be better than if an indi-vidual had undertaken the developmental work unassisted.

Herein, then, lay a great challenge: if a large group of individuals were to share a common vision of a framework and if they were to practice their communication skills within the terms of this frame-work, then as a group — or an organism — they could function more efficiently than the most skilled individual among them![1] Although doomed to be always inefficient when compared to the instant relays of the human brain, the organization would be compensated by the fact that the group would enjoy a wider knowledge and competence than did any one individual.

With careful training a team could learn to behave like an intelli-gent organism rather than as an unruly gang of individualists stepping on each other's toes. There would be ample opportunities for tactical or stylistic interpretations of the work at hand — these would be part of the excitement of working together. The essential ingredient, though, would be that communication between team members would have to occur in relation to a commonly held framework — a point that was perfectly and cogently illustrated by the Apollo moon shots. A large number of people from disparate specialties — metallurgy, energy, astronomy, physiology, computer science, and so on — had a shared mental model of the problem at hand. They didn't have diver-gent views on the fundamentals of the project — the distance to the moon, the lack of atmosphere there, the relatively lower gravity, etc. Consequently, they could pool and combine their skills so successful-ly that they eventually managed to run an electric car on the moon.

No one individual working in isolation could have accomplished such an exquisitely complex project. (Our real problem was that we were not using electric cars here on Earth where, socially and economically, they would be more useful!)

We already had some experience with shared mental models. Even if we weren't necessarily cooperating on a project, we still functioned together in complex systems where shared mental models are necessary for responsible attitudes. When we drive, for instance, we are generally not alone in the traffic. And though it may seem chaotic at times, the whole traffic system wouldn't work unless we all had a shared mental model of its rules. Police remove people who believe, for instance, that a red light means "go" or that it is okay to drive on whatever side of the road you want (in other words, those who violate the "trunk and branches" principles of the system). But beyond being expected to adhere to the traffic laws, we are each allowed to develop our personal driving style and to go wherever we want (part of the "foliage" of the system). I thought that if we could only find and collectively agree on some basic principles for sustainability, then we could use them to guide us into the future.

Consensus on the Right Level

I thought that my reflections on systems thinking had uncovered a basis for ultimate consensus work. I knew some people would argue that "efforts to agree on everything" were bad, because we should always be free thinkers or because polarities are good for creativity. Indeed, polarities are wonderful, since they provide us with the beauty of diversity, the excitement of tensions, and the fruitfulness of creativity. It was unbearable, however, when polarities about survival issues were based on poor thinking, incorrect knowledge, and misunderstanding.

When we were talking about the governing principles of complex systems or of complex projects in complex systems, consensus seemed a very good idea, indeed, because:

1. on those levels, our task was simply about understanding the fundaments of a system, and consequently,

2. its complexities could be managed in a much more elegant way than by trial and error, and

3. on those levels, we could go beyond values and cooperate even if

there were polarities on more individual levels (just as soccer players or hockey players can cooperate while representing opposing teams).

That seemed relevant to what I wanted to do.

Understanding the basic principles of a system goes beyond values: either energy and matter disappear in chemical processes or they don't. Either we are all constituted of cells or we are not. Basic knowledge — about the principles of harmony in music, for instance — offers the player the freedom to improvise. Conversely, not understanding the basic principles leads to being a slave to mediocrity. Surely, given the increasing seriousness of the situation, understanding was preferable.

Scientists and Consensus

Where was science in all this? Scientists were trained to deal with complex systems in systematic ways. Did that make scientists automatically helpful in the public debate? Were their training and experiences of using teamwork on complex systems automatically applicable when they were invited into the public debate? The answer depended on how the debate was framed.

A politician, for instance, wanted to know what to do with PCB (polychlorinated biphenyl). He turned to a group of scientists, dashed right into the "leaves" of interrelationships, and posed the following question: "Is it true that it is PCB that makes the wombs of seals in the Baltic grow together, thereby destroying this species' ability to reproduce?"

The result was a chaotic fight. "Yes, that is clearly proven," said one scientist.

"No, that is not scientifically demonstrated. It is claims of that kind that destroy the reputation of science," said another.

"We have identified a substance that is much more important than PCB, and nobody listens to us," said a third scientist. And so on.

The politician shrugged his shoulders. How could he use this information to make relevant decisions? He prepared to leave the room. Only seconds later, he was convinced to give the group of scientists one more chance, only this time the questions were to be framed in a way that made sense for the system he wanted to handle: the system having to do with decision making.

So the questions began again:

Q. "Is PCB a substance that is naturally occurring in nature, or is it foreign to nature?"

A. "It is foreign to nature," all the scientists agreed.

Q. "Is it easily degradable or persistent?"

A. "It is relatively very persistent; the compound is consciously designed that way." All the scientists again agreed.

Q. "Does this mean, that as long as we use it on a large scale in society, outside of rigorously controlled technical systems, it will continue to increase in concentrations in the biosphere and in ways that are very difficult to foresee?"

A. "That is correct," said all the scientists.

Q. "Are there any tools by which you scientists can foresee the safe thresholds in different sites of the biosphere for such persistent compounds in nature?"

A. "Oh no," the group of scientists said, "that is impossible because of the complexity of all the pollutants and their possible interference with one another and with the complexity of ecosystems. At best, we would be able to explore the mechanisms of damage in nature once damage had occurred, but even that would be difficult."

Q. "Can society then go on using PCB but in technical systems that are rigorously controlled to prohibit leakage into nature?"

A. "No, not if we want to maintain prosperity and, in the long run, survive. The same goes for other persistent compounds foreign to nature."

The politician felt a minor dizziness. Had he experienced all this on the same day?

The paradox was that a consensus process of this kind — one structured in line with principles that were relevant for decision making — often creates much more demanding and radical standpoints than any individual scientist would expect. The problem we had with sustainability was not our knowledge — science had brought about an impressive amount of that. The problem was that we didn't structure it in a way that was relevant for society. So we didn't ask the right questions.

Summary and Conclusion

I was ready to summarize my findings and use them for the consensus process I had decided to facilitate.

1. Systems are held together by a fixed framework of fundamental, interrelated principles, as well as by a wealth of details that comply with the rules of the framework.
2. The structure of a tree makes a good and easily transmittable metaphor for a complex system. The trunk and branches represent a system's framework of basic principles, and the leaves correspond to its details.
3. The human brain seems programmed to discern the totality of things by searching out principles at the "trunk and branch" level first and then projecting that understanding when called upon to handle the "leaves" of details.
4. Although the individual brain seems to be programmed to automatically organize data about complex systems into ordered structures, large groups of people often neglect to do so. Systems thinking seems to be less about teaching the individual anything and more about teaching groups what seems entirely obvious to the individual.
5. My effort to achieve consensus, first among scientists and then among business people, would be characterized by a continued search for basic principles that could later serve individuals as a guide to creativity on sustainability matters.

A plan started to evolve. I would ask fellow scientists in Sweden to be partners in a dialog. We would withdraw from the detailed levels of our scientific frontiers a bit, look with a bird's eye on the totality of our present non-sustainable path, and then elaborate irrefutable principle structures. We would then translate those into terms that we believed would be comprehensible and smart for decision making in business and politics. After that, we would ask advice of leaders in business and politics, instead of attacking them.

The group I had in mind would not be another talk club. Instead, The Natural Step was to evolve into an ongoing and growing dialog group whose specific purpose was to find guiding principles for sustainability that were neutral to political or religious beliefs.

The public debate was obsessed with disagreement. So the Natural Step was going to do the opposite: find areas of knowledge where we could agree. (Afterward it struck me that such knowledge was fruitful when dealing with polarities as well: when we understand what we hold in common, true polarities become much more visible.)

The Natural Step was going to have an inviting attitude, so that we would be able to learn from anyone who wanted to take part in the search for "trunks and branches." We were going to be non-prescriptive: individuals would be free to apply what we learned to their particular circumstances. And we were going to celebrate each step of the way.

CHAPTER 3

THE LAUNCH

IN AUGUST 1988, I sat down at my computer and wrote a manifesto that I felt might earn consensus from the Swedish scientific community. It took its starting point in the cell. Thus I made my beginning right in the field of my own research — healthy and malignant cells — and went on to discuss the crude mechanisms of environmental degradation.

The cells that constitute animal and plant life, I argued, are incapable of even very simple opinions on economic or political matters. They are concerned only with the fundamental conditions for life. We can neither ask nor convince our cells to survive without phosphates or to process mercury or to try to break down PCB. Yet cells dictate our potential for health and prosperity. Therefore, it is up to us to devise a system that absolutely respects their conditions. I figured that my argument might make an excellent starting point for the systems perspective we had to learn and that it could provide a way out of the deadlocks — the so-called conflicts of interest — that were so agonizing for most of us to watch.

Everyone should be able to speak for the cell, to take its perspective. Even heads of state, national economists, and CEOs of big multinationals were made up of cells, and I had an inkling that they, no less than anyone else, would be inspired by a few tales from the microscopic world. The infinitely complex communication systems both within and outside a cell, its unrivaled capabilities in precision manufacturing at the molecular level, and its systematic way of transferring the blueprints of life into the future were all wonderful secrets that spoke with great conviction and power of our kinship with nature.

From that starting point, it was easy to go on and describe the cycles of nature that have been the engine of evolution and to talk about society's dependence on healthy ecosystems. Since the psychological root cause of people's immobility seemed to come from a "What can I do alone?" attitude of helplessness (what I called "The Thumbelina Attitude," from the fairy tale figure no bigger than a thumb), I elaborated ideas on how to present non-sustainability from a "trunk and branch" perspective, and on what premises we might join forces to escape the dilemma. The manifesto ended with a call for cooperation at the societal level — at least on things we could agree on.

My first move was to present my plan and the manuscript to Björn Wallgren, then head of the scientific department of the Swedish Environmental Protection Agency. He had an impeccable reputation as a friendly and intelligent chemist with integrity. He received me at his office, smoked his pipe, laughed, and told me in a friendly way that the task I had taken on was perhaps not possible. But then he said that he would support me all the way regardless. He also brought a couple of his peers into the picture: Bo Ohlson from the largest Swedish NGO (non-governmental organization) for protection of the environment (Swedish Society for Nature Conservation), a leading expert on the problems we were going to have to deal with; and Erik Arrhenius (Björn's previous boss), professor at the Stockholm University's Department for Management of Natural Resources.

I realized I needed more help, and I decided to ask a close peer in cancer science, Stefan Einhorn, to merge forces with Björn, Bo, Erik, and me. I had authored a number of articles on cancer science with Stefan; we had jointly brought a student to PhD; and we had a lot of fun when we where working together. I knew that Stefan would not say no.

I felt a bit encouraged and sent the first draft of the manuscript out to a number of peers in various fields of science, telling them that I planned to mail it to all Swedish households from us collectively. And I explained the need for merging forces on true and comprehensive principles.

For any doctor of science, it is irresistible not to go for all the flaws and errors when receiving something from another doctor who claims that he or she has discovered something that is "true." So, when the manuscript returned to the "editorial group" — Björn, Bo, Erik, Stefan and me —it had gained weight from the correction of all its mistakes.

We repeated the whole procedure, taking all the points of view into account and following the initial plan to go for "the trunk and branches" and avoid bickering about such details among "the leaves" that were of no relevance to the big picture. In this way, we built up a network of well-respected scientists from Sweden.

The group's first challenge was to reach unity or consensus on the educational program that I had already drafted. I sent out that manuscript, took heed of comments, wrote additional drafts, and expanded the circle of scientists to include physicists, medical doctors, chemists, biologists, and so on. As we proceeded with the arduous work of correcting, altering, and proofing the manuscript, more and more participants were drawn in — people from the major educational associations, a growing number of scientists, and researchers and teachers from schools and universities. And after 21 drafts, the manuscript was finalized in December 1988. Every sentence had been polished and honed until the ideas seemed, to us, inspirational. By that time, about 50 of the country's best scientists were part of the primary network — the Advisory Council — and it was becoming almost impossible for anyone to dismiss the importance of what we were doing.

Undoubtedly I underestimated the task and probably (most probably) would not have the power to do what we did again. I was obsessed. I got wonderful help from Stefan and my new friends in the editorial group, and I never found the time to feel sorry for myself.

My initial hopes had come true. Surprisingly, although about 50 scientists stood behind it, the manuscript had not been diluted into something toothless; in fact, quite the contrary had happened. And I had learned that it was easier to reach consensus on very demanding and challenging principles than on details — even those of relatively minor importance.

Somewhere near the beginning of this process, I had presented myself to Lill Lindfors (one of Sweden's most loved entertainers) and said, "All these scientists and I are going to launch an ongoing dialog in Sweden to make the public dialog on sustainable development more effective. If we succeed, would you like to be part of it?" She said yes, and I asked her whom she would like to have with her on stage at that time. She gave me their names, and I phoned them up and said, "Lill and I and all these scientists are.... Would you like to be part of it?"

Then I went to Sven Melander, the head of Swedish TV Channel 1 and said, "All these entertainers and scientists and I are.... Could you give us a permit to celebrate the launch of this project with a TV broadcast to all Swedish homes?" This was in September 1988. Mr.

Melander laughed and didn't believe that this would be possible. Certainly, I was not sure myself. But he said yes and gave me a few months to finance the whole project: the costs of the TV broadcast and the mailing of a booklet and audiocassette to all Swedish households and money for follow-up projects to give leverage to the event. He set the broadcast date for the end of April (1989) — a Swedish holiday in which we celebrate the return of light after the long winter.

I went to the government's Department of Education next and presented them with the same story. "Channel 1 and I and…. Would you like to have this booklet and audiocassette of scientifically agreed-upon knowledge mailed free of charge to all schools?" Their question, of course, was the same as all the others had asked me: how could I afford to do what I proposed? I replied that this had not yet been solved but that expense was not the issue. I just wanted to know whether or not we would get their support if we succeeded in getting the money together.

I figured that my strategy would achieve two things. First, by building on the premise of success (nobody wants to be part of a failure), we would be more likely to find out if people liked the idea as such. Second, since our starting point was success, it would be easier to be full-heartedly positive and to use that energy to build momentum. The only drawback was that dangling "if we succeed": we would have to do it all ourselves. But I was obsessed and I didn't care.

I approached the Swedish king after that. It may seem be surprising that I could just "go and ask the King," but Swedish society is relatively open. (Since then, we have approached a number of politicians the same way, including the Swedish prime minister, and it has worked each time.) It certainly helped that I could tell the King's personal assistant that "the government and I…." Still, I was surprised when I was invited to see the King and Queen in the royal castle to present my project.

On the day of my visit, a guard adjusted his steps to fit the rhythm of mine as together we marched down long corridors and through many doors. Finally I was let into a lecture room. As I sat there on my own, thinking about what I was doing and of my peers at the cancer ward and my safe work at the laboratory, I seriously wondered if I was sane. There I was, waiting for their Majesties King Carl Gustaf and Queen Silvia of Sweden, and the legitimacy to do so had been given to me by me.

The routine with which I had started to feel comfortable helped me out when I responded to the King's questions: "I really don't know, Your Majesty, but if Your Majesty stands behind this, I figure that its chances will be so much greater." He said yes, and I was later invited to a dinner at the castle, which told me that he had no regrets. Since then, the Swedish king has helped us many times on policy matters and with advice and promotion on international matters. He has even taken the initiative on one TNS project — King Carl Gustaf's Challenge — a competition for Swedish municipalities.

Finally, I turned to the sponsors and said, "The King and the government and I...." With the main consensus document in place and with high-level support, I knew it was time to start wooing people in the business sector. The aim was to build up a network of business corporations and other firms from as wide a background as possible, thus emphasizing the universal nature of our quest. It was also important that the products and activities of these firms did not have a negative impact on our credibility.

Eventually, a list was drawn up of private and public companies, charities, trade unions, and even the church: Folksam, KF (the largest supermarket chain in Sweden), Nordbanken (Nordic Bank), SJ (Swedish Rail), The Swedish Cancer Fund, Lions Club, three trade unions — Metall, Fabriks, and TCO — and the Swedish Church. We invited the chairmen of these organizations to join an *ad hoc* sponsoring group. We also invited them to join the prospective board of The Natural Step and to reap whatever benefits they could from the future activities of the Foundation. In my experience, hard-pressed managers and other corporate people were as capable as anyone else of having a vision of a better future. And contrary to popular opinion, many of them were prepared to make personal sacrifices even when there was not a hint of profit in the air (depending, of course, on the magnitude of the sacrifice).

The support of all the sponsors was very invigorating. In fact everything had gone almost too smoothly. And I finally hit a serious obstacle. (With the benefits of hindsight, it now seems rather obvious.) Every time I had asked our sponsors how much they would contribute, I had received the same answer: "That depends on what you get from the others." In the end I was running blindly from one sponsor to another, and the whole project was in a state of limbo.

There seemed to be no way out. I had no money at all, and all of my peers were watching. So were the scientists I had never met but who trusted that I hadn't wasted their time by having them read the manuscript. So was the government, and so was the King. I started to sweat at night.

The solution to the problem came to me late one night (or, rather, early one morning). Conscious of the whole machine that I had set in motion without a single penny in my pocket, I suffered one of my many restless moments. The next day I phoned the secretaries of all the men in question and announced that I was convening a general meeting. I set a date and time in November 1988 but did not dare to confirm; instead I wrote a grateful letter with the complete send list, thanking everyone for agreeing to come. And everyone came!

The meeting took place at Arlanda Airport (its participants have been known as "The Arlanda Group" ever since). Some of the exchanges during this fateful meeting will be forever lodged in my mind. The discussion centered on the difficulty of entering into a project that in spite of the high cost to sponsors would grant no exclusive marketing rights: no one company would be able to claim that they were the official or chief sponsor. Yet, no matter how we looked at it, we would need several sponsors if we were to going to be able to pay the substantial costs for the mail-out and subsequent projects (40 million SEK — about $US 5 million).

When Stig Larsson, CEO of Swedish Railways, took the floor, it seemed to me that he single-handedly saved the project from disintegration. He said, "We have a problem that is even greater than the difficulty of finding the money. If we don't support this project, which has such great potential for the future, who else will? And how can we then be sure that the project will fall into good hands?"

Larsson's comment broke the impasse, and then suddenly there was a second surprise. Leif Lewin from KF, a warm and grandfatherly man, threw me a friendly glance and with a look at the other men around the table said, "Isn't it about time that we let this doctor off the hook? He certainly can't read the atmosphere of this meeting; he isn't used to board meetings." And then he turned to me directly and continued, "You're going to get this money, you see."

I still don't understand how he could have said that at the time. But since no one opposed him, the decision was, in fact, taken. They needed some more time to determine how much each would put into the pot, but they agreed to take a personal responsibility for the project. And with their names on a piece of paper, the German printer (4.3

million booklets and audiocassettes couldn't be printed in a few weeks in Sweden) would agree to start the presses.

Weeks of agony and sleeplessness suddenly dissolved into huge joy and gratitude. I realized that all I had to do was continue to weld the raw forces of vision to the common practice of will. The working method and overriding motto of The Natural Step (both then and now) was to "find principle fundaments of indisputable relevance, and thereafter ask the advice of others on how to apply them."

In April 1989, we held our TV broadcast. The King, Mr. Perez de Cuellar (Secretary General of the UN), and Astrid Lindgren (author of the Pippi Longstocking books) congratulated us, and all the entertainers joined in a cabaret. One week later, we mailed the booklet and audiocassette to all Swedish homes and households.

Today the dialog goes on. We have a growing number of scientific publications and doctoral dissertations describing the TNS framework, its evolution, and its implementation. And we have a growing number of case studies from the universities, business corporations, and municipalities around the world that are applying The Natural Step. I am happier than ever, but no less terrified than I was in the beginning.

PART TWO

"Everything-Ology"

CHAPTER 4

THE SCIENTIFIC EXPERIENCE

THE FASCINATION THE SWEDISH public felt when they encountered the "Big Mailing" was great but certainly no greater than my own. Along with extremely smart and helpful scientists, I had been on a journey that had increased in beauty and magic since I started to realize my dream. My reward was a journey into a worldview that was more comprehensible than the one I had had before.

My new peers and I needed to describe the prerequisites for the existence of life before it would be meaningful to discuss sustainable development on a new, more comprehensible level. For fun, we coined the term "everything-ology" as the working title for this new field of competence. It created a necessary platform for the elaboration of principles, strategies, and programs that later evolved from The Natural Step dialog between scientists and decision makers.

The "Big Mailing" provided an abridged version of the following worldview:

Life is the eternal tide of decay and reconstruction. We live in a continuous conversion of organized matter into waste. Indeed, we could perceive the whole system of life and industry and everything that moves as propellers taking power from a continuous stream of decay. The stream is essential to life. Of course, so is the ongoing reconstruction of waste back into resources again. To reverse the stream of decay in any given system, though, energy in a usable form must be introduced from outside the system.

The Pixies in the Box

Let us conduct a thought experiment. Imagine an enormous box without a lid. Inside are all the natural resources that we consume today in the course of our economic activities: coal, oil, wheat fields, fish-stocked lakes, waterfalls from a dam driving a turbine, and so on.

Now imagine that a gang of pixies is allowed into the box. Their avowed purpose is to make things as pleasant as possible in the limited space available. (In a very real sense mankind does actually live inside a box like this! Earth, after all, is a system limited by size, and gravity holds all things in place as surely as if we did live within walls. Our box does not have a lid — we gain energy from the sun outside and give it off again into the cool universe in the form of heat radiation.)

Continuing with our thought experiment, imagine that the walls of the box are insulated so that neither light nor heat can get through. A well-fitting lid is fixed on top so that the home of the pixies is, to all intents and purposes, hermetically sealed. The pixies now rapidly — and rather painfully — begin to understand the main tenets of thermodynamics.

First, they have to start using artificial light, even by day. In the early stages, the waterfall generated electricity, but once the water had fallen to the bottom of the box it stayed there. Previously, of course, sunlight had raised it up again and "the bill" for expended energy was paid from "outside." In the same way, the pixies soon realize that once the firewood has been used up it will not come back and neither will food once it has been eaten.

The pixies' next painful insight is that nothing — neither materials nor energy — can disappear within the sealed box. All the smoke, sewage, heat, etc. generated by all other processes remain in the box. Every attempt to restore the earlier and more pleasant state of things — for example, by carrying water back up to the dam — results in dire failure. Besides, all that work requires the consumption of even larger amounts of food, leading to the dispersal of even more bodily waste. And nothing escapes from the box.

Other attempts to tidy up the mess and restore order quickly point to a host of new "bills" that the pixies leave unpaid. The vacuum cleaner wears out, and a new one has to be manufactured in a smoking, spitting factory. Like everything else, the pollution from its production stays in the box. The same goes for vacuum cleaner bags — both the new ones that have to be manufactured and the old ones that are thrown on a dump at the back of the box. Then the cleaner's shirt starts to wear out and, as a result of all his sweaty work, needs to be washed in a machine of limited life span which, furthermore, requires energy to function. The laundry requires detergent that comes from another production facility; this powder and the dirty wash water are flushed out of a pipe and then dispersed within the box.

Suddenly the awful truth dawns on the pixies: they are doomed to destruction. Their sealed environment allows no access to outside sources of energy, so the usual processes of reconstruction cannot even partially offset the normal processes of decay. Hence the whole system will run down rather rapidly. Ultimately, everything, even their own bodies, will dissolve into a diffuse soup at the bottom of the box with a cloud of gas above it. All differences or contrasts will be resolved: no energy-binding chemical compounds will be found and no differences of temperature. Chaos will have arrived — the principle of absolute poverty and death.

The pixies have experienced the operation of a dramatic yet very concrete set of principles that have important implications in "the real world."

The Conservation Laws

Scientific Principle # 1: Energy cannot disappear or be created. This is the first law of thermodynamics and it applies universally. Scientists often remind people that for normal chemical reactions, the same applies to matter.[1] Both energy and matter may (and constantly do) change form, but the total amount of each remains constant. In other words, nothing disappears. The pixies felt the effects of this law when they discovered that the heat and smoke generated by combustion or the making of vacuum cleaners hung in the air forever. We feel its effects in the "real world" when the gasoline we burn is dispersed into the air as gas emissions and simply produces new forms of compounds.

Scientific Principle #2: Energy and matter tend to disperse. The second law of thermodynamics, the entropy law (expressed here in a popularized way), also applies universally. Although the total quantity of energy remains constant, the quantity of energy available in a useful form decreases with each transformation and tends to dissipate through a system (as when chemical energy transforms to heat energy, for example). In all systems, there is always a cost for any process to take place (even if we were to have access to ideal technologies — which we don't). The second law of thermodynamics [the entropy law] is the physicist's way of describing the irreversibility of energy transformation in all processes. It is also one of the few indisputable ways of defining time. The energy released in a combustion process cannot be used to bring the fumes back into the same amount of fuel again. Water in a waterfall cannot create electricity enough to pump the same amount of water back into the dam again. Time cannot go backward. The same law explains why batteries cannot recharge themselves or why perpetual motion machines are impossible.

Some people regard the entropy law as an enemy because it lies behind such things as the rusting of cars and the aging process. But it is really one of the many prerequisites for life itself. Remember the fairy tale about a king who wanted time to stop so that he wouldn't grow old? His wish came true. But the birds suddenly stopped singing, and the king encountered the sterile state of death. (His next wish was obvious.)

As the pixies discovered when they burned the firewood, energy in the form of heat dissipated rapidly. Once dispersed, that energy was no longer useful. The ash and smoke that was really the transformed matter of the wood also dissipated.

Because their system was completely sealed, the pixies had trouble with accumulating heat and also with waste matter. For us, the fact that energy changes into heat radiation is not too serious a problem. Heat leaves the Earth's atmosphere at the same time as we are provided with new solar energy. However, dispersed matter can become an environmental problem because gravity retains it in the atmosphere. We have considerable problems with residual particulate matter from wood and coal burning, for instance (as well as with a host of other pollutants).

Scientific Principle #3: Material value is measured in the concentration and structure of matter.[2] As matter transforms and spontaneously disperses, it becomes less ordered. But matter in a lesser state of order is not as easily used as matter in a higher state of order. Thus the value of matter — either biological or economic — increases as its concentration rises.

We do not really ever consume matter, as such; rather we consume its concentration and structure and purity — some particular quality that is of functional or economic use. When we eat, for instance, we consume a food's chemical energy quality (the sun's energy that is bound within it plus its concentration of valuable building blocks for life such as certain minerals, plus purity). The more concentrated the energy quality of a particular food, the more biologically valuable it is.

Similarly we find a gold ingot more economically valuable than an identical amount of gold dispersed in nature. If we add form to matter — in other words, give it structure — its quality or value goes up even more: a gold ring commands a higher price per gram than the gold ingot.

Scientific Principle #4: Plant cells, assisted by the external energy of the sun, create a net increase in concentration and structure on Earth. Photosynthesis is the primary process upon which all biological processes on Earth ultimately depend. Through photosynthesis, plants use the solar energy that flows continuously into the Earth's systems to gather dispersed matter and assemble it in new, complicated structures. In other words, plants access energy from outside Earth's systems and return dispersed materials to available forms — a unique accomplishment that makes them the primary producers of the planet (although we have started to mimic nature here and there. Human solar-driven processes can also create a net increase in concentration and structure. Take, for instance, solar-powered vehicles transporting materials for recycling).

Cells

All living things are made up of cells. Bacteria and amoeba are single-celled organisms, whereas more complicated species, such as humans, consist of billions of cells reacting within a single system. The first cell was formed in water about three-and-a-half billion years ago — such a marvelously improbable occurrence that many cell biologists have fallen into religious musings trying to explain it. And the reverence and love for life we learn when observing a cell is further heightened when we take into account the interplay of billions of cells within one body or, indeed, the interrelationship of all living things on Earth.

Cells themselves are made up of organelles — various organ-like structures that function similarly to the way the stomach, lungs, skeleton, and blood vessels function in our bodies. Each organelle is an infinitely complex structure, useless by itself in exactly the same way that human lungs, for instance, could not possibly work independently of the other organs.

The nucleus is the central organelle of any cell and, in many ways, does the work of a brain. The nucleus contains the genes that control our vital functions. Human genes have been inherited, adapted, and changed from those of the various species that make up our ancestry.

Each gene is responsible for the production of a different protein, and life is steered by these proteins. Some proteins are simply building blocks in the body; others are enzymes and hormones that affect the growth and development of the body, determine our sex, regulate the rate of cell division, and so on. We commonly associate genetic information with such external physical characteristics as eye color, but genetic activity actually controls everything in our bodies, ensuring that each cell is continually doing what is best for the body as a whole.

Plant cells' great precision and capacity for production have always kept the world tidy in spite of humans and other mammals. The leftovers of our meals, the ash and smoke of our fires, the ruins of abandoned settlements — from such things life has always sprung anew. Plant cells convert waste products from animals into carbohydrates, fats, and proteins; when the cells reach twice their original size, they divide. They are incalculably more efficient than people at building up new resources, and collect molecules one by one from our garbage and even position atoms as required. But at no point do they use more raw materials than they need.

According to the law of thermodynamics, disorder (entropy) has to increase somewhere else as it decreases here, and not even the plant kingdom can override this natural law. In spatial terms, plants exist on Earth between the sun and the universe. Once they have consumed the ordered quality of sun energy, plants give off heat that escapes into the universe. In other words, the plants are part of a system in which the sun is the energy source and the universe the "cooler." Although we don't experience the consequences — at least not in a time perspective that is relevant for humanity — the ordered quality of energy from "the sun-space battery" is slowly being consumed (the "cost" of the energy transfer) as the sun runs down and will slowly lose its ability to provide us with the right temperature. Hence no natural law is being contravened.

Evolution

For millions of years, the second law of thermodynamics has seemingly been reversed in one tiny place — this thin shell, this home of life that we call the biosphere. The first plant cell came into being some 3,500 million years ago in a highly disorganized and even toxic atmosphere. A host of molecules was used up fitting atoms into the growing chemistry of life — complex structures of essential proteins, carbohydrates, and fats — and in this way the levels of disorganized matter in the atmosphere steadily fell. As the cells started making their presence felt, the atmosphere gradually became cleaner and more welcoming for higher forms of life.

Some toxic substances that became attached to the first primitive cells — including heavy metals such as mercury, lead, and cadmium — could not be used as building blocks for life. Sedimentation and fossilization processes carried those substances deep beneath the surface of the earth with the dead cells that would eventually be converted into oil, coal, and other deposits. (Some of these deposits form a kind of storage facility for ores.)

It took more than 3,000 million years for our primitive forebears to prepare the Earth for higher life. During that time and using the continuous ordered energy flow of the sun, cells gathered and deposited minerals, cleaned the sea and land, produced oxygen and food, and changed the fundamental equation between ordered and disordered matter. Once the plant cells had multiplied and the Earth was clean enough and its atmosphere rich enough in oxygen, new and more complicated plant-eating creatures could develop: the animals.

Animals could not photosynthesize, but they could digest plant matter and thus convert solar energy for survival, growth, and mobility. Unlike plants, animals are net producers of waste, even when sleeping. However, waste products from animals were the raw materials for survival and growth for plant cells. Thus began a regenerative cycle between plants and animals that gave rise to an ever-greater diversity of species (including humans) and that continues to provide enough food and oxygen to sustain life for all. Indeed, we owe our continued existence to all the biogeochemical cycles of nature: the cycle of resources and waste between plants and animals; the water cycle that provides the "bloodstream" of the system; and the sedimentation processes, volcanic eruptions, and weathering processes that process matter between the biosphere and the Earth's crust.

Reverse Evolution

The disturbing fact was that over the past 100 years or so, we had reversed the evolutionary process and were traveling backward at blistering speed toward a disorganized and toxic biosphere. The message of the "Big Mailing" was clear: primary production and the ecocycles could no longer "pay the bills" and reverse the tide. Waste products from chimneys, sewage pipes, dumps, and slag heaps were taking their toll. We were actively seeking out, extracting, and scattering mineral deposits that had been hidden away during geological times in the form of oil and coal. We were releasing heavy metals such as lead, mercury, and cadmium that could never be broken down by nature since they are elements. We were manufacturing persistent compounds foreign to nature (certain pesticides, additives in plastics, anti-flammables, coolants, and so on) that cells had never encountered before and of which the normal base-line concentrations were consequently zero. Through over-harvesting and displacement of natural systems, we were destroying habitats and species that had preceded us. In short, we were well on our way to bringing about extinction to all advanced life forms, including our own.

Our prosperity depends entirely on abundant, well-ordered natural resources. As soon as we plunder them, the "bills" start to come in. For instance, it had already become more resource expensive to conduct a commercial fisheries industry: greater areas had to be covered just to find the fish because pollution and over-fishing had decimated fish stocks. We were using progressively more energy and raw materials to get food on the table, because our industrial society was not particularly resource efficient. Acidified lakes had to be dosed with lime at regular intervals; landfill sites had to have safety systems installed; waste products from mining had to be buried; and CFCs in dumped refrigerators had to be safeguarded. The costs of municipal water treatment plants had skyrocketed; the procurement of land for dumps had increased; and acid rain damage to property, agriculture, and forestry had intensified. Until we actually attacked the root of the problem, these costs would continue to escalate. Thus far we had mainly been paying to treat symptoms. And on a metaphoric level, we were not paying down the principle on any of our environmental "bills" but were transferring payments from one place to another or putting them off for future payment.

Unless we halted the destruction of the environment, we were headed for a disastrous endpoint: toxic waste, poverty, and social despair. Politically this issue was usually dealt with as if the alternatives would be green leaves, happy birds, and poor people on the one hand (sustainability) and somewhat dirtier leaves and not-so-happy birds but rich people on the other (non-sustainability). But non-sustainability really meant that we would lose it all.

The "Big Mailing" made the point that there really should be no conflict between environmental and economic interests, since our affluence depended on nature's ability to recycle waste into resources and provide us with life-sustaining resources such as clean water and air. If we could agree on that basic fact, we argued, then time frames, economic negotiations, and strategies for change could follow. And progressive economists and entrepreneurs were beginning to "get it." Ecology was slowly starting to change orthodox economic practice.

Thus the scientists behind the "Big Mailing" collectively and with a united voice provided hard evidence that a paradigm shift was needed. (Previously, diverging views among scientists about detailed problems had created the impression that we could not agree on anything at all.) We also suggested that firms and people who wanted to be part of the solution rather than part of the problem could probably count on various kinds of increasing support in the future — proactivity was likely to pay off, in other words, whether motivated by altruism or self-interest. The dialog and ongoing learning process between science and decision makers had begun.

CHAPTER 5

THE SOCIAL EXPERIENCE

BEFORE THE "BIG MAILING," specialists in communication and marketing told us that the impact from a mailing addressed to everyone — not to a specific target group — would be small. Less than one percent of the Swedish population was likely to pay any attention at all, they said. However, people had never before received a booklet and an audiocassette in the mail free of charge and delivered simultaneously as the result of a private initiative. Suddenly TNS was on TV and radio and in newspapers everywhere. We met with more and more decision makers in business and politics who wanted to hear my story. More people became curious enough to go through the material, and a Gallup poll showed that around 15 percent of the Swedish adult population had really studied it — a lot of people in absolute terms. But the major impact was to be found in the follow-up.

My dream was to continue the learning experience and ongoing dialog between scientists and decision makers with the whole Swedish population as witness. I figured that it would work two ways: my growing dialog would be empowered and challenged by being watched by the public, and the public would watch us as long as relevant and comprehensive results continued to come out. In this way, more people would be challenged and recruited into the process.

On a very conscious level, I realized that I needed to stay the same on a personal level if I was to continue my work. If I started to confuse myself with the consensus-result from so many people, that would be the end of it. I was proud to have served as the initiator and the facilitator, and that was okay. But I wanted to remain only that. The mentors and benefactors of the Arlanda Group continued to meet with me, of course, since our cooperation had led to spectacular results so far.

On a partly intuitive, partly conscious level, I understood the wisdom of remaining the "absent-minded professor." In fact, it made my work much easier: I could concentrate completely on science and the dialog with decision makers. Also, I thought that as long as my deficient experience in business and relative ignorance about how society at large was organized was allowed to show and thereby communicate helplessness, it would foster the feeling of responsibility of the Arlanda Group. A sense of shared responsibility would drive them to come up with smart ideas for projects to communicate the next steps of The Natural Step to the Swedish community. It worked beautifully. Each individual of the Arlanda Group had his or her competence, and my peers in the science network had theirs. I was the happy facilitator in the middle, and together, we enjoyed learning.

Hans Dahlberg became my primary mentor in business matters. Hans was a member of the Arlanda Group, CEO of Folksam (Sweden's largest insurance company), and the first person from business to whom I introduced my plans when I was preparing the "Big Mailing." He not only gave me advice on how to approach the other CEOs but also realized that I would need help in the follow-up to the "Big Mailing."

To best use the momentum we had built up, we needed to work on a broad scale, and if I were coordinating it all alone — well that would be the end of it. So Hans recruited a competent project leader, Per Uno Alm (PUA). PUA was running a consulting bureau at the time, and Hans knew him to be a clever and devoted young man from business.

PUA and I soon developed a friendship, and without him I would not have managed to make much out of the launch. PUA allocated his business office to The Natural Step, and suddenly there was the nice voice of PUA's secretary announcing, "The Natural Step" when anybody phoned us. The Arlanda Group turned into a sort of TNS *ad hoc* board; PUA was invited to become the CEO of TNS; and I remained its absent-minded scientist and homemade philosophical leader. The money I got from lecturing about the "Big Mailing" had started to create an income, and PUA (who was now also part of the Arlanda Group) soon started to identify new projects of potential significance for the newly born TNS organization.

At first, I tried to do it all: develop new projects within The Natural Step with PUA, take care of the patients at my cancer section, and run my scientific cancer cell projects at the laboratory. After a bit more than a year of this, my wife said that it was all ridiculous — *I* was not sustainable! So I left my clinical practice and tried to keep up with my two remaining duties. The Natural Step continued to take off, and eventually I had to choose again — this time between The Natural Step and what was left of my previous professional life in cancer science.

When it started to become obvious to me that I would have to leave my work in cancer science, I felt a sorrow in my heart that is difficult to describe. I had spent most of my conscious professional life reaching the position I was in. I had wonderful peers at the lab and at the ward, loved the challenges and progress of the work, and felt as if the patients needed me. Yet here I was, prepared to leave it for good.

The workload was too much — my wife could smell burning rubber from my study! So after my last student had defended his doctoral dissertation and before I made the mistake of taking on yet another PhD student, I went to my boss, professor Gösta Gahrton (head of the clinic for Internal Medicine at Huddinge Hospital) and told him that I needed to resign. I had feared this moment, and in my mind I had repeated my arguments over and over again to make him accept and endorse my decision. I guess it was me I needed to convince, because Gösta just smiled in a friendly way and said that he had been waiting for this conversation since the "Big Mailing" well over a year before. (He had known before I did!) That was a wonderful moment, and I will never forget the gratitude I felt to Gösta for making it easy on me — I had certainly made it hard enough on myself for both of us.

Within a couple of years, TNS had launched a number of public follow-up projects:

- The Youth Parliament for Protection of the Environment. PUA and I contacted the Swedish students' federation and with them elaborated a project plan to educate about sustainability annually in all Swedish schools. Students coordinate a central summit of about 400 students from different schools to run workshops, interview business leaders, and present the results on the public TV's education channel (that way, students outside the central summit can also take an active part). Business corporations — some from the original Arlanda Group — sponsor the project, and the number of firms involved in the dialog expands each year. An annual event involving around 50,000 students each year, the Youth Parliament for Protection of the Environment celebrated its ten-year anniversary in 1999.

- The King's Challenge (a contest for Swedish municipalities). The Swedish King took the initiative to have TNS run this contest every three years. The municipality that has taken the most convincing initiatives to become a sustainable region of Sweden wins the Challenge. The winning municipality receives the award from the King's hand at a ceremony where scientists gather to talk about sustainability from a municipality perspective. The third contest was run in the spring of 2000.

- The Environmental Hunt. In teams of 15, people from companies and municipalities along with their suppliers and clients have fun competing and learning systems thinking in line with the TNS Framework.

- Two train exhibitions. "Eco-motifs" traveled through Swedish cities to display how business corporations were working with sustainability issues in line with the TNS Framework. Each car was "owned" by a certain business corporation, and each of them — Electrolux, IKEA, Swedish McDonald's, Scandic Hotels, Siemens, Swedish Farmer's Federation, JM Construction, Hemköp and KF (supermarkets), and Swedish Rail — demonstrated how they had interpreted the TNS Framework in their business activities.

- Foundations of professional associations. Named by their professional identities — "Engineers for the Environment," "Medical Doctors for the Environment," "Swedish Food for the Environment," "Communicators for the Environment," and so on — these different associations have the same shared mental model for communicating (the TNS Framework; see Chapter 10) but were developing their own specific professional conclusions from it. The associations were set up to be independent and traditional democratic membership organizations. The idea was to stimulate people to apply their professional expertise to the protection of the environment and not just pay others to do it for them (paying membership fees to NGOs like Greenpeace, for example).

- Publication of *The Natural Step*, a national journal.

- Seminars for politicians, site visits to the Minister for the Environment for business leaders who apply the TNS Framework, debate articles, books, and so on.

Projects of this kind helped to increase the visibility of TNS and its basic information, which was the intention, of course.

At the same time, the struggle for money had begun. Many of the projects were creating some income (far from all of them), but it was not sufficient to support professionals to work at an office full-time. And we were slowly running out of the money we had raised in the "Big Mailing" budget. In fact, the problem was growing daily, and I had not understood that we had a problem until after the mailing. The budget was substantially smaller than we had planned (because the agreement at the Arlanda meeting to pay the bill for the mailing and raise some surplus money for the follow-up was not quite met). In fact, we were about 12 million Swedish crowns ($US1.5 million) short.

All this was completely new to me. I had been working at a university hospital, spoiled by the fact that all bills were paid as long as I did my best scientifically and clinically. Suddenly I was professionally worrying about money and business and the mass media and....

Outer turbulence was mirrored by inner turbulence. I felt fear and a subconscious anxiety that was difficult to explain. The money didn't bother me too much, because I had a feeling that the momentum we had created would solve that issue one way or another. And I had an almost blind trust in the business people of the Arlanda Group.

The anxiety seemed more related to cultural shock. Where I came from, it was not considered "serious" – that is, altogether trustworthy – to pay attention to how much the public understands of science: to make the public understand inherently required simplification, and this is not scientific. To a certain extent I agreed with that. But there was more to it than that. The struggle to make intellectually difficult issues easier to understand is a demanding task in itself. It forces you to really think through the intellectual context, particularly since you cannot use the jargon of the specific fields of science. I knew I would be working in a very public arena, and I wasn't sure I was up to the task.

I comforted myself with thoughts of two earlier experiences that told me I probably didn't need to worry. The first occurred one day when I came home late from work. My oldest son Markus (then seven years old) asked me why I came home so late from the lab every evening. I certainly couldn't tell him Dad was trying to induce differentiation in primary malignant cells from patients with chronic lymphocytic leukemia and myelodysplastic syndromes. So I started to explain what I had been doing as systematically and comprehensively as I could, deleting all words that a seven-year-old could not understand. As I talked, it occurred to me for the first time that I didn't understand myself what I was doing so late at night at the lab. I was shocked. The scientific jargon had helped me bypass some essential elements of understanding, and I could hear how shallow it all sounded when I couldn't use those words. From then on, I made sure I was able to describe what I was doing in clear, everyday language.

The second experience occurred as I was planning my first scientific presentation to my older colleagues in medical science. I spotted a very strange and ugly plan in my own head: it was as if I were consciously planning to present my findings in a somewhat fuzzy way. The aim was simple — if I was not completely clear, then the risk of being revealed as a superficial beginner in science would naturally be smaller. I even remember thinking that the experienced audience could probably develop some meaningful thoughts in their own minds — triggered by my not completely clear presentation.

Once these vague thoughts reached my consciousness, I put words to them and didn't like what I heard. I made a decision: I would present what I had found in my studies and what I had thought exactly as they appeared to me. And I would include the childish metaphors I had invented to make it more understandable.

After my presentation, a number of scientists came up to me. "We understood 100 percent of what was said, which is, in fact, unusual when you learn about other people's scientific work. Thanks for a very clear presentation. By the way, you have misunderstood this part of it. If you want us to, we can help you in our lab to make a part-study and elaborate this further...." I decided then that I had found my way: I was going to try never to pretend to be smarter than I was, and I was always going to try to present things the way they appeared to me. (After all, being corrected by more experienced colleagues and peers was really not that bad.)

My musings were all very comforting, but I was still in shock. There would be no more deep discussions with my peers in medical science about frontline cancer research. Everything I did now was based on shaky ground, and the reason was simple: the intellectual tradition in the new scientific field "systems thinking in sustainable development" was not very long or very deep. I decided that for each public project PUA was initiating, I needed to accomplish some new intellectual breakthrough to make up for it. So it was that a couple of months after the "Big Mailing," I met with my mentor in multidisciplinary science, Karl-Erik Eriksson.

I first met Karl-Erik Eriksson, professor of theoretical physics at the Institution of Physical Resource Theory at Chalmers University and his student John Holmberg at a seminar at Orsa (a beautiful place a few hours north of Stockholm). I had been invited to the seminar after the meeting agenda had been prepared (people in the green movement had only learned about me since the "Big Mailing"), and I was allowed only a short time right before the lunch break that, accordingly, was shortened because of me.

Karl-Erik and John found it amusing when one of the organizers dropped all my slides onto the floor just as my presentation was about to start. People were tired and hungry, were looking ahead to a shortened lunch break, and my slides were scattered on the floor. So I thanked the organizing committee for having confidence in my ability to pull it off in spite of the poor conditions. Karl-Erik found this even more amusing, and he approached me after the meeting.

I learned that John was working along exactly the same lines as I was. The three of us merged forces from that day and have been close partners and friends ever since. John soon became my closest peer as I developed my ideas and eventually wrote his own doctoral dissertation in fields where I had taken active part.

If you are concerned about your intellectual education, you are fine with Karl-Erik! (He was the youngest and smartest Swedish professor in theoretical physics from the beginning of his career.) Through intellectually demanding conversations, and by helping me produce scientific articles on new ways of structuring information on sustainable development, he calmed my tense academic nerves. All of this led to the launch of some other projects that balanced the more public ones (to the benefit of my well-being):

- Production of publications in scientific journals on the principle understanding of sustainability and sustainable development.

- Consensus seminars among Swedish experts in various societal sectors that were critical of sustainability. After some years, we came up with consensus documents in a number of areas such as agriculture, metal flows, energy sources, and forestry.

- *The Swedish People's Environmental Encyclopedia.* This project was the result of collaboration between the scientists in the TNS network and publisher Nationalencyklopedin/Bra Böcker. Some well-known parliamentary politicians invited the scientists in the TNS network (at the time well over 100) to come to a meeting in the Swedish Parliament. I made a presentation on how the TNS scientific dialog had proceeded since the "Big Mailing," and we invited the scientists to write an encyclopedia on the environment and on sustainable development that would further the idea of consensus and complete the debates on controversial details.

- Doctoral dissertations. In 1999, four doctoral dissertations describing and elaborating on the intellectual framework of TNS were published: two in physics in Sweden (John Holmberg and Christian Azar at Chalmers in Göteborg); and two in social sciences (Hilary Bradbury at MIT in Boston, and Brian Nattras at the University of British Columbia in Canada). At least four more were in process in the year 2000. Since then, scientists outside of Sweden helped further elaborate the Swedish TNS Framework and reached consensus on the new and more refined versions of it (scientists in the US, Australia, New Zealand and England).

Eventually in 1995 I was appointed adjunct professor of Physical Resource Theory at Karl-Erik's institution and found a new academic home there.

Communication Tools

It may appear that everything developed smoothly, guided by some inner sense that effectively protected TNS from making mistakes in the outer world. I only wish that this had been true. It soon became apparent that you cannot avoid resistance no matter how hard you try to stay focused on the issues ("Play the ball, not the player.") and no matter how hard you try to be pleasant and non-adversarial. I am hot-tempered by nature and soon learned the hard way how little a reactive attitude is likely to achieve in reaching goals. Out of need, then, I developed some communication tools that helped when I needed to handle myself in tense situations. Along with my peers in the growing scientific network, I referred to the most important of those tools as "The Simplicity without Reduction Strategy," "The Yes, and Technique," and "The Asking Advice Attitude."

The Simplicity without Reduction Strategy. As soon as resistance arose from anywhere, I learned to apply my reflections on systems thinking by searching for overarching principles in order to resolve the issue (escaping from the "leaves" and looking for the "trunk and branches"). Eventually, this process became more or less spontaneous and automatic.

The term "simplicity" referred to the fact that it is easier to reach understanding, and eventually consensus, if you first discover basic principles. "Without reduction" meant that the search for basic principles was not to reduce or overlook any of the complexity in the system, thus distinguishing "simplicity" from "simplifying." In fact, "simplicity without reduction" is the opposite of simplifying. Out of respect for complexity, it advocates the strategy of identifying the basic principles first. Only then is it meaningful to start finding how much can be agreed to on more detailed levels ("trunk, branches and leaves").

The Yes, and Technique. "The Yes, and Technique" acknowledges another's point of view and then broadens the discussion. By starting your sentences with "yes" (even in dialogs with antagonists), you are forced to endorse some aspects of what you hear. Some aspects most likely are true. Then, when you continue your sentence with "and," you expand the perspective and bring in other aspects that are needed to foster a more subtle comprehension of the problem at hand. Thereafter you may come up with a couple of suggestions. In this way, the conversation becomes a dialog. Listening not only occurs but also gets confirmed in the ears of your antagonist as a necessary aspect of communication. For instance, if you are talking about biofuels, somebody may say, "No, no, no, they are much too expensive." If you reply, "Would you rather die in a non-sustainable world?" then you are unlikely to have a successful dialog. A better answer would be, "Yes, you are absolutely right. And not only that, their availability is very low, too. I have seen some methods to deal with this problem. For instance, some firms use a small number of biofueled cars just to prepare the market. And differentiated taxes may be an option if...."

The Asking Advice Attitude. "The Yes, and Technique" (not "Yes, but," which everyone knows means "no") can become even more powerful if you leave off the "and" and ask for advice instead. This attitude is particularly useful when the resistance is harsh. Rather than delivering suggestions of how to solve a problem, you can ask people — even antagonists — for advice. Using the preceding example, you would say something like, "Yes, you are absolutely right. You know what we are trying to do. Do you have any suggestions of what would be appropriate measures in this case?"

A number of results generally follow when we ask for someone's advice:

- It defuses the aggression of opponents.

- It always produces an answer. I don't know why, but if somebody says, "Could you give me some advice?" it probably flies in the face of some rule of behavioral science to simply reply, "No!"

- The person realizes others are watching or listening and finds himself or herself in the position of having to explain in a clear way.

- What people say is almost never the same as it would have been had it been obtained under duress. Defensive statements usually contain sweeping value judgments, whereas a non-confrontational approach actually reveals the true underlying cause of resistance.

- The advice is often of a very high quality or reveals a misunderstanding that may have arisen from your own way of communicating.

- You gain an ally instead of an opponent.

- By engaging the other person, you foster a sense of shared responsibility and not dispute.

These three communication tools could go a long way in encouraging dialog. But they couldn't guarantee it, as I soon found out.

When "The Yes, and Technique" Didn't Help

A few days before the Arlanda meeting, just before we agreed to launch TNS through the "Big Mailing," I ran into my first big crisis that was potentially dangerous for the whole enterprise. The head of environmental affairs at one of the Swedish trade unions didn't like me at all and convinced his firm to refuse my proposal to be a part of the TNS dialog. Klas (the man's first name) was not only concerned about his own firm but regarded it as his personal responsibility to put an end to TNS anywhere. He phoned up all the CEOs that he knew I had contacted and told them that the scientific arguments we presented were flawed. According to Klas, there was no extinction of species, no loss of rainforests, no accumulation of pollutants in our ecosystems, and — overall — mankind had never been happier anywhere.

I heard rumors about Klas's actions from some of the CEOs who were supporting me, met with Klas, and tried "The Yes, and

Technique" without success. He had already made up his mind. I didn't understand him. He didn't enjoy the discussion about principles at all but hid among the "leaves" as soon as the dialog started. He seemed to take the whole thing on a personal level, and I felt that I was not very effective in getting him interested in the "trunk, branches, and leaves" of systems thinking. No platforms of mutual understanding were built — we didn't get anywhere. "The Yes, and Technique" didn't help. Not even "The Asking Advice Attitude" helped: the advice was that I should lay off.

One day I was called to a board meeting at the bank that was planning to support the "Big Mailing" with a major grant. I was going to give a brief presentation, and then they were going to decide on a grant of 10 million Swedish crowns ($US1.3 million). Just before the meeting started, Klas entered the room. He had been invited by the chairman of the board to present his criticism officially.

Klas was invited to start the meeting and he did. For well over 15 minutes, he spoke fast and in many, many words about all the flaws in the manuscript that TNS was going to mail to Swedish households. I recognized Klas's diffuse way of arguing — supporting the wrong meaning with the wrong arguments.

I had plenty of time to plan my countermove, but I didn't know what good this would do me. What was I to do? "The Yes, and Technique" wouldn't get me anywhere, because it had already proven insufficient with Klas, and this was not about dialog with Klas anymore. But if I started to argue about details, explaining how Klas was wrong about this and that, I would be doing exactly what TNS was tailor-made to avoid. It would be like demonstrating to the board that dialog on these matters doesn't actually work. It was all about philosophy and personal trust, and I would only have a few minutes to give them my case, and then a decision was going to be made.

Although I was embarrassed to be accused of being a complete intellectual failure, and by an attack that was personal and that gave no room for a fruitful dialog, I looked up and watched the eyes around the table. They all looked bored when Klas spoke. The talk wasn't all that inspiring, but their boredom still surprised me, since 10 million crowns were at stake. I figured that this sum didn't sound as impressive to a bank as it did to me. A plan evolved in my head that was hardly built on "The Yes, and Technique."

Eventually Klas was done, and the chairman asked me if I had any comments. I said in a deliberately slow and firm voice, "Having heard Klas's long talk, you may believe that he had a bad day today. Maybe you think that Klas is not always this vague and unclear and difficult to understand. However, you are wrong. Klas is always this flaky." Then I turned to Klas and said, "You are unique, Klas."

The whole board burst out laughing. Suddenly the voice of an old man materialized from a telephone loudspeaker on the table — one of the board members was obviously in another city. "Yes, I must say that I had difficulty staying awake during that long presentation," the voice said. More laughs. The chairman asked Klas if he had anything to add. Since he didn't, he was asked to leave the room. The laughter continued as the door closed behind him. Nobody asked any intellectual questions — they had found the confidence they needed on some other level.

I felt a combination of victory and failure. TNS had encountered some resistance and found itself in a situation where no standard tools or intellectual arguments or sophisticated attitudes would help. Although the situation wasn't pleasant, it was in a way a useful experience, almost like an initiation rite: a kind of "welcome to reality." Although I don't regret my response — I was fighting for the life of TNS, and I can still think of no option that would have had a better chance of succeeding — I still feel bad about this moment. "The Yes, and Technique" is impressively effective, but there are times when people simply don't want to discover areas of agreement; persisting with it at that point just jeopardizes credibility — there is always a limit.

Two further battles in the early years deserve mention, because they both helped shape my attitude for the future of TNS. The first occurred during the second "Youth Parliament for Protection of the Environment." The students were going to interview the heads of environment from Sweden's parliamentary political parties and broadcast the interviews on TV.

Students — even preschool children — understand and respect that adults have divergent standpoints and values in different matters. But when it comes to the laws of nature and some very basic conclusions from them, it should be possible to reach consensus. Obvious as it may seem, this is not what the Swedish public debate had transmitted to the people at the time. It was rather as if there were different laws of nature, depending on which political party you talked to (something that made the rest of us uneasy). Anyway, this project was intended to change that.

In preparation for the broadcast, I educated the politicians in two consecutive seminars about the main scientific contents of the TNS standpoint thus far (very similar to the information presented in Chapter 4). The idea was to put everyone on the same scientific map. But one of the parties didn't send its representative to these preparatory seminars. On the contrary, the head of environment of this party didn't turn up until it was time for the broadcast. I took him aside and briefed him on what the rest of us had agreed to do: the politicians were going to affirm the agreed-upon laws of nature and state that ecocycles were the fundament for our lives. From there, the interviews were going to explore different political means of integrating societal flows into the cycles of nature. The response I got from the errant politician was, "All the talk about natural cycles has become something of a dogma. And mankind has been forced to abandon many dogmas, including the one about the Earth being flat."

I was so perplexed by his words that I forgot myself and let my debating instincts take over. First of all I put a question to him: "So you mean that if one accepts a generally accepted notion without prior involvement in the idea from a scientific standpoint, this can be counted as a subscribing to a dogma?"

"Precisely," came the reply.

"So you're still keeping an open mind, then? Perhaps the Earth is flat?"

A long silence followed. I kept quiet, not wishing to throw any lifelines to my opponent. When the answer finally came, it was tentative, yet with an attempt at scholarly open-mindedness. Fingertips poised against fingertips, the man replied, "Now that's an interesting question." There was laughter among the people who heard this, and again I felt ashamed of my sense of triumph.

Shortly afterward I realized that we had lost all sense of communication. Any potential for further discussion with this politician, no doubt a man of both talent and influence, had been lost. I had fixed us both into entrenched positions — precisely what The Natural Step culture aims not to do.

The next early battle was a major blow that definitely confronted TNS with crude reality, serving as the most violent rite of initiation to that point. A few months after the "Big Mailing," I was phoned up by a journalist from one of the leading Swedish daily newspapers, *Svenska Dagbladet*. We met, and the journalist posed questions about the financing of the "Big Mailing." I told her about this and how the CEOs had merged forces to support TNS. She asked me about the sum for the mailing but never confronted me with the budget and the reason behind the deficit in it. Quite the contrary, she seemed content with each answer. I was left with a feeling that everything was fine.

A couple of days later, I found myself in the headlines of this paper. Although the article didn't say so explicitly, it implied that I was a cheater with a hidden agenda who had started TNS to make loads of money; the gap in the budget had probably even disappeared into my pockets from our initial project — the "Big Mailing."

On the same day that the paper came out, a radio broadcast on Radio Stockholm tried to protect me. It was said that certainly I was worth some money, considering what I had accomplished, and that it was all because of envy that the journalist didn't want me to make money. The broadcast was well meant, but it didn't particularly make my case any stronger. It's okay to make money if you say that you want to, up front, but you cannot claim to be working only for an ideal at the same time: you have to make up your mind.

My immediate reaction to the article was a desire to fight back — I wanted to phone up the journalist and ask her, "What the hell...." Fortunately, the CEOs of the Arlanda Group invited me to my life's first crisis meeting. One of them hauled up an overhead picture from his briefcase. Its headline read: "The Handling of Mass Media Crises." Underneath were two bullets:

- Don't say a word.
- Put all papers on the table.

I was convinced by very friendly but very firm voices around the table that I was not to say *anything* to journalists. Whatever they asked me, my answer was to be the same: "All papers will be put on the table within a week." Since I didn't say anything but this, and since all the CEOs did the same, there was nothing to write about.

During the week that followed, every bill and every book and every account (even my personal accounts) related to TNS were turned inside out. The Natural Step project — patronized by the Swedish king — certainly deserved certain unusual countermoves at a moment like this. Every supplier to the project kindly opened all their books and accounts, and an independent accountant bureau, headed by one of the highest lawyers in the country, presented a report within a week. The report concluded that not one single crown had disappeared and that the business aspect of TNS had been run in an elegant and cost-efficient way. And no money had been given to me.

It turned out that the journalist had confused "budgetary deficit" with "cash flow problem" and concluded that there was a story to be told. The deficit in the budget existed because one of the firms had not provided the project with the money it had promised at the Arlanda meeting. The bank that handled the money refused to comment when asked about it, claiming confidentiality. The journalist was not convinced there was nothing amiss and decided to take a chance. I had suffered the result.

The end of this story told me that sometimes you end up in situations where neither skilful routines nor smart improvising will be of any help — you simply need good luck. Although the paper had to publish a denial, admitting that it had been wrong, TNS was still short of money to make any substantial follow-up. In fact, we lacked around 12 million crowns ($US 1.6 million). This was a great risk to us, because the "Big Mailing" needed a substantial follow-up to be perceived as serious.

At about this same time (1990), TNS had applied for money from the State's Lottery. Each year in Sweden, the government allowed various idealistic organizations to apply for the proceeds from one of its lotteries, and if you got it, about 10 million crowns ($US 1.3 million) would feed your enterprise. This sum would cover most of our budget deficit, and the stakes were high. However, we were a young organization and the competition was too stiff to give us any hope: a number of altruistic and well-known organizations were our competitors, and I had already heard that the application from TNS was not too convincing. I started to prepare for defeat.

Unbeknownst to us, three ministers had decided to fight for TNS because of the negative newspaper article. They argued that TNS was a grassroots movement at last gathering scientists into a dialog that promised to be meaningful to Swedish society. We had been seriously attacked on false grounds and needed support. The upshot was that 10 million Swedish crowns were handed over through the State's Lottery to TNS.

It was later confirmed that if the newspaper had not attacked us, there was no way we would have been granted the money. Our application to get the lottery was simply not solid enough in itself, but the attack had, in an indirect way, demonstrated the need for an organization of our type. The deficit in our budget was now almost completely covered. And I decided that reality was able to beat fiction any time.

The mental costs of swinging between despair and pride like this were substantial. One day I was in the headlines as a dishonest man with a hidden agenda. The next I was receiving 10 million crowns from the State's Lottery and learning that my work had been named "The Best Social Invention of the Year"[1] And before I knew it, I was attending a private Mass in the Vatican. The Pope questioned me in much the same way as the King of Sweden had once done. I felt slightly dislocated by the whole experience (and for many years had a small crucifix above my bed to prove that it had all been true).

On a personal level, I learned that you cannot make any major impact to change established ideas unless you are prepared to sacrifice your innocence. You can reach far with consensus, and I really believe that consensus provides the main hope for our future. However it's also war out there, and there is only one way to stay alive if you take part in it. Whether you win the battles or not, stay closely linked to those friends and family members who can support you when you are right and, more importantly, correct you when you are wrong and still love you. I honestly don't believe that there is any other way for a normal human being to be a public figure and still maintain his or her personal integrity.

If you don't get substantial help from people who know who you are, and who can bring you down to earth in a loving way, well, before you know it, you don't recognize yourself anymore. Out of exhaustion, the temptation to play roles gets to you: "What did I say last time, when people liked my reply so much?" It's when you start referring to yourself, rather than bringing up authentic materials from your soul, that the dying starts. It must be consciously fought back, and for that your dear ones and close friends are your only allies.

Organizational and personal challenges aside, it was becoming clearer and clearer to me that already existing knowledge really was enough to induce substantial change, and that most people only need to be allowed into the dialog to be prepared to act. The greatest challenge seemed to be how to gather and disseminate knowledge in a relevant and inspiring way — a challenge at least as important as conducting research to acquire new knowledge.

Traditional environmental organizations had done tremendous work in mobilizing people to wake up (and still do). But blaming polluters and expecting environmental pressure groups to do the work on society's behalf wasn't going to be enough. What I had been working with was not necessarily another organization — I had really not planned for TNS to become an organization — but a new mental attitude to complete the work of environmental NGOs. I believe that the simplicity, beauty, and necessity of the TNS idea itself convinced our sponsors and attracted new recruits in a steady stream — people eager to put their competence in service to nature.

CHAPTER 6

THE SYSTEM CONDITIONS
FOR SUSTAINABILITY

THE SCIENTIFIC STORY IN the "Big Mailing" provided a compelling and relevant context for dialog. I lectured about it to larger and larger audiences and introduced it to business corporations outside the Arlanda Group and to municipalities. But the knowledge we had achieved could not be used immediately for operational planning: there was still a huge gap between the overall picture — the "everything-ology" that we had worked with — and the concrete planning that was taking place on Monday morning in the firms I visited. It became more and more obvious that although the story about life can bring soul to sustainable development, sustainable development must take its operational starting point in principles and not from a story — no matter how wonderful and demanding the story may be.

We had a firm scientific foundation on which to build (Chapter 4). What we needed was an overall model of the sustainable society that would be a relevant starting point for planning in business and politics. The question was how to derive one. A collaborative effort by Karl-Erik and me was to provide the answer.

Shortly after I met Karl-Erik and John in Orsa, they discovered that I needed a more subtle understanding of thermodynamics before I would be ready to really apply it. And they, in turn, discovered that they needed a more thorough understanding of the biological conditions for life. As a result, Karl-Erik and I authored and published a scientific article together in the journal *Reviews in Oncology* of which I was then chief editor.[1] We called the article "From Big Bang to Sustainable Societies," and in it we described the scientific creation myth, from Big Bang through physical evolution to biological evolution and eventually to the development of sustainable society from the current non-sustainable one. That article provided us with the raw materials we needed. We came up with a thermodynamic model of the sustainable society that fit into the cycles of nature in an integrated way.

The Sustainable Society

In the sustainable society, flows of matter are balanced or, at least, not systematically unbalanced. Natural cycles surround society and define the limits within which we have to live. The sustainable society lives partly on flows from nature's production and partly on smaller flows of metals and minerals from the Earth's crust. Plants build up enough renewable resources to satisfy their consumption by animals and humans. A proportion of natural resources — atoms dispersed 3.5 billion years ago but now concentrated and structured into what we refer to as meat, fish, timber, pulp, fuels, medicines, and so forth — are guided in an organized way into society. Since (in the sustainable society) the rate of this flow does not exceed the rate of regeneration of resources, it can be regarded as an "interest rate" from nature rather than as a systematic toll from its "capital."

Resources are recycled and used efficiently so that human needs can be fulfilled effectively. Some matter can be brought up from the Earth's crust as resources (from mining and drilling for petroleum, for instance), but most mineral flows are recycled within the society. Some of the flows into society end up as very long-lasting structures, such as buildings (that might be recycled into new buildings). Because of the second law of thermodynamics, such structures also shed considerable flows of corroded and cracked matter back into the ecosystems. These flows of slowly degraded resources are accompanied by some flows that are large (even in a short-term perspective), such as consumed foods and fuels, which quickly end up in nature as building blocks for new resources in primary production: fumes and body waste become new forests and plants and algae and animals. A tiny part of the societal waste can also enter the slow geological sedimentation processes. The atmosphere and waters and soils are thereby kept clean, and at the same time we get a sustainable flow of resources to meet our needs.

Deducing the System Conditions

We now had a model of the sustainable society. TNS produced a scientific consensus document on the societal use of energy (the second after the "Big Mailing"), based on the article I wrote with Karl-Erik, and defended it in a hearing with Swedish parliamentary politicians. Our model, however, lacked the principles that could define the sustainable society. Instead, we had a figure, and flows in this figure, and a long story to explain what those flows meant. It was interesting, but not very helpful. We needed solid and clear principles that could help us to understand the underlying problems behind our current non-sustainability and to envision solutions and futures that would really be sustainable (not just a bit less non-sustainable than what we already had).

I was dumb enough to stare at the model, off and on, for well over a year without seeing how it could help me find first order principles for sustainability. No matter where I started, I ended up in a story of explanations rather than in principles that could be used for planning. In hindsight, I cannot understand why it took so long. Eventually, the obvious loomed out of the mist of traditional thinking: we hadn't needed to talk about sustainability until mankind had started down a non-sustainable path. If destruction was the problem, well, then we should study the principles for that destruction. And rather than go directly from the model into an attempt to define principles for sustainability, it would be more helpful to apply the model to identify basic destructive principles and then define sustainability as "non-non-sustainability."

The strategy recommended itself for at least a couple of reasons. As it is generally easier to destroy something than to build it, principles for destruction should also be easier to determine. Furthermore, such an approach excluded the need to bring in a great number of conditions for sustainability that humanity could not influence and consequently did not need to relate to in this context (the sun, the distance between the sun and the Earth, gravity, the principle of matter conservation, and so on). Thus the solution should be simpler and, at the same time, relevant for decision making.

The connection points between society and ecosystems as represented in the model yielded the principles of destruction. There seemed to be only three basic mechanisms by which human society could damage nature:

1. Nature was damaged if concentrations of substances were continually rising because they were being dispersed outside the Earth's crust faster than they were returned to it (or re-deposited), leading to a net input of elements into the biosphere (elements never break down).

2. Nature was damaged if concentrations of substances produced by society (combinations of elements) were continually rising because the rate at which they were dispersed exceeded the rate at which they could be broken down and built into new resources by nature (or deposited in the Earth's crust).

3. Nature was damaged if the basis for the natural cycles and biological diversity was continuously diminishing through physical means such as extraction or by manipulation of ecosystems. Examples of extraction included such actions as clearcutting timber on too-large areas or catching fish at a faster rate than nature could regenerate them. Ecosystem manipulation included such things as altering the water table, causing soil erosion through poor management of forests and cropland, risking accidental outcomes from the use of genetically modified organisms (GMOs), or covering fertile land with asphalt.

Later it occurred to me that the human brain, programmed to understand basic principles of complex systems, would easily have grasped the preceding principles without the model that we used. It would have been enough just to play around with a bizarre thought experiment.

Suppose that a group of consultants from outer space were called in by humanity to help us destroy the Earth. It would be a natural thing for those consultants to stop by at the moon and get an overview of the system before they decided how to destroy it from within. (Few consultants would start "among the leaves" and dash down to Earth to study details of the possible deleterious effects of anti-flammables, for instance). It wouldn't take them long to come up with the same solid strategies we did using our sustainability model.

First, it would be obvious from the moon that matter could not escape but had to remain and disperse through the biosphere. If people were encouraged to dissipate materials without constraints, then that process could easily be accelerated. And if they could be convinced to go after elements in the Earth's crust that were normally scarce in nature and use them in wasteful ways, then all the better. That way, as with adding more and more ink to a bathtub of water, nature would become "bluer and bluer" with mercury, cadmium, copper, zinc, radioactive isotopes, and so on. It would also be good to arrange for an increase of more abundant elements. But in order to bring about an increase in concentrations of such elements, the Earth's inhabitants should be motivated to bring up large quantities from underground and waste it quickly — burning off large quantities of coal and petroleum daily for years, for instance.

Second, it wouldn't take long to see that producing new compounds would also make the biosphere "bluer." The smartest strategy would be to go for persistent compounds foreign to nature — compounds that nature can neither assimilate into its production nor degrade into compounds that can be assimilated. CFCs, PCB, bromine organic anti-flammables, dioxins.... But large emissions of more abundant compounds such as nitrogen oxides (NO_x) would also do the job.

Third, given how vulnerable the Earth looks from space, it would be immediately obvious that one of the easiest things to do would be to simply remove nature with various tools such as asphalt machines, chainsaws, digging machines, too-large fish boats, and so on.

The consultants wouldn't be very clever unless they also tried to figure out some internal principle in society that could directly hurt its inhabitants, particularly if this principle could at the same time serve as a driver behind the other three mechanisms for destruction. The consultants would soon realize that the ultimate internal principle would simply be for people to waste human resources and avoid taking responsibility for humanity at large. An internal use of resources that was inefficient to meet human needs and inequitable on the global scale could act as a driver of the three ecological mechanisms at the same time as it hampered social sustainability in a more direct way.

Finally, before coming down to Earth to deliver their advice on how to destroy the conditions for life and prosperity, the outer space consultants would zoom in on human societies to see how people were doing on their own. They would be puzzled. Why would they even have been called for? People on Earth seemed to be doing it all themselves.

Sustainability: The Four System Conditions, Objectives, and Practices

Once we had determined the four basic mechanisms by which human society could damage nature, we could define the four system conditions required for sustainability and the objectives and some of the practices that could bring it about. The results were as follows:

SYSTEM CONDITION 1:
In the sustainable society, nature is not subject to systematically increasing concentrations of substances extracted from the Earth's crust.

Ultimate Sustainability Objective for an Individual Organization: "Eliminate our contribution to systematic increases in concentrations from the Earth's crust."

Suggested Practices: Substitute certain minerals that are scarce in nature with others that are more abundant, use all mined materials efficiently, and systematically reduce dependence on fossil fuels.

SYSTEM CONDITION 2:
In the sustainable society, nature is not subject to systematically increasing concentrations of substances produced by society.

Ultimate Sustainability Objective for an Individual Organization: "Eliminate our contribution to systematic increases in concentrations of substances produced by society."

Suggested Practices: Systematically substitute certain persistent and unnatural compounds with ones that are normally abundant or that break down more easily in nature, and use all substances produced by society efficiently.

SYSTEM CONDITION 3:
In the sustainable society, nature is not subject to systematically increasing degradation by physical means.

Ultimate Sustainability Objective for an Individual Organization: "Eliminate our contribution to the systematic physical degradation of nature that we bring about through overharvesting, introductions, and other forms of modification."

Suggested Practices: Draw resources only from well-managed ecosystems, systematically pursue the most productive and efficient use both of those resources and of land, and exercise caution in all kinds of modifications of nature.

SYSTEM CONDITION 4:
In the sustainable society, human needs are met worldwide.

Ultimate Sustainability Objective for an Individual Organization: "Contribute as much as we can to meeting human needs in our society and worldwide, over and above all the substitutions and measures taken in meeting the first three objectives."

As with the other three system conditions, the remedy for the destructive mechanisms of a socially non-sustainable society lies in its opposite: meeting human needs worldwide would counteract the waste of human potential. People actually are quite good at things like staying alive and healthy, and being social and kind — if they only get the chance and are allowed to reflect on and influence their own situation. Culturally we believe that it is much nicer to love people and be fair to them than the opposite. So the fourth system condition for sustainability also happens to be a shared cultural value.

Granted, it will be harder to know whether or not human needs are really being met in an efficient way — harder than to reveal whether or not cadmium compounds are increasing in human bodies and ecosystems, for instance. However, this objective is as relevant as the other three. The difficulty of assessing something does not mean that it is principally wrong or of no practical importance. For pedestrians, looking both ways before crossing the street is a fundamental principle if they want to stay alive, yet the principle is extremely difficult to validate by scientific methods!

Suggested Practices: Use all of our resources efficiently, fairly, and responsibly so that the needs of all people on whom we have an impact now and the future needs of those not yet born stand the best chance of being met.

If the Four System Conditions were met, then we have sustainability. But as long as the system conditions were violated (trunk and branches), we could expect a more and more complicated pathology of effects in nature as well as in society (the foliage). And the problems would grow, spreading locally, regionally, and globally. Eventually, we would reverse the process of evolution.

Our work to this point had in no way been rocket science. Quite the contrary, our long and in-depth considerations had led us to something very simple — in fact it was so simple that we suspected that was why it took so long. Our access to system conditions that didn't overlap but covered relevant aspects of sustainability helped to organize information in a way that was more relevant for decision making. The system conditions were not there instead of any other information but to structure information. Previously we had sought knowledge but had been drowning in information. Structuring the information prevented that and made us see the upstream causes of problems — the relatively few first order mechanisms by which the myriad of problems evolved downstream.

Karl-Erik encouraged me to write a book about The Natural Step and the systems perspective that had evolved after the "Big Mailing." Soon after the book was published, John defended his doctoral dissertation in which he had elaborated the scientific perspective on the same findings. Since then, we have coauthored several scientific articles and have re-written the phrasing of the system conditions several times in order to make them even sharper, less open to misunderstanding, and more hands-on applicable for society and for scientific studies of various problem areas in society.

Applying the System Conditions for Systems Thinking

The system conditions applied to systems thinking enabled a shift in focus: we could look at the upstream causes of environmental problems rather than at its downstream symptoms. The problem with the public debate thus far was not that we had learned about the negative effects in nature and society from our system errors upstream. The problem was that we did so *instead* of drawing the conclusions on the level of principles. This lack of a principle understanding had also seriously affected our authorities and business community. Thus intelligent decision makers had difficulty coming to grips with the situation.

The primary problem with heavy metals (System Condition 1) or persistent compounds foreign to nature (System Condition 2) was not about the exact mechanisms by which they exert their negative effects. The primary problem was that they were allowed to increase in concentration and eventually exceed their ecotoxic thresholds. And the primary problem with allowing ourselves to encroach more and more on our vital life-sustaining resource base (System Condition 3) was not about the exact importance of each lost species or ecological productive unit. Similarly, the primary problem with continuing to spend resources without a perception of the global human situation (System Condition 4) was not about trying to understand all the social problems that will lead to. Unfortunately, however, this was not how the public debate went.

We ought to have been saying that we had failed to ask the right questions about matter from the Earth's crust and that the result was a systematic increase in concentrations of matter from there into the biosphere. Then all the concrete examples of that central problem would have been meaningful and would have stressed the importance of it. But *instead* we only said "greenhouse effect," "sulfuric acid rain," "phosphates in lakes," "heavy metals in sludge," "cadmium in our kidneys," and so on — adding more and more problems from "among the leaves" to the list. In the same way, we didn't say that we had failed to ask relevant questions about chemicals so that the concentration of thousands of them was increasing systematically. *Instead* we said "nitrogen compounds in sea water," "nitrogen acid rain," "ozone depletion," "hormone disrupters," "anti-flammables in our blood," "pesticides from South Asia in Antarctica," and so on and so forth — adding more and more impacts from this principle error to our list of problems. We rarely heard anybody say that we were physically encroaching more and more on the remaining life-supporting systems. *Instead* we said "loss of groundwater reserves," "deforestation," "erosion," "extinction of species," "reduction of fish stock," and "monocultures." Finally we seldom talked about the failure of our time to constitute institutions and measures to efficiently take care of each other and meet human needs worldwide. *Instead* we said "crime," "eco-fugitives," "costs of the UN," "terrorism," "alienation," and "crises on the stock market." Consequently, decision makers based programs for sustainable development on chaotic information about impacts and effects "among the leaves" rather than on an understanding of relatively robust "trunk and branch" principles upon which the details should be projected.

Seen from a solutions perspective, the system conditions could be presented in the following way:

SYSTEM CONDITION 1:

In the sustainable society, nature is not subject to systematically increasing concentrations of substances extracted from the Earth's crust. In a sustainable society, all materials taken from the Earth's crust are handled in such a way that concentrations of metals, minerals, and fossil fuel fumes do not build up in nature. Some metals — the scarce metals that normally occur in very low concentrations in nature — are gradually phased out from large-scale societal use since the probability of rising concentrations of such metals in nature is extremely high. In a sustainable society there is no longer any need for mining or extraction of the kind that has no other purpose than short-term dispersal in society (unlike the current reality with phosphate, for example, or with fossil fuels such as oil and coal). Metals are high-performing resources, but they are also relatively resource demanding — for instance, it requires higher amounts of energy and fossil fuels to mine and refine metals than to recycle scrap. Therefore in a sustainable society, metals are properly recycled.

Nature cannot sustain systematic increases of any substance. Every single atom of mercury, lead, zinc, copper, or coal that we extract from the Earth's crust must end up somewhere. If we continue as before, levels of substances from the Earth's crust will continue to increase. We are currently experiencing, among other effects, rising levels of heavy metals in the soil, phosphate in lakes, sulfuric acid in forests, carbon dioxide in the atmosphere, and cadmium in our kidneys. And metals that are either not recycled or recycled so poorly that they cannot be directly reused for their original purpose add to the rising concentration levels. Complexity and time-lags make it difficult to predict at what stage damage sets in. Each substance has its own limit, but this limit is usually unknown until the damage has actually occurred. Even after we have recognized the problems caused by rising concentrations of substances from the Earth's crust and have cut down levels of extraction from mines, many substances will continue to build up in nature.[2] This is because society has already amassed huge quantities of materials from mines, many of which are not common in nature.

Sustainable options are to switch to renewable fuels and materials such as wood, fibers, ceramics, glass, and so forth. We can also discriminate in favor of metals commonly found in nature. The more common a metal is in nature, the more freely we can use and recycle it without fear of rising concentrations. Aluminum and iron, for instance, are considerably more common in nature than are copper and cadmium. Using such metals efficiently and establishing sophisticated recycling systems are other ways to avoid rising concentrations in nature. Even in a sustainable society, it may be necessary to increase the mining of particular substances in the short term — for example, certain rare metals needed in solar cells (to be recycled later, of course). Long-term effects of such mining would be beneficial, as solar cells reduce the need for nonrenewable fuels.

SYSTEM CONDITION 2:

In the sustainable society, nature is not subject to systematically increasing concentrations of substances produced by society. In a sustainable society we do not manufacture substances, either intentionally or unintentionally, at a faster rate than they can be broken down and integrated into the natural cycles or returned to the Earth's crust. This applies to the manufacture of chemicals, medicines, additives in plastics, and other substances. It also applies to incineration.

Just as with System Condition 1, System Condition 2 puts special emphasis on substances that are unusual in nature or in normal circumstances are not found there at all. These substances must have the ability to break down quickly in nature into substances that are found there. If we have to use a substance that is both non-biodegradable and not common in nature, we have to establish sophisticated methods for preventing its leakage into nature. Many people believe that this is because "artificial" compounds are bad and "natural" compounds are always good and harmless. This is not true, of course — just think about bacterial toxins or venom from snakes, for instance.

The less abundant something is normally in nature, the greater the risk of getting increased concentrations of it as it leaks from society. That potentially creates two problems: first, the bodies of nature (including our own) react to changes of concentrations, not to the absolute amounts of a substance *per se*. And second, if the compound doesn't exist normally in nature, then the risk of eco-toxicity is relatively greater because evolution has had no reason to develop mechanisms to deal with it. We know about several examples of this problem: there are a number of non-biodegradable substances not found in nature, such as chlorofluorocarbons (CFCs), polychlorinated biphenols (PCBs), some pesticides, dioxins, bromide anti-flammables, and chlorinated paraffins.

If we continue as before, levels of substances produced by society will continue to rise. Complexity and time-lags make it difficult to predict at what level damage is caused. Each substance has its own limit, but this limit is often unknown until the damage has already occurred.

Sustainable options include phasing out substances that do not readily biodegrade and are not commonly found in nature. It may also be necessary to control a range of other substances that, even though biodegradable, are nevertheless building up in nature because of excessively high volumes in use. By using substances efficiently and establishing sophisticated recycling systems, the need for substances produced by society will be reduced. Even in a sustainable society, it may be necessary to occasionally use non-biodegradable substances not normally found in nature —for instance, important pharmaceuticals (which can later be recycled from bodily secretions) — though that choice would apply only if there are no better alternatives that are safe to use without constant monitoring.

SYSTEM CONDITION 3:

In the sustainable society, nature is not subject to systematically increasing degradation by physical means. In a sustainable society we do not affect the ecosystems physically in a way that impedes nature's biodiversity or its capacity for production. We live on the "interest" that nature gives us, not its "capital." In a sustainable society there is enough space for animals and plants to live unaffected by human activity. Agriculture and forestry are not practiced in ways that lead to a loss of nutrients, extinction of species, or sinking sub-soil water levels. Nor do we allow more and more roads and construction to displace nature or nature's processes.

Examples of problems are the clearcutting of forests, desertification, loss of nutrients, over-fishing in seas and lakes, damage to sub-soil water flows, mass tourism in pristine areas of nature, and construction of roads and buildings on fertile land.

If we continue as before, nature's capacity will be reduced in functions such as waste processing, the building of resources that society needs, and the provision of a host of "free services" crucial to the survival of life (for instance, clean air and potable water).

Biodiversity must not systematically diminish; diversity is an important defense strategy for nature in the face of change. New species and substances are being discovered every day, and they often offer enormous potential benefits in areas such as medicine, materials technology, and food. Finally, nature with its wonderful diversity of species has a value in its own right — something most people feel instinctively. We have still classified but a small part of the planet's biodiversity and associated functions in nature, and we simply have an ethical obligation to preserve what is there. A true "win-win" situation: what we do to nature we do to ourselves.

Sustainable options are to buy food from farms that grow crops sustainably and obtain raw materials from environmentally managed forestry plantations. By locating new factories on the foundations of old ones and planning all construction with respect for nature, we can minimize our presence in nature. Another sustainable option is to become more efficient — for example, companies can plan strategically to reduce the need for land-consuming, long distance transportation.

SYSTEM CONDITION 4:

In the sustainable society, human needs are met worldwide. In sustainable societies, within the constraints given by the first three system conditions, as much human benefit as possible is created from each thing taken from or released into nature. At the same time, resources are distributed fairly and efficiently enough to ensure that at least the basic human needs are satisfied in all areas of the world.

System Condition 4 has a unique role. It recognizes people's constant striving to improve the ways in which we satisfy both our own needs and those of other people. For companies, this is largely a matter of getting better at giving customers what they want, while using fewer resources. The fourth system condition is in itself basic to sustainable development in a direct way (social sustainability) but it is also a precondition for being able to achieve success with the first three system conditions. Growing social tensions from non-equity and other examples of disrespect for human values hamper our chances to enter a transition to ecological sustainability successfully.

Examples of problems currently associated with System Condition 4 are: the increasing gap between the poor and the rich, famine, the loss of a sense of meaning and of cultural values, alienation, crime, the misdirection of enormous amounts of resources (including time spent in traffic jams and such, instead of working or being with our children), increasing costs to sustain the UN, and on and on.

If we continue as before, wasting human resources on a global scale and failing to implement social sustainability, then it will be difficult or even impossible for mankind to comply with the ecological System Conditions 1 to 3. The loss of cultural meaning will hamper our belief in the future — both rich and poor will suffer from this — and will increase the risk that low expectations will be self-fulfilling.

Sustainable options include various measures to inject human values into everyday business in a very substantial way. Services rather than commodities must be prioritized to identify more efficient ways of meeting human needs on the global level. This means identifying means of selling "light" rather than "kilowatt hours," "cold food at home" rather than "refrigerators," "fast and nutritious food" rather than "hamburgers," and so forth. Furthermore, it means allowing the resources that can be freed by more sophisticated methods to meet the same needs. For instance, allocate the fuels no longer being used in the rich world as a result of smarter ways of doing business to the developing world to meet their justifiable demands to be recruited into the world's economy. The rationale is simple for any firm with global interests — the developing world has tomorrow's neighbors, markets, and partners. Fairness will be an increasingly important component of sustainable businesses.

Humans are social by nature, and fairness is a shared value; it is also a very rational part of System Condition 4 for sustainability. "Fairness" in this context refers to a hypothetical situation in which at least the most basic of human needs are being fulfilled globally. At the moment, 20 percent of the world's people are using more than 80 percent of the resources, while the poorest 20 percent are malnourished and do not have access to safe drinking water. People living in poverty are obviously less able to think about their future or, indeed, about environmental ideas such as the system conditions. Achieving resource savings in specific technical areas or within national borders is therefore never going to be enough. Resource savings must occur globally.

Taken as a whole, the system conditions provided a framework for understanding problems as well as for coming up with solutions. Each of the system conditions led to a number of suggestions of how to change practices. For instance society could substitute metals and compounds (System Conditions 1 and 2), change management routines for fertile areas (System Condition 3), and find new and more subtle ways to satisfy human needs on a higher and wider level (System Condition 4).

These various kinds of informed substitutions — so-called transmaterializations — were all well and good. But the same purpose could be achieved indirectly by decreasing the amount of metals, chemicals, and renewable resources needed for the same human utility — what ecologically oriented literature refers to as "demateriliza-tion." If, for instance, we wanted to decrease the risk of a certain chemical increasing in concentration in nature, we could substitute another chemical in its place that was more biodegradable (transmaterialization) at the same time that we avoided wasting it and recycled it when finished (dematerialization). Thus dematerialization not only complied with ecological constraints (System Conditions 1 to 3) but could also be used to mobilize resource flows for a more equal distribution (System Condition 4).

Thanks to the dialog with all the firms and universities and my peers at TNS, and to Karl-Erik and John who gave us intellectual support and coaching, we were ready to continue the dialog with decision makers. But this time we would be operating from a higher platform of knowledge than had evolved from the "Big Mailing." Our work would eventually lead us to the complete TNS Framework (see Chapter 10) and to a thorough understanding of how this framework related to the work of others (see Appendix 3).

PART THREE

Walking the Talk

CHAPTER 7

IKEA: CREATIVITY AND BOLDNESS

L ENNART DAHLGREN (vice president at IKEA) and Russel Johnson (global head of quality at the same company) approached me in 1990, in the early days, for help in overcoming some resistance they had encountered within their own management team against proactive measures. They had received the "Big Mailing" along with all other Swedes, had asked around, and had gotten the impression that I would be the man to deal with this resistance. The problem was not so much a negative attitude toward sustainability as such but rather the feeling that such issues could hardly be converted in a meaningful way into everyday business practices. A couple of peers felt that sustainable development was an altogether flaky business, but Lennart and Russel doubted that it needed be that way.

I met Lennart and Russel in one of the world's largest IKEA stores — just next to Huddinge Hospital. Even at my first impression, I was surprised about something that later on proved to be an essential part of IKEA's core values. Even though the two represented IKEA at the global top management level, they were still completely open, relaxed, and friendly, and their personal attitudes were free of presumptuousness. Their appearance was "Swedish-normal" — buttoned-down, while professionally focused. I found the combination compelling. To me, they provided an institutional role model for TNS from the beginning. Yet I had no idea how much these two men and their colleagues would mean to me personally, as well as professionally.

They wanted to hear my view on sustainability in firms and how this view had evolved since the "Big Mailing." They also told me about some of their problems — for instance, the "flakiness" label that was attached to sustainable development in business. I don't remember my own answers, but apparently I passed the test. Within a couple of months, I was lecturing the top management team of the IKEA

Group, including the CEO, Anders Moberg, for a full day at the international IKEA headquarters in Humlebeck outside Copenhagen.

I knew that I knew less about furniture than anyone else in IKEA's management team (perhaps the leading team in the world in this field), so humility came naturally to me in this situation. What could I possibly say to these people that would really help them to provide furniture to people sustainably? Now was the moment of truth. This was the first "client" for TNS, and all the thinking and self-convincing talks I had had with my peers were now to be tested in real life. Would the systems perspective be helpful, or would it all end up in embarrassment?

If I failed here, at one of the most successful entrepreneurial Swedish companies of modern time, then the near future for The Natural Step would be much more doubtful. Yet I was more focused than nervous, probably because all the members of the IKEA management team were exhibiting the same relaxed everyday attitude that I had found in Lennart and Russel. Their CEO Anders Moberg, was no exception. It probably also helped that I had told them all, up front, that I needed to learn just as much as they did, and that this was about a serious dialog rather than about teaching. So I talked about systems thinking in general — driving cars and learning a language, and so on (see Chapter 2) — which they were already experts in. I talked about the need for teams to agree on overall principles to be able to perform as well as individuals when it came to systems thinking and systems planning. And I went through evolution, drawing my naïve symbols for the developing species on the white board. I didn't have any professional slides of course, and the latter, Russel and Lennart told me later, may in fact have enhanced the success we were going to celebrate that day. It helped to communicate that we were in this uncertainty together.

After presenting the system conditions, and the need to ask relevant "upstream" questions that were guided by them, I talked about role models and obstacles. The role model is not a firm that takes one large quantum leap to sustainability overnight, I told them. The role model doesn't just sit at a distance and point at the obstacles, saying, "If those obstacles were not there, well, then we would also go in that direction." The role model does what can be done within the given restrictions, moving up to the obstacles so that a momentum in the right direction is created. The more firms that do the same, the harder the pressure on the obstacles. And *vice versa*. If nobody does anything because of the obstacles, nothing happens. That's why role models are essential for society at large.

I gave examples of what I meant by obstacles: that customers to IKEA would not use checklists with system conditions when they were evaluating the money value they got from IKEA; many measures in line with the system conditions would be more expensive; some colleagues within IKEA would provide resistance based on the premises that proactivity is synonymous with "sandals, bikes with flower stickers, and communism" (I could hear laughter here, which was a relief).

In a sort of reverse psychology, I stressed the importance of not neglecting the obstacles. Trying to sweep those under the carpet would be the worst mistake the green movement could make. The reason was simple, I argued. If we succeeded in hiding or diminishing the obstacles and succeeded in making proactive firms more enthusiastic about entering the arena of sustainable development, then eventually they would hit their heads anyway, and we would actually have created a way of getting rid of role models. But if you could see the obstacles clearly, you could approach them gently and start applying some pressure on them in a planned way. And if more role models started doing the same — perhaps by merging forces — the obstacles could be removed.

I thought that my message came through beautifully, but I immediately ran into some resistance. One of the managers reacted with a long and impressive lecture.

> One of IKEA's leading core values is to 'create a better everyday life for the many people.' To that end, our prices — and costs — must be the lowest on the market. You have now told us (he held four angry fingers in the air, one for each system condition) that we are to:
>
> 1. Cease using scarce metals, like lead, in our furniture. And find substitutes for those. And we must recycle the more abundant metals that we keep in our lines, presumably by asking our clients to bring their old furniture for recycling. And we have to cease using petroleum and natural gas as raw materials for plastics, and tell the chemists that we want them to produce plastics from renewables — for instance, charcoal and water. And then happily pay for all these changes.

2. For the same reasons, we are not only going to phase out chemicals that have ended up on the EPA's list, but happily submit ourselves to ask chemists to get rid of all persistent compounds foreign to nature in glues, paints, plastic additives, and so on, and so on. And find good functional substitutes and pay for that as well.

3. And when we buy wood for production of furniture, we have to request sustainable harvesting methods in forestry. Which costs more, of course. And we have to phase out wood from rainforests as long as it is part of deforestation, and find expensive substitutes, for instance, wood from cherry trees. Which will not only be more expensive, but also run into the fourth system condition on the global level, since many poor people in the developing world are surviving from logging in rainforests.

4. We will simply be obliged to help poor people in rainforest areas to establish sustainable forestry, for instance, through plantations. And to help them establish a sustainable society of their own, we need to add social costs to the prices we pay for logging. And here in Sweden, our stores are located far outside of the city nuclei, needing long transports to shuffle furniture between factories and clients, helping to create traffic jams. We would simply need to help clients organize more efficient transports for people as well as goods — perhaps through buses and trucks owned or leased by IKEA.

Who do you think will pay for all this? The EPA? The government? No, it will be the client. So we will be more expensive than our competitors, and if we put this into practice, we will have destroyed our core values. Thank you.

The "thank-you" sank in. Simply not knowing what to say made it easy to remember the "Yes, and Technique": "Yes, I understand your point perfectly well. And I have no idea how to solve it (because I hadn't). And it would be ridiculous for me to stand — a medical doctor — in front of the world's leading team for sales of furniture, and explain how to do business in this arena. I am sorry, but I cannot answer. Is there anyone else?" The "Yes, and Technique," combined with the "Asking Advice Attitude" paid off right away.

Another manager turned directly to his critical colleague, and said: "We only need to develop the sustainable sofa, in small production volumes to begin with, and then have the lowest prices on both alternatives. Later on, when production volumes go up for the new sofa, costs and prices will drop, and the transition is made."

I saw a faint blush on the cheeks of the first manager, because the answer was so simple. And I felt gratitude of course, because a potentially dangerous blind alley turned into a challenging possibility. The open attitude created a very nice response, and all the managers teamed up for proactivity — the people who had served as devil's advocates turned around and declared this openly during the seminar.

A couple of years later, on October 6, 1993, at a business seminar in Stockholm, which TNS organized jointly with *Veckans Affärer* (the largest weekly business journal in Sweden), I heard Ingvar Kamprad, the founder and Chairman of IKEA, say something like, "IKEA plans to introduce furniture in line with the system conditions, step by step, and then to start discouraging the customer from buying the old type of furniture. 'These are the old-timers on their way out,' we'll say, 'but these new lines have qualities that are not only inherent in the furniture, but to our whole habitat. Of course they are a little bit more expensive, but you cannot find them cheaper anywhere else.'"

IKEA implemented the strategy we talked about on that first day of our cooperation. They developed an exclusive line of furniture, the "Gustavian line," which was so exclusive that no customer asked questions about the marginal extra cost for environmental concerns. It was hidden in the exclusiveness. However, the problem was how to communicate this during the transition time. If the customer learned that this and that line of furniture had become very "sustainable," then what were the clients to believe about the other lines? Wouldn't this be counterproductive? Such concerns have led IKEA to complete the strategy of quantum leaps when possible, with small but systematic steps for all the other lines. In fact, the latter has become a relatively stronger strategy over time.

After the initial management seminar was completed, on day two of my trip to IKEA's head office, Lennart and Russel asked how much they owed me. I was embarrassed to talk about money, but managed to say something like, "5,000 crowns or so ($US 600)." When Lennart intervened, "No, no," I continued, "or whatever you think it was worth."

"No," he said, "you don't understand. If you don't charge in a professional manner, you will never be able to pull this off, and TNS will die. You need money if you are to disseminate this dialog and give more people access to it. And if you don't do that, it will be as wasteful as anything you have talked about during this seminar. You must charge us at least 25,000 crowns ($US 3000)."

This conversation was followed up by a harsh letter from Lennart and Russel to the Arlanda Group — the board of TNS. They made it clear to the board that unless they developed a professional business strategy for TNS, they were going to lose its first entrepreneur (me) from burnout.

Since that day, there have been many, many reasons for the rest of the TNS board and me to be grateful to IKEA. Not only because of their protective attitude to TNS and me, but also because of their skilful intellectual partnership and for applying the intellectual achievements in concrete business practice. Their first move was to ask TNS to help them produce teaching material for their own teachers — overheads, materials for break-out sessions, videos, booklets, and so on. Ten years later, about 400 teachers (IKEA managers) applied this material to educate about 50,000 employees around the world.

I started to admire the creativity and boldness that came from the process. The systems perspective had become so much richer with the concrete inputs from IKEA, and it had started to evolve into a sort of overall description to the game called "sustainable development." It started to appear like the text on the box of a family game, and IKEA treated it that way. It turned out to be more fun to play the game now, when the players shared the same idea of what it was all about. Evidently it was more fun to apply the system conditions to tackle problems upstream than to just talk about one problem at a time as if there were no principle connectedness between them. And this shared structuring of thoughts was obviously helpful for community building. More and more exciting examples of this were referred back to me from Russel and Lennart.

One day, for instance, IKEA personnel had built a stage mock-up of a bank inside the Swedish head office in Älmhult, with a sign above the counter explaining what it was all about: "The Bank of Ideas." Personnel dropped ideas into the "bank." In this way, various ideas triggered by the TNS systems perspective, such as new systems for logistics or waste management, as well as for new products, came to the attention of the management. And smart ideas that could be put into early business practices were celebrated and award-ed. Bicycles and even an electric car could be seen among the awards for good ideas. I asked Russel to get a picture of the "bank." The main reason for this, besides using it as an example of a creative atmosphere, was that I liked the sign, "varning för smärtsamma kon-sultförsök" ("warning for painful consultant experiments"). It sim-ply meant that this game — thinking upstream to phase out non-sus-tainable activities — must be played by the firm as a team, and not handed over to consultants.

IKEA produced a booklet named "Trash is cash" that explained that waste equals costs, because it reveals that something is wrong. Why not reduce the waste or use it for something else and reduce costs at the same time? The story behind the booklet deserves to be told. Roger Johansson was the manager of the Gothenburg IKEA ware-house. One day the phone rang in Roger's office, and he heard an upset voice in the other end: "Do you remember the entrepreneur who promised to empty the garbage dumpster twice a week instead of only once a week?"

"Of course I do. It wasn't that long ago."

"Well, anyway, he doesn't do it. So it's now flooded with garbage, which pollutes the parking lot down here, just outside our entrance."

Roger felt his pulse rate and blood pressure rise, and he started to dial the number to the waste management firm. While he was dialing, it struck him that it had taken him only around 30 seconds to end up "among the leaves," downstream, trying to empty the garbage dumpster more often. So he hung up before there was an answer and started to think (which he had promised himself to do). Had he dou-bled the turnover at IKEA in Gothenburg, leading to a correspon-ding doubling of the waste? Unfortunately not. He came up with a better idea than emptying the dumpster more often and phoned up his colleague.

"Turn it upside down," Roger said.

"Excuse me?"

"Turn the dumpster upside down and pour all the garbage out on the parking lot."

"Well, you're the boss...."

Then Roger phoned up middle managers — purchasers and other people who, in different ways, were influencing the material flows at

IKEA — and they all went down to the parking lot to take a walk in the garbage. "Metals, System Condition 1, that could be sold as scrap instead of wasted? The same goes for wallpaper and fine paper: System Condition 3. Waste from our customer restaurant, mixed with chemicals that we have not analyzed with reference to System Condition 2?" and so on and so forth.

The flows were analyzed; some of them could be sold as scrap, others composted. Still others could be reduced by not bringing them in into IKEA's economic domain in the first place. Roger broke the figures down into economic figures: "+" for sales of scrap or a phased-out need to purchase, and "–" for the costs of certain procedures to sort out chemicals (for instance, so that the scrap could be sold). He implemented a sophisticated program for "upstream" waste management, and the booklet "Trash Is Cash" was produced.

The year before Roger implemented this new program, the costs for waste management amounted to 250,000 Swedish Crowns (SEK) ($US 30,000). The year after, they were down to 0 SEK, and the next year gave a profit of 40,000 SEK ($US 5,000). When I told this story the first time in the US, I messed up and said that the name of the booklet was "Cash Is Trash" — something that may have helped spread the misunderstanding that "environment" and "communism" walk hand in hand.

Anyway, IKEA had shown that there is much more to it. And they had started to refine the planning instrument that was based on the system conditions. They realized how important it is not only to critically assess today's flows with regard to the system conditions, but also to critically assess possible solutions in the same way. This was to avoid blind alleys further down the road.

Together with IKEA, by studying the way they were applying the system conditions, we started to develop a more complete framework and a manual to go with it. This manual was later on called "A, B, C, D Analysis" (see Chapter 10).

The methodology by which IKEA introduced their particular brand of low-energy lamps on the market is one example of how to apply the systems conditions for planning. Russel Johnsson, the head of environmental affairs at that time, presented the story.

> Replacing an incandescent lamp with a CFL will produce
> considerable savings in energy consumption and electricity
> costs (roughly a factor of 5) and a considerable increase in

product life (a factor of 8 to10). But the high price has been an obstacle for private households to prove these facts to themselves in practice. The typical price level in Sweden at the time was 120 SEK ($US 15) for an 11W CFL (corresponding to 60W incandescent lamp). The reason for the high price has evidently been that the lamp manufacturing giants have large production facilities for incandescent lamps and don't want to compete with themselves by marketing CFLs at low prices. The problem is even more complex, since CFLs, unlike incandescent lamps, contain mercury.

"The tradeoff problem is among higher use of mercury (System Condition 1), lower expenditure of energy (mainly System Conditions 1 and 2), and higher costs for the lamps lowering their availability to the public (System Condition 4). A more creative methodology than trying to estimate if the impacts outweigh the benefit is to start the planning procedure from a point where the tradeoffs don't exist — backcasting from the system conditions to find a strategy to comply with them [see Chapter 10].

"In short, these were our moves: We identified a producer who could provide a good enough combination of the listed criteria to serve as a platform. We wanted a good reliable CFL lamp with a maximum of three milligrams of mercury. That would be comparable to the requirements in the European Union environmental labeling system for such lamps, which is a maximum of six milligrams of mercury (factor 3). A Chinese manufacturer, outstanding both from product design and production technology points of view, could meet those requirements at the same time that he was competitive enough on price. We let this producer and his competitors know that as long as he was ahead of his competitors on price, energy expenditure, and mercury contents, he would continue to have business with IKEA.

"During the fall of 1997 we started the Swedish marketing campaign of CFLs. It consisted of the following steps, which would take us further in the right direction:
1. Price cuts of one-third for the 11 W (about $US 5) and less than one-half for the other lamp sizes. (In the year 2000,

the price was cut even further — one-tenth of the price in 1997).

2. Cooperation with the largest Swedish environmental organization, The Swedish Society for Nature Conservation (SSNC), around a public information campaign about energy (and cost) saving possibilities for the households.

3. Advertising in all major daily newspapers, offering all households free of charge (during a two-week period) an 11W CFL in IKEA's stores in order to convince themselves that CFL was a very profitable choice for their homes. Somewhere near 600,000 lamps were given away. Sweden's population was about nine million.

4. Before launching the campaign we, together with SSNC technical experts, visited our CFL supplier in China. We met their management and made a thorough review of the factory, with a special focus on the company's environmental management system and practices, work, workers' conditions, and so on. We also visited the supplier's RD&E department and discussed possibilities for further reduction of the mercury content and other potential environmental improvements. We documented our visit on video, and edited videocassettes were later distributed to all IKEA's Swedish stores.

5. We informed customers about the very serious environmental dangers of mercury and offered to take back (free of charge) all their mercury-containing used light sources at IKEA stores. We made a contract with a major recycling company (RagnSells) to take care of all such returned light sources, including all those we generated ourselves in stores, warehouses, and offices. Ninety-eight to 99 percent of the mercury is recovered by a specialist company in Germany. Together with SSNC we made a thorough review of this company also and documented it on the same videocassette we made about China.

"As a result of this campaign, private household sales of CFLs in Sweden increased considerably. The competition had to decrease their prices, and our CFL sales increased. We think that our campaign was good for everybody — for the customers and for the country (we need to save energy in

order to close down nuclear reactors) — except for the manufacturers and importers of incandescent lamps. We
calculated that if every Swedish household replaced 20
pieces of 60W incandescent lamps with 11W CFLs, the
resulting yearly energy savings would equal the production
of one of the Swedish nuclear reactors. Mercury contents are
decreasing systematically, but the goal, of course, is zero
mercury in the lamps."

So, envisioning future success and planning from there is a way of
finding strategies to get there (backcasting: see Chapter 10). IKEA
takes it seriously. One day, when I was going back to the Swedish
head office to deliver a seminar for green managers, I found the roof
and the front wall of the Swedish head office's main building covered in photovoltaics. This shows employees in a concrete way that
what we are heading for is not edible roots in cages, but something
that can look more sophisticated than we have today. In Ingvar
Kamprad's words: 'Most things still remain to be done: a glorious
future.'"

In 1996, TNS invited Swedish Prime Minister Ingvar Carlsson to a
meeting with a number of CEOs and other managers who had gar-
nered experience of the TNS framework in their businesses —
Electrolux, Scandic Hotels, Swedish McDonald's, Hemköp and KF,
JM construction, and The Swedish Farmers' Federation. The meeting
was at Electrolux, and its host was its CEO, Leif Johansson. After an
initial presentation of the TNS systems perspective and how this was
applied in business, Ingvar Carlsson asked the managers around the
table how deep was the conviction of their respective companies. The
vice president of IKEA, Lennart Dahlgren, responded: "If the management of IKEA would try to cut down on environmental ambitions,
we would be run over by our own employees and face a revolution —
it has become that deeply inherent in the way we think." Though I
was doubtful — leadership and systems thinking within the firm can
disappear much faster than it takes to build it — I was grateful for
Lennart's devotion.

So, the initial dialog with IKEA expanded to more and more companies and was further developed in cooperation with them.
Together, we had discovered how non-overlapping principles for successful planning in any complex system could be elaborated into a

concrete framework for decision making. Before going into more detail, let us look at a few more examples of the same kind of thinking.

CHAPTER 8

SCANDIC AND SÅNGA SÄBY:
TEST PILOTS FOR SUSTAINABILITY

SCANDIC HOTELS IS THE LARGEST hotel chain in Northern Europe. In the early '90s, it had suffered from weak core values, had lost confidence in what they were doing, was at the edge of bankruptcy, and had fired the previous management team. The new executive, Roland Nilsson and his close peer Ola Ivarsson, head of purchasing and head of environment (an interesting combination for "upstream thinkers") had decided to change Scandic Hotels.

The previous mixture of luxury and medium-class hotels did not present the image of a focused and well thought through business idea. Roland felt that the quality of service was key, and that this quality must be built on some deeper values that didn't exist in the firm at the time. Not even the sumptuous and sterile luxury of their finest hotels could substitute for good core values. The atmosphere, which was going to be achieved with better training, needed to be more home-like and modest. Scandic was going to be transformed into the "IKEA of hotels," and the overall guiding spirit was to communicate *"värdegemenskap"* — shared values with the customers.

After a management seminar with TNS, Roland and Ola decided that TNS's non-prescriptive focus on principles, in combination with the support of individual creativity, provided an excellent tool for the creation of community building and teamwork. Furthermore, TNS's focus on sustainability —the strongest long-term trend — was complying with Scandic's ideas of "sharing the customers' values."

Our experience with IKEA helped us to serve Scandic with a somewhat higher level of professionalism and speed. This, combined with Roland's and Ola's passion to transform Scandic's problems and the personnel's happy relief at the challenging new atmosphere, created a pace of transition that I didn't believe was possible.

Our presentation to the management team was in February 1992. Teaching material, based on the TNS systems perspective, was ready in May. By August, all several thousand employees had gone through the training. And in November, still within the first year of cooperation with TNS, Scandic had launched 1,500 measures in line with the TNS Framework — measures that were invented by Scandic personnel. Those measures had potential for further development (that is, were not early steps into blind alleys) and also were all "low-hanging fruit" — they brought money into the process through various kinds of savings (see Chapter 10).

All new Scandic hotel rooms were built in line with the TNS Framework. For instance, Scandic changed from PVC to wood on walls and floors in order to comply with System Conditions 1 and 2. On the floor, the switch also saved resources that could be used in better ways for the service of guests, since a wooden floor could be sanded several times and required fewer chemicals to clean and maintain (System Condition 4). They also used wooden furniture.

Ola had consciously played the game "sustainable development" with the system conditions as guiding principles. After educating the personnel in the systems perspective, he encouraged individual creativity that could be triggered from the principle understanding. Information structures had been created by which the management team could learn about the good ideas that evolved.

Ideas were disseminated by various means — in newsletters, competitions, awards, celebrations, and through the creation of organizational structures for follow-up. Ola thanked the personnel for all the ideas that had been implemented and that everybody could see at the hotel: new materials, new chemicals, low-energy lamps, a device to turn off lights when nobody was in the room, a dispenser system for soap and shampoo, new transport routines, new purchase routines, and so on.

At the same time, the "too-high-hanging fruit" (see Chapter 10) was also explained: "These suggested measures are too expensive to be launched within such a short time, but we haven't forgotten them. This is the list." One year later, 500 measures from this list had been launched. Ola calculated profits from everything possible — mainly savings on energy and chemicals. In addition, a number of firms started holding their conferences at Scandic, based on the "shared value" spirit.

Ola was a tough negotiator. His job as head of purchasing was tailor-made for applying the TNS "upstream" perspective. One of his first moves was to change the routine for the purchase of laundry and dishwashing chemicals, such as detergents. "What gets in, gets out," he said, "so let's focus on what gets in." At the time, traditional counterarguments for "green" chemicals were that they were more expensive and sometimes didn't work as well.

Ola looked into the current routine and found a pronounced diversity among Scandic's different hotels regarding all the different brands of chemicals that they used. If he considered high-quality "green" chemicals that also had relatively low prices and then calculated the mean cost if they were to be used at all Scandic Hotels, that mean cost would be slightly lower than the actual mean cost for all the diverse chemicals they were currently using. The reason for this was simple: several of the "non-green" chemicals were quite expensive — the poor performance with regard to the system conditions was not always compensated for by a low price.

Ola's discovery led to yet another opportunity: through joint purchases of the most price-worthy green line of chemicals from all hotels, the costs could be reduced even further. It was true that Scandic could have applied the same strategy to purchase the single lowest-cost chemicals on the market, and saved even more in the short term. But this would, in the longer term, cost more in internal as well as external contradictions, since it would fly in the face of the new core values. So the relative improvement in costs as well as in total quality could be celebrated and used as encouragement to discover more of the same.

Another example of creativity came from Ola's negotiations with Tvätman, the company that took care of Scandic's laundry.

"We don't want you to use any persistent unnatural chemicals when you wash our laundry," Ola told them.

"Don't worry," they said, "we have taken the TNS training as well, and the work is already done."

"Then we want you to phase out whiteners as well as bleaches from the washing powder you use," Ola said.

"But our whiteners and bleaches are not a problem with regard to System Condition 2, as they are not persistent and foreign to nature," countered Tvätman.

"Yes," said Ola, "but we think that there is a conflict with the fourth principle, since they are probably unnecessary and hence the resources could be used in a better way for our guests."

"But if we delete whiteners as well as bleaches," Tvätman said, "your linen will turn grayish over time. Let's at least try to delete them one at a time."

"No, we want to take the whole step right away," Ola persisted. "We don't believe that our guests will carry sheets with them from home and hold them up against our sheets at the hotel to compare the whiteness. People probably want the sheets to look fresh, smell fresh, and be clean. And that's enough."

"Well, let's try," Tvätman conceded, "but the cost will be somewhat higher."

"No," said Ola, "we want you to apply the same washing methods as before but without whiteners and bleaches — we expect a lower cost."

The change in the washing routine was made. What happened? After several years, not one single guest has made any complaints!

By the year 2000, Scandic was doing very well economically and showed no signs of declining. The TNS systems perspective was communicated internally as well as externally. Hotel guests could read about the system conditions in their hotel rooms, and in some hotels, the framework was even displayed at the reception counter. "Our long-term goal is to phase out all contributions to the violation of the system conditions; we have taken these measures already, are working with these things now, and will do these things later."

Scandic also entered the Stockholm stock market and started to expand through purchase and cooperation with other hotels (for instance, it purchased the Finnish hotel chain Arctia), and in the year 2001, Scandic — now a comet amongst Swedish public companies — was purchased by Hilton. In one way this could be promising, since it opens up opportunities to spread the systems perspective to more hotels. On the other hand, there is also a threat, of course.

What will happen in the long run if business expands beyond the "human" perspectives, and if the driver of business is short-term stock share values rather than core values? Will it be possible to maintain the atmosphere of "shared values with the customer" that made Scandic into what it was in the early days of the new millennium? Nobody knows, of course. If they succeed, the good and educative atmosphere might find an even wider market. Roland and Ola are probably the men to pull it off, but they have also told me that "sometimes it is more difficult outside of Scandic, and it doesn't happen by itself." Afterward, when you have partnered long enough with friends on the barricades, you start to worry and take on a personal feeling of responsibility.

There is a conference hotel outside of Stockholm, Sånga-Säby Courses and Conferences. It is the champion in the world when it comes to sustainable development in hotels. Sånga is owned by the Swedish Farmers' Federation, another organization that works with the TNS systems perspective. The pattern of their process was almost identical to that of Scandic's. The business was so lousy a few years ago that the Farmers Federation was considering closing the facility down. The competition in this field of business is extremely tough in Sweden — there are almost as many hotel beds in conference hotels as there are Swedes. A new management team was employed, and Mats Fack, CEO with his close colleague Jimmy Sjöblom, head of environmental affairs, transformed the firm within a couple of years. The core value that was to provide the competitive edge was plain sustainability awareness. They were simply going to become the best in this arena.

The TNS Framework was made a part of the community process, and the employees were educated and trusted to come up with the solutions themselves. Mats and Jimmy didn't want the personnel to come up only with solutions but also with ways to monitor the progress with reference to the system conditions. How could this or that unwanted flow be measured, for instance, and what would be the ultimate indicator to demonstrate its systematic phase-out of it? According to Jimmy, the critical flows with reference to the system conditions will be measured if the person in charge of the respective flows — for instance, purchasers who buy items containing unnecessary heavy metals or persistent compounds foreign to nature — is designing the methods for the monitoring.

Jimmy's and Mats's own work also became much more pleasant. Rather than chasing people and controlling them, the two served as sounding boards for suggestions and then received clear and comprehensible figures to be collected into the annual environmental report. This report displayed the relevant indicators for each system condition at Sånga, and demonstrated how much the organization had approached compliance with the systems conditions.

Today, renewable energy is running the whole facility. Energy is saved through heat pumps, good insulation, sensors that turn the lights off if nobody is in the room, and so forth (mainly System Conditions 1 and 2). Persistent compounds foreign to nature are phased out from the chemicals used (System Condition 2). Even the wood for the latest hotel building on the facility is FSC-labeled,[1] and the purchase of food is made from farms with proactive management (mainly System Condition 3). Waste is sorted, and the non-sorted waste currently amounts to 98 grams (3-1/2 ounces) per person per hotel night, to be further reduced to zero according to Mats (System Conditions 1 to 3).

In 1998, Sånga had much proof of their success. Business was going very well, and the personnel were proud to work at Sånga. They had received the first ISO 14001 certificate among hotels, had been awarded the first "Nordic Swan" symbol among hotels (a Nordic eco-label for environmental performance), and, finally had been awarded "Worlds Champion" of green management by the international GREEN GLOBE.

Although Scandic and Sånga are in the same market in principle, they are not competing for the same customers. Sånga attracts people who want to enjoy calmness surrounded by nature during conferences that last long enough to allow this to happen. Scandic attracts anyone who needs a hotel, as well as business people who want to run effective conference agendas without necessarily changing the big city pace. Yet, the two hotels — sharing the same "language" for sustainable development — are highly aware of each other. Sånga, with its small scale and relatively higher "mobility," is the aggressive test pilot whereas Scandic checks out how things can be run on a larger industrial scale. Both hotels feel that the TNS Framework has been essential as a shared mental model for community building and teamwork.

CHAPTER 9

ICA/ELECTROLUX:
TRENDSETTING TEAMWORK

T HE ICA CHAIN OF STORES (one of the three leading supermarket chains in Sweden) and their suppliers had suddenly come to realize that they had been running "into the walls of the funnel" for a considerable period of time. Along with other players in the market, ICA had contributed to society's violation of System Condition 2 through the use of CFCs in their refrigerators and freezers, both as a coolant and as an insulating material. "Farther out in the foliage," the problem manifested itself in damage done to the ozone layer once CFCs leaked out (everything disperses but nothing disappears) and found their way into the stratosphere. It was now an urgent matter for ICA to clean up its operation in head-to-head competition with the rest of the food retailing sector. With an increasing number of alarming reports in the national press, the problem was being recognized as acute.

ICA plunged head over heels into a solution: an investment of at least one billion SEK (about $US 125 million) in refrigeration technology produced by Electrolux — a cooling system based on HCFCs, both in coolants and in insulation. This was a prime case of problem solving at the "foliage" level. While HCFCs are certainly less damaging to the ozone layer, they nevertheless directly contravene System Condition 2: being long-lived and synthetic, HCFCs would increase in concentration in the atmosphere, just like CFCs, if they were to be applied on a large scale.

Yet, for ICA there seemed to be no other solution. CFCs and the damage they were doing to the ozone layer was an acute problem. Because ICA's management had been trained in TNS systems thinking, they wanted the additional benefit of a Natural Step seminar. This event served as an interesting pilot project in the Swedish marketplace, and "everybody" was there — representatives from the Swedish Society for Nature Conservation, Swedish EPA, and The Swedish Association of Refrigeration. And, of course since it was about a business deal in the 1 billion SEK range ($US125 million), the ICA board was there. Electrolux had sent two representatives who were perceived to be knowledgeable on coolants.

After a thorough review of the TNS Framework, the speaker gave way, and Rolf-Erik Hjertberg, Chairman of ICA, began by directing the following question at the two Electrolux representatives. "Does the use of HCFCs contravene System Condition 2, or is it the case that HCFCs or degraded components of it can be used as building blocks in natural cycles?"

The answer from Electrolux came from out in "the foliage." "The whole point about HCFCs is that they contain substantially fewer chlorine atoms and hence are far less damaging to the ozone layer."

But Hjertberg was not about to give in without a fight: "That was not my question. I wanted to know whether HCFCs will accumulate in the ecosystem just like CFCs, so that one day levels will approach currently unknown tolerance levels that should not be exceeded in the atmosphere?"

Another "foliage" comment was offered as an answer: "Obviously the technical systems have to be sealed so that they don't leak."

ICA's Chairman did not quite see it this way: "But wasn't that also the case with CFCs currently being used?" (Everything has a tendency to disperse, and the real question was whether HCFCs after their dispersal could be processed in the ecosystem or if they were going to accumulate and throw a spanner in the works as CFCs had done.)

At this point, a representative from the Swedish Society for Nature Conservation contributed to the dialog with the following remark: "We already know about one problem with HCFCs — they are greenhouse gases and will exacerbate the problem as long as they continue to be used. This shortcoming has been recognized by their manufacturer, Dupont, and the decision has already been made to withdraw them from production in the future."

It was now becoming apparent to ICA's management that HCFCs were about to follow the same route taken by CFCs in the 1980s. In practice, society had accumulated an enormous debt from CFCs, which were now slowly leaking from refrigerators and other equipment lying disused in dumps. No one could even say with conviction that "things have gone well up until now." Production schedules for CFCs were systematically being shortened from year to year. Originally scheduled to be phased out a few years into the next millennium, at the 1991 Copenhagen Agreement it was declared that CFCs had to be axed immediately, as the ozone problem had become acute.

An investment in HCFCs, which contravene System Condition 2, would have coupled ICA to an unsatisfactory technology with a limited shelf-life. ICA felt that the gigantic task before them was now to woo more than 2,600 shops (many of them small and with low profit margins) away from CFCs and to look for ways to avoid the path of HCFCs (which some 150 shops had already been advised to adopt).

Certainly there is no official committee prepared to take the rap for economic hardships suffered by companies that make mistakes in their planning, and obviously it is wholly misguided to invest in outmoded legislation or obsolete market forces. ICA's management came to an immediate decision not to repeat the same mistake, preferring to revise their strategy and make different choices in their action plan.

I noted a clear irritation on the part of the ICA management that they had already advised some of their shops to make costly investments in a technology with no future — one that had no justification whatsoever in terms of the recently discovered TNS framework. They were frustrated at being in the hands of a small group of multinational refrigeration experts, who had persistently put ecologically ludicrous substances into the market.

To get away from their most serious short-term problems and work toward full compliance with the system conditions was neither an easy nor a cheap road for ICA. Yet there was no hesitation in their decision. What follow are the general step-by-step measures developed through backcasting from the TNS framework and outlined by the ICA management. They were communicated both internally in the organization and outward to heighten public awareness.

- Seal all refrigeration facilities;
- Change to HCFCs in existing systems only in cases where there is no other alternative;
- Change to non-CFC gas in existing systems, but view even these as transitional solutions as long as they are not compatible with the TNS Framework. Substitute the refrigeration/freezing systems and examine the possibilities of using ammonia and other systems consistent with ecocyclic principles; and

- Change to an entirely new method of food preservation if solutions were not ultimately satisfactory.

ICA management charged their technical attachés with watching international events. An intiative was made to hold an international conference, and a network was established within the food retailing sector to stay abreast of the latest technological advances. Above all, ICA prioritized their resources first to evaluate and then proceed with CFC substitution. They did so more quickly than anyone else in their business. For ICA, the acute problem of CFCs (a major "foliage" problem) led to the development of an entire action program in accordance with the TNS Framework. There was never a question of "foliage" solutions — they were always fully aware of the "trunk," or basic issues.

During this whole exchange, The Natural Step was obviously in danger of becoming a bad guy in the eyes of Electrolux. However, their reaction was quite the opposite of what we had feared. In fact, Electrolux was now also feeling that they had run "straight into the walls of the funnel," and this feeling was intensified when Greenpeace publicly dumped CFC-based refrigerators outside the main entrance to the company's headquarters only a few weeks later.

The Natural Step had not tried to influence or lobby ICA in any way. What we had done, in effect, was to provide the intellectual tools required for a thoughtful response and some help with the later planning work. All the rest, and certainly the very competent decision to proceed, came from ICA.

Before very long, Electrolux management was showing us that they, too, were made of sterner stuff than some might think. Gustaf Uggla, the corporation's public relations manager, arranged for me to meet the production chief of white goods to discuss the system conditions with him. This first meeting was so positive that they contacted me again, and this time invited me to meet the management. On this second occasion, the company's managing director was there, as were technical development and marketing and public relations people. We proceeded as in the meeting with ICA's managers — that is, we outlined the planning instrument and thereafter left the discussion completely open.

As always, discussions began "in the foliage": "You see, Electrolux uses a technique during the application of insulation layers that gives our refrigerators better insulation properties than any of our competitors," one of the technicians told me. "Because of this, our refrigerators use less energy than theirs. And this is in spite of the fact that as early as 1989, we took the first steps to phase out CFCs by reducing the CFC component in insulation layers by 50 percent. You are obviously aware of the fact that energy is largely generated by the burning of fossil fuels, which causes a global net increase in greenhouse gases. So the superior insulating properties in Electrolux refrigerators is a positive factor in the whole greenhouse problem, not a negative factor as indicated by that woman from EPA who attended the seminar."

I answered as follows: "So you mean we simply have to take the rough with the smooth? By flying in the face of System Condition 2 you comply with System Condition 1?"

"Yes," the technician said, "but there is an even more decisive factor. The major environmental impact of a refrigerator is not during its manufacture, because we only produce each fridge once, but during its long period of use when it is continually using energy — day in and day out for years."

This was logical and could have been confirmed by any life cycle assessment. However, the argument did not provide any kind of hope for the future, so I simply pointed to the picture of the framework that was attached to the wall and said: "It sounds very good that you have full control of today's situation. But then what?"

What do you mean, 'then what'?" he asked.

"Well, applying backcasting, HCFCs will probably not be in the picture once the Electrolux of the future has developed refrigerators that comply with the system conditions. This compels us to pose the obvious question: what in present-day Electrolux planning will facilitate the phasing out of HCFCs tomorrow? Aren't you investing quite heavily in HCFC technology?"

A long silence followed this, after which a question was put in return to me: "Do you think it's easy making refrigerators?"

Of course I swore on my life that such a thought would never have occurred to me, and I assured them that I had the greatest respect for their competence and for the thorny nature of the problem.

A week later I was once again contacted by the public relations director, Gustaf Uggla, who briefed me on the feedback from the meeting and told me about the proposals that were now being tabled. Apparently during earlier research and development in the 1980s and early 1990s, Electrolux had identified what equipment and investments would be needed to change from CFCs via HCFC to a completely CFC-free substance known as R134a. Now the management team had come to a new decision regarding their white goods. In forthcoming structural reforms, they would pass over the HCFC stage and go directly for R134a in the compressor and later to pentane in the insulation layer. During the transitional phase, Electrolux would use R134a in their manufacturing process.

Gustav Uggla explained this to me on the phone: "Through the childishly easy-to-understand TNS Framework, we have resolved a two-year-old in-house fight at Electrolux. We are still talking about a substance which is long-lived and unnatural and which therefore contravenes System Condition 2. However, this move does tackle the acute ozone problem because R134a is entirely free of chlorine. Furthermore, it sits comfortably in the action program because, technically and economically, it facilitates the next developmental phase, which will use isobutane mixtures as cooling agents. Insulation will be achieved by the use of pentane. In other words, Electrolux has put forward a plan which phases out all long-lived and unnatural synthetics. In the production volumes currently being projected, there will be no build-up of isobutane and pentane in the ecosystem. Nor will Electrolux need to use raw material resources in future production. Even the metal in Electrolux's refrigerators will be incorporated into technical cycles, and because the company plans to introduce more compact infrastructure by fostering local flows between customers and recycling factories, the company, in effect, will have formed a plan that integrates its whole refrigerator manufacturing process within the TNS Framework."

I wondered why Electrolux wouldn't simply bypass R134a and go straight to isobutane. The reason was that some problems remained before the butane mixture in the coolant could be made safe (the gas is explosive). And if eco-labeled Electrolux fridges were ever to start exploding in the faces of their customers, then the company could hardly be said to have encouraged a brisk development toward an environmentally friendly white goods market!

I was proud of the Electrolux management for quickly setting out on a new course, and my suggestion that Electrolux should be named Winner of that year's Natural Step Environment Prize won swift approval. They received the award on Swedish TV.

A few months later, CFCs disappeared from all coolants in Electrolux's new refrigerators. Within another six months, the first insulation layers were manufactured by pentane blowing, making Electrolux the first large white goods manufacturer to market entirely freon-free refrigerators/freezers.

Because the compass course had been properly set, Electrolux had actually been able to go faster and eventually overtake its own goals on the journey. And the changes at Electrolux put pressure on all of its major competitors to follow its lead. Electrolux was a company that had set a truly good example.

CHAPTER 10

THE TNS FRAMEWORK
(A, B, C, D ANALYSIS)

THE EARLY BUSINESS EXPERIENCES, such as the way IKEA used their newly acquired systems perspective, had revealed some very concrete benefits from being able to define the endpoint of planning (sustainability) on the principle level. If such principles were to be met, it would be rational to understand current problems from that particular perspective. That way people could discover the root causes of problems and not just the symptoms associated with non-sustainable activities. As IKEA discovered, the main problem with PCB was not the exact mechanisms by which it hampered the reproductive ability of marine mammals, for example. The problem, rather, was that PCB was inherently linked to a much more fundamental problem that preceded its toxic effects: it was tailor-made to increase in concentration in the biosphere as long as it was used on a large scale in society. (Matter has a tendency to disperse, but doesn't disappear. PCB is foreign to nature, so it is not used in natural cycles; it has base-line levels that normally equal zero; and it is persistent, so it doesn't degrade. Furthermore, its eco-toxic thresholds could not be foreseen due to complexity.)

Understanding at the level of principle, then, makes it possible to not only phase out persistent unnatural compounds with known deleterious effects. It also makes it possible to design a policy to phase out *all* persistent unnatural compounds that are not safeguarded in very rigorous technical systems. And even more importantly, when new compounds are substituted for old ones, previous principle mistakes can be avoided.

Planning ahead from a starting point of success in the future is called "backcasting." The term, coined by Dr. Robinson at the University of British Columbia , simply refers to "looking back from

101

the future." I am often asked whether it is always easy to determine if something is completely foreign to nature or to draw the exact line for "persistence." The answer is No, of course, but the principle is relevant in spite of that. Furthermore it puts the burden of proof on the manufacturer, not on Greenpeace or anyone else. I believe that in the future, chemists will be a proud professional group who won't dream of suggesting the launch of new compounds into the market without having crystal-clear views on these aspects.

Forecasting

The most common way of planning is to look in the rear view mirror, analyze what is happening in the present, and try to remedy perceived problems in the future. We call this "forecasting." As a planning technique, projecting the present into the future has many disadvantages. Perhaps its most crucial flaw is that whatever seems important in the present comes to define the future. Traditional planning is planning according to prevailing conditions. In practice, this means that planning strategies will be based on present-day tax levels, present-day costs for sustainable technology, present-day fuels, and present-day energy systems. This is particularly risky because many of the trends are the main drivers of the problems. Thus, we risk taking today's problems into the future.

Backcasting

Firms such as IKEA and Scandic discovered that when the Natural Step Framework was used, operations could be specified with the help of a "future perspective." To begin with, they envisaged a successful result in the future. Then they asked what they could do today to reach that goal?

Backcasting is especially effective if there is a high level of complexity, a pressing need for fundamental change, or if dominant trends are part of the problem.[1] As all three of these are currently very much in evidence, backcasting can play a useful role in planning for a sustainable future.

When I was contemplating all the smart ideas that employees at IKEA and Scandic developed from the idea of complying with the system conditions in the future, it struck me that individuals apply backcasting from principles all the time and are generally very clever at it. Let's say that a family was going to move from Chicago into a new house in Miami, because the family members had found new jobs there. Moving the household is in fact a complex project, with many details that must be aligned within a set of guiding principles. First the new house must be located in a place that makes it possible for the family members to get to their jobs and back. Second they must be able to afford the new living quarters. Third it must meet certain individual minimum requirements (number of bedrooms, for example). Fourth the house itself must meet certain overall demands (provide a decent and safe enough indoor environment).

The four principles are functionally different, and to be successful the family must plan from a backcasting perspective where all the principles are met. They would have to decide how to make all details in the planning coherent with those principles. The first principle, for instance, could be met with public transport (which might limit which areas to live in) or with one or more cars (which expands the possible area but may negatively influence the second principle. That in turn may alter the options for meeting the third and fourth principles.) If the family is not aware of the principles of the project and not clever enough to organize the details in a dynamic way so that they fit all principles, they might end up in a castle in New Jersey they can't afford, trying to figure out what went wrong. This generally doesn't happen when individuals are planning their own lives, because individuals are clever in systems planning and because the consequences of failure are often very direct. (And besides, there is no one else to blame!)

The first step in the planning process for a firm that wants to enter a process of sustainable development is to design the overall objectives for the firm. This is done as a "translation process" that moves from the system conditions for sustainability in the whole biosphere to the objectives of the individual firm (see Chapter 6). An important point is that the objectives and guidelines can then be the same for all firms, including suppliers, clients, and partners. All firms can have a "shared language" by which to support each other's transition. The ultimate objective of any firm is to not contribute to the violation of the system conditions.

The way that shared language could change the thinking of decision makers was fascinating to study in itself and provided more and more essential material for the endless dialog I had with John Holmberg. We didn't just "think" to describe essential elements of sustainable development; we were obsessed by the idea of studying thinking as such —

considering it from a point outside of the thinking. In this way the "TNS language for sustainable development" developed and became richer. The way smart strategists think can be structured as something John and I named the "A, B, C, D Analysis."

A, B, C, D Analysis

The TNS Framework seemed to allow teams to appear as even smarter than individuals when it came to systems planning (see Chapter 2). Using the shared framework of future success principles (the system conditions), teams came up with solutions — steps that moved as clearly in the right direction as was typical for individual planners. At TNS we studied the teamwork and came up with a model that described what took place. Think of it as the manual for the TNS Framework, or the text on the box of the family game "sustainable development," describing the principles of success and a strategy to comply with those principles.

A. Sharing the Natural Step Framework

Discuss the framework among all participants. Discuss the funnel, the mechanisms by which firms that hit its walls may suffer economic consequences, the system conditions that define the opening of the funnel, and the self-benefit that lies in strategies to avoid the walls.

B. How does the organization look today?

Analyze current operations in relation to the system conditions with the help of an environmental review. Map out flows of raw materials and energy that are critical with reference to the system conditions. By attacking the root causes, it ought to be possible for smart decision makers in business and politics to prevent damage before it has even happened. This could occur by asking smarter questions, guided by the system conditions. Rather than only asking questions such as, "Do we emit greenhouse gases or toxic metals or CFCs" and "Do we buy wood from rainforests," etc., it seems relevant to ask questions like, "Are we dependent on buying anything from the Earth's crust? If so, are we going to use that material to build up technical structures that we will hand over to our children? Or is the reason for the mining that we need to cover losses of those materials? Are those materials scarce or abundant in nature, and how does that influence our policy as regards the full life cycle of the materials?

"Are we dependent on buying or producing chemicals that are persistent and foreign to nature? If so, how are those compounds safeguarded so that they cannot leak out into nature (a demanding task in consideration of the second law of thermodynamics)? Are we emitting naturally occurring chemicals that are increasing in concentration in nature due to very large societal emissions?

"Are we dependent on buying renewable materials from suppliers that don't take care of their ecosystems and that don't have management systems for that purpose? Are we expanding our needs for land-consuming road transports that could be exchanged for other business strategies such as licensing?

"Are we dependent on any activities that don't put our clients, personnel, and humanity at large, in focus? Are we fair, also, to suppliers who perhaps live in developing parts of the world? Are there competitors who are learning how to meet the same human needs in much smarter and less resource-demanding ways than we do at present?"

Questions of this kind, organized in line with the system conditions, lead to a list of flows and activities that are critical with reference to the system conditions. At this point, smart indicators to determine these flows are also considered, as well as people who are primarily responsible for the flows, and who can, consequently, directly influence the future in these respects. In addition, when tools are selected and designed, backcasting from the system conditions should be done (see Appendix 3): "If in the future we are going to comply with the system conditions, how shall we select and design tools to monitor a phase-out of our critical flows, and help us get there?"

C. How does the organization look in a sustainable society?

Using the application of the system conditions, analyze how operations will look in a sustainable society. The creative process of identifying the critical problems in today's activities — the "B-list" — triggers creativity for identifying solutions. The process is run as a traditional brainstorming session, where it is forbidden to criticize each other with comments such as, "That solution only works in other cultures," or "That is unrealistic since it is too expensive," and so on. As long as something is a theoretically possible solution to the problems in B, it should be made part of the C-list. There are no restrictions at this point other than the system conditions. The same framework is applied when it comes to solutions as to the identification of problems.

D. Solutions from the C-list are prioritized into an early activity program for change.

There are three criteria by which solutions with high priority are selected. The criteria are investigated by three questions:

- **Direction.** Does the measure go in the right direction — that is, is it helpful in reducing the firm's contribution to societal violation of the system conditions? Since this is the lens through which the C-list is produced, this only means that the measure is critically assessed once more — in relation to all System Conditions — before being actually decided.

- **Platform.** Is the measure technically flexible so that it can be further developed with reference to the other options on the C-list? That is, it should serve as a "flexible platform" for further measures and not be a blind alley. Consider an example from ICA (a supermarket chain in Sweden, see previous chapter). They considered investing very large amounts of money in a recycling plant — tailor-made to collect mercury and cadmium in household batteries. That went in the right direction, since recycling of mercury and cadmium batteries slows down the leakage of these heavy metals into nature (responding "Yes" to the first question). However, from a backcasting perspective, it wouldn't serve as a platform to further development (responding "No" to the second question). Since mercury and cadmium are heavy metals that are normally very scarce in nature, it would be a very costly thing to safeguard flows between households, shops, and manufacturers in the future. So ICA realized that it would be smarter to invest the money in environmentally much sounder battery technologies that didn't need to be safeguarded so rigorously (and expensively).

- **Low-hanging fruit.** Is it likely that the measure will give a good return on investment — that is, be sound from a business perspective.

It is the combination of "Yes" to all those three questions that provides the strategy: measures that can serve as steppingstones in the right direction are launched, and since they are representing sound business at the same time, money will feed the subsequent steps.

The Framework Applied for Scientific Purposes

The business experiences at IKEA, Scandic, and Electrolux were paralleled by a very deep ongoing scientific development. John and I responded to more and more questions and criticism from an expanding group from the international scientific community, who had learned about TNS and our work. This triggered a very creative process, in which John and I reshaped the wording of the system conditions over and over again to avoid misunderstanding and to make them even more robust to build from. And it led to the first doctoral dissertations in which the TNS Framework played an essential role.

I was proud when John Holmberg defended his doctoral dissertation in 1995: "Socio-Ecological Principles and Indicators for Sustainability." John's dissertation definitely placed systems thinking into the Swedish scientific arena. Later on, our close peer Christian Azar, at the same institution, defended his dissertation: "Long-term Environmental Problems, Economic Measures, and Physical Indicators." It was also influenced by systems thinking, and contained a chapter about indicators that were built on the TNS Framework.

More scientific articles from our institution came out as the consequence of these dissertations. For example how to apply the TNS Framework for the development of indicators in municipalities, or how to follow a product "from the cradle to the grave" — that is, how to use the TNS Framework for life cycle assessment (LCA). We have also used the TNS Framework to study how various tools for sustainable development relate to sustainability: Ecological Footprinting together with Professor Mathis Wackernagel, for example and the Factor 4 and Factor 10 concepts together with Professor Weizsäcker and professor Bio Schmidt Bleek (see references in Appendix 3).

Two new doctoral dissertations are currently in process as a joint venture between TNS, my institution at Chalmers, and the University of Karlskrona. The PhD students, Ulrika Lundberg and Sophie Byggeth, are studying various aspects of product development and how the A, B, C, D Analysis can be applied to bring a sustainability perspective into product development at the early stages of planning as well as throughout the production cycle. This cooperation is the fruit of my growing friendship and partnership with Dr. Göran Broman, Sophie Byggeth's teacher.

Göran has successfully made the TNS Framework a mandatory part of the curriculum for engineers at his university in Karlskrona. "I cannot see how you can become an engineer in our times, without having an idea of the serious challenges of these times and a sound strategic perception of how to tackle them," he says. Göran's intelligence, honesty (also to himself) and loyalty have influenced me on such a deep level that I have difficulty describing them. A person being "close to perfect" is great to be with in reality, but how do you make it interesting to read about (or even believable)? Göran is constantly critical, keeping you on your toes, but he is constitutionally unable to be that way for any purpose other than to bring issues further.

We have also begun to see scientific papers and doctoral dissertations produced outside of Sweden. Hilary Bradbury from MIT wrote a dissertation on the social aspects of the TNS "learning story," drawing on in-depth interviews with people who were part of the start-up period (including my wife). Brian Nattras from the University of British Columbia produced a doctoral dissertation on the implementation process of TNS in four firms (Scandic Hotels, IKEA, the US carpet tile company Interface, and the US forestry company Collins Pine).

The Framework for Scientific Consensus

I used what we had learned about applying the framework in business in attempts to deal with larger business examples. I selected a number of societal areas with profound problems from a sustainability perspective and tried to mimic the process I had witnessed in business. I turned to various stakeholders — mainly scientists and practitioners — and asked them to help me enter a consensus process on areas such as the energy sector, metal flows, agriculture, and forestry. In retrospect, the early attempts with energy and metals are not all that impressive examples of how to use the TNS Framework. But as the framework developed into a more and more refined model for planning, later achievements in agriculture and forestry made quite good examples of how the A, B, C, D Analysis can be of value also for scientists in a consensus process.

Politically, the most interesting of those consensus documents was the one on agriculture (see Appendix 1). This field had been the subject of very strong controversy in the Swedish public debate on sustainability issues for many decades, and the relationship between "ecological farmers" and the more traditional "industrial farmers" was a hot issue in the early '90s, to say the least. For a long time, both sides had written debate articles and called each other names. Now, representatives from both parties had accepted my invitation to be partners in an intellectual process. The tension, based on those traditional polarities, was easily detected around the table when representatives from the ecological farmers were confronted with agronomists and practitioners from the industrial farmers' community.

The TNS Framework and the A, B, C, D Analysis were presented and then applied to the problems of today's farming. At the time, I was quite ignorant about agriculture. In a way, this came in handy for my role as chairman in the consensus process. First everything needed to be explained very clearly to make a medical doctor understand: agricultural jargon had to be replaced by quite neutral words. Second the perspective was new to the debaters. Everything — problems as well as solutions — was to be looked at through the lens of the TNS system conditions, which helped reduce the loaded words and perspectives that otherwise would have carried emotional tension from fights that had been going on for years between "green" and "industrial" farmers.

Although a number of months were spent on some arguments and fights, the process became more and more balanced, and after a two-year period the logos of TNS, the Swedish Farmers' Federation, and the Swedish Society for Organic Farming were on the same consensus document that suggested quite radical changes in Swedish farming. And more interestingly, the process had substantially helped The Swedish Farmers Federation to change not only their scientific programs but also their business programs.

The Scientific Consensus Process

The experiences that followed from all the scientific consensus documents can be summarized into the following "manual."

One or a few persons may want to apply the TNS Framework and its A, B, C, D Analysis to a certain problem area. The crucial element in this initial stage is to find possibilities for the TNS Framework to resolve various types of resistance to proactivity through the discovery of neutral/logical/self-interest arguments. This is achieved through an emphatic "looking at the problem from the eyes of the antagonists, but through the lens of the TNS Framework."

A little larger group of five to ten people (not more) is then addressed and asked to constitute the editorial team together with the initiator(s). This group then discusses the TNS Framework, so that it can be the shared mental model for the work to come.

Members of the editorial team should share some of the following qualities. They should be perceived to be technically and politically knowledgeable in the area. They should have personal integrity and be creative; they should like goals and sound logical thinking more than personal prestige; and they should have a reasonably good name in the eyes of the "sounding board" (see below). In my experience, those qualities are much more important than having a "politically representative selection of the community" at this primary stage in the process. By this I mean that the intellectual work must get started, and if skeptical people are present even before the problems have been structured in a meaningful way, the sensitive initiation process may be hampered.

If the members of the editorial team are smart enough and knowledgeable enough and have enough personal integrity, they generally have no problem coming up with a reasonably fair presentation of the most commonly applied counterarguments. This is key to being able to go for emphatic solutions. In my opinion, the "political" aspects of the editorial team should be considered only to avoid such an unbalanced selection of people that it would later be difficult to get a politically representative "sounding board" to support the work. Often this is less of a problem than it may seem. Most scientists, officers at EPA and other specialists, are not politically loaded. But they are often surprisingly knowledgeable about politics.

A secretary (sometimes the initiator, sometimes somebody elected in the group) assumes the task of writing each new version of the developing document. These versions are produced after each meeting, perhaps once every month or every two months. It could also be a little more often, but the writing takes time if it is to be good, and each member in the editorial group should get some time to consider the text before the next meeting.

Eventually, when the editorial team feels enthusiastic about its text, the text is disseminated to a larger "sounding board." Now the project changes character, and needs to become more political.

The people on the "sounding board" should have respected names and be selected for their integrity in combination with their political stands. "Would the name of Mr. or Ms. So-and-so be helpful in bringing around a consensus on this issue?" At this point, the document is of good quality and (A) presents the TNS Framework and its application to the problem area, including its background, why an analysis of this kind is needed, any restrictions (what you have not studied, for example), and finally, the analysis; (B) presents today's problems with reference to the system conditions, one by one; (C) presents various alternative measures to solve the problem; and (D) presents some suggestions for getting there — that is, ways to pick the potential solutions in a "flexible platform/low-hanging fruit" way.

When the documents are disseminated to the "sounding board," we ask for comments and pose the following question: "Provided that we pay attention to your comments to your satisfaction, are you behind this document?" The editorial team is now handling all the comments from the "sounding board" (not the secretary on his or her own).

We found it to be very important that the group be working together person-to-person at this final stage. The points must be handled in a way that satisfies the persons behind them, without jeopardizing the overall philosophy of the document. It's a lot to think about, and it requires a creative and experienced team to deal with it.

The final version is then once again disseminated to the "sounding board." After the final endorsement it is published, along with the names of the editorial board and the "sounding board," plus a description of the methodology.

Three experiences are worth mentioning:

1. The process tends to make a political impact even before the document is published. People start to talk about it before publication, particularly if the editorial team happens to be constituted of interesting enough people. The reason for this is simple: the process is at least as important as the document. Everybody around the table learns during the process and starts talking to their influential peers about what they have come to think about. This is enhanced even more, of course, when the larger "sounding board" is invited into the process.

2. Generally, the document does not create any turbulence in the mass media. You might expect that it would, but the mass media are generally not so interested in consensus. Quite the contrary; the Swedish experience is that the documents tend to "sneak in under the radar" as they find their way to the tables of decision makers. This is a more subtle way to make a difference.

3. A lot of the success is dependent on the people who take part. This goes for the chairman, too. (Often this is the same person as

the initiator of the process, but it doesn't have to be.) The chairman of the meetings has a key role, at least in the beginning. If he or she is prepared to take all the punishment with a smile and without losing focus, the whole process is a piece of cake. If he or she loses track of the goal and starts getting personally involved in turf wars over details, the project will probably fail. The reason is that he or she must have authority at meetings, without bullying the participants (they must be respected from the heart, which is why the selection of those people is so important). He or she must really master not only the TNS Framework but also how to apply it, so that he or she can always see the possibility of merging divergent points of view into one new platform, applying "Simplicity without Reduction." The latter is often the only option, since it is usually a doomed ambition to try to convince people to endorse an old, unchanged, inflamed, and conflicting standpoint about various specific details. The attempt must be to discover principles for shared understanding during meetings, so that the editorial board feels enthusiasm for the process and its flow. The intellectual satisfaction of fast progress is the reward for the editorial board. In fact, if you have no money, and if the participants are active in the sustainability field anyway, it may be the only reward.

The consensus process is difficult, but when it works, it is beautiful, particularly since it has a tendency to become autonomous. The main difficulties occur when you start out. If it works in the beginning, then the participants adapt the technique afterward. And then the chairman can sit back and enjoy the ride.

THE MCDONALD'S CASE

IN 1992 A MUNICIPALITY outside of Gothenburg, Mölndal, received an award from TNS for its bold activities against the local McDonald's restaurant. The municipality tested Swedish law by suing McDonald's to try to force them into using reusable packaging — the local waste produced was not compatible with the Agenda 21 work of the municipality. To us at TNS, it seemed important to give the award to Mölndal before the case went to court, because we were not out to detect winners and losers but to find actors in society who had vision and were bold enough to act in spite of the unavoidable uncertainty inherent in the untraditional methods used. McDonald's complied without going to court.

A year later, Paul Lederhausen approached me, the entrepreneur who introduced McDonald's to Sweden. He attended a seminar that another of our clients, Ekoxen hotels, was running to build up momentum for their own transition. Mr. Lederhausen told me that he appreciated the constructive attitude I had displayed during my presentation, although of course he didn't like it that we had rewarded Mölndal for suing them. But now he needed some help and wanted to know if TNS could provide it.

"No matter what we do, we get punished for it," he said. "It is as if McDonald's is the traditional Swedish symbol for a superficial and unethical business corporation, in spite of our trying hard to improve on social as well as ecological values. Whatever we do, we get discouraged. It is as if our critics need a scapegoat, because they don't want us to improve. Recently, we switched from plastic covers on our hamburgers to paper covers to improve our environmental performance. It didn't take more than a couple of weeks for a Swedish professor to appear on national TV and explain that paper weighs more than plastic. In turn, this means that the transports of all the paper

113

covers will consume more fossil fuel than we have saved as raw material for the previous production of plastic. So, according to the professor, we have lost ground from an ecological perspective. Whatever we do, we get punished. What shall we do?"

I responded that the reason for the frustration was probably that in spite of a real intention to improve, they had no clear understanding of the goal. Consequently, the change of material didn't represent a step planned through backcasting from an imagined future success, but was rather an *ad-hoc* activity. So the change of plastic to paper could not be explained as a natural step towards sustainable business activities. Which, in turn, made it difficult to answer the professor.

My conversation with Mr. Lederhausen led to a business seminar a couple of months later, with the management team of Swedish McDonald's at their head office outside of Stockholm. Mr. Lederhausen — who would soon retire — was present, as was his son Mats, soon to take over as CEO of McDonald's. I remember that I reflected on the difficult task Mats had. There was turbulence, not to say a crisis, around as well as within McDonald's, and here he was — the future CEO, appointed by "Dad." Could his beginning be any harder? Would the rest of the personnel follow him?

Since that seminar, TNS in Sweden and Swedish McDonald's have been close peers on the barricades for a sustainable future. We have learned from each other, exchanged experiences, and shared the pain that always follows from doing something different. At TNS, we have been surprized to find McDonald's climb from the bottom on a Gallup poll with regard to the market's perception of social and ecological standards, to become one of Sweden's three most-respected companies in their field. Through a systematic step-by-step approach, Swedish McDonald's has turned to renewable energy, purchases as much food as possible from farms with clear management programs for sustainable development, has developed recycling programs in all its restaurants, and has had the US management team traveling across the Atlantic to learn what was going on in the remote little part of the world we call Sweden.

When this process had been going on for a couple of years, Mats Lederhausen, the new CEO, phoned me up and asked me the following peculiar question, "Do we need hamburgers at all in the sustainable society?" Although I realized it was Mats's normal way of being challenging — it was a rhetorical question that didn't reveal his own opinion — it told me how deep the process can go if you have a framework that allows you to come up with all the questions yourself. You don't need to think very long about what would have happened if I had asked that question to Mr. Lederhausen when he phoned me up that day, complaining about what the professor had said at Swedish TV. If I had asked, "Do we need hamburgers at all?" that would certainly have been the end of discussion. However, when the CEO asks the same question a few years later, there is power in it. It told me something about the mark of a truly professional manager. Such a manager asks: "What am I doing here; what is the real purpose of it all; and, based on such considerations, on what premises can my assumptions be questioned?" It is doubtful whether systematic incremental improvements can follow from any other attitude.

I didn't answer Mats's question, of course, but took it as a stimulating starting point for a dialog. The process that Mats had initiated led to the introduction of even more radical purchase routines for meat and to the introduction of "veg-burgers." And it led to something that probably puts Swedish McDonald's in a unique global position as one of the most radical firms working toward sustainable development. The head of environmental affairs, Bertil Rosquist, came up with the brilliant idea of "pathfinder" documents.

The McDonald's Pathfinder Documents

One of the major problems for firms that have embarked on a course toward sustainability is to know where to draw the boundaries around their own company with regard to the issue of responsibility. It is virtually impossible to be sustainable — even if you are doing everything you can — because we live in a society where virtually nothing is planned in a sustainable way. How can you, for instance, call a course "sustainable development" if all the transport of your goods is performed with today's means of transportation?

Bertil's solution came from the TNS Framework's focus on process toward the system conditions, and from the phrasing of the overall environmental policy to "phase out McDonald's contribution to society's violation of the system conditions."

Bertil started the process by investigating the societal areas where McDonald's is influencing society the most. The results were:

- Energy and transportation, since they purchase so many services of that kind;

- Agriculture, since they sell food;
- Construction, since McDonald's and/or their franchisers own the restaurants;
- Packaging, since the food business has strict rules about packaging; and
- Chemicals and detergents, since the food business has strict rules about sanitation.

Bertil now entered a process in which McDonald's, together with TNS and a number of other external experts within the respective fields, produced A, B, C, D documents — the so-called Pathfinder Documents — within each of the five areas. The idea was to sketch out today's problems and solutions and then to recruit the suppliers into the process. They were invited to a kick-off once the draft documents were produced.

The implicit attitude was: "Dear suppliers, you have always been good and loyal to us. So we want to keep on doing business with you. We are in a tricky stage of transition — there is a funnel that will heavily influence the way we do business tomorrow. We have, to the best of our capacity, produced some thoughts about today's problems within your fields of competence. We have also considered some possible steps to solve those problems, along with some ideas of high-priority measures. We would like to support you in that direction by doing business with you. If you find any errors in these documents, please help us to correct them, and if you see anything we have forgotten, please add it."

I found this to be a nice and inviting way of introducing the suppliers into a systematic and comprehensive dialog. And it was smart — McDonald's could take a wider responsibility for their business with relatively less work. This was because responsibility was shared in a fair way.

The documents were handed out at the kick-off together with the suppliers. One of them said, "I deliver chemicals to McDonald's in Sweden. It is stated in the Pathfinder Document on Chemicals that I am supposed to phase out all chemicals that are persistent and foreign to nature. But today I can only guarantee that my chemicals are not toxic. How long do I get to make certain that I don't violate System Condition 2?"

My colleague Jonas Oldmark, who attended this meeting, was worried because he didn't have a clue how he would have responded to this question. But the response from McDonald's top management was warm and direct: "We leave that to you, since you are a pro on chemicals — let it take as long as it takes. Just be transparent with us and keep us informed of your progress."

Of course! Jonas watched the supplier, and the response sunk in as intended. It was a friendly response, because it transmitted trust in the supplier. Yet it was as tough as it gets. The responsibility was completely handed over to the supplier. In combination with the lack of a time frame, Jonas felt that this was the perfect way to keep the supplier on his toes.

Today, Mats Lederhausen, the previous CEO of Swedish McDonald's, has become senior vice president of McDonald's Corporation. He is head of corporate strategy and gives advice about a broad array of issues to the senior management team. Recently, I heard McDonald's Chairman Jack Greenberg say on a video to the European suppliers: "McDonald's has now entered a process toward sustainability. McDonald's in Sweden, working together with the Swedish environmental organization TNS, is one of our role models."

Since this book is a personal testimony, I can mention some reflections that are only personal and that have very little to do with the TNS ambition to teach systems thinking. Swedish McDonald's is one of the most ethical companies I have ever come across. By "ethical" I mean their willingness to struggle in the direction of what they say, and to do so even if it hurts at times and costs some sacrifice. I have thought a lot about this, and what a wonderful part of life it is to be surprised every now and then.

The people who run Swedish McDonald's are simply honorable and decent. But maybe the high moral standards of Swedish McDonald's can also, somewhat paradoxically, be attributed to the low expectations people have of them in this area. McDonald's is often used as an example of a superficial firm, with only commercial interests. It was like that in Sweden too, not so many years ago. I believe that it is easier to reflect on ethics, and to realize the need to fight for them, if they are questioned. And *vice versa*. If you work in a firm where everybody takes ethics for granted, then there is still the need to bring it into focus.

PART FOUR

The Next Step

CHAPTER 12

GOING INTERNATIONAL

THE WORLD NEEDED GOOD EXAMPLES and role models on all levels and scales — business, municipalities, and nations — and it needed them more than ever. I had seen the possibilities for my own country to take a lead in this area. Sweden is beautiful, with its huge areas of natural landscape. And I believe that this landscape is endemic to the culture of its inhabitants, who love outdoor activities like sailing and hiking. Sweden is also a relatively small and homogeneous nation that is highly industrialized. And it has a surprising number of very large business corporations with high visibility that are deeply involved in international trade. The country has an international reputation for social responsibility. If Sweden couldn't make it, what country could?

I used the argument about Sweden as a role model a lot during my lectures, as a challenge, and to find yet another argument for proactivity for the people I tried to recruit to the TNS network dialog in Sweden. But it never occurred to me, other than as a superficial intellectual perception, that a national role model is in fact no role model at all unless people from other countries learn about it. However, the need for role models and leadership was so strong at the time that many people *wanted* to discover role models. So I found more and more articles in international journals about TNS.[1] Before I knew it, I was invited to talk about the Swedish TNS experience abroad.

At first the Arlanda Group — the TNS board — was hesitant, to say the least. The same goes for the business leaders of some of the firms we worked with. Many thought that TNS was much too weak to carry the burden of my traveling around the world. Furthermore, even the "soul" of The Natural Step was at risk. Its spontaneous innocence and positive belief in dialog and in people might die in some traditional and slimmed-down "business consultant role" if we were to be too heavily exposed out there. I could even be "hijacked" by US business leaders, and find myself a new job in the US.

However, the chance of my permanently leaving Sweden physically or emotionally, no matter how much attention we got abroad, was zero. When I travel, I start to long for my home as soon as I pass my mailbox. My family and I are deeply and irreversibly rooted where we live today. So, I wasn't concerned about the risks. But though my reasoning was different from the board's, I agreed with them. I simply didn't want to travel, so at first, our joint and convenient decision was that I was to continue to take care of the interest that was raised in Sweden, and the "international wake" of this Swedish role model was to be taken care of by somebody else, or by itself.

And in 1995 there was an international case to build on. The Foster Foundation in Australia (amongst other things devoted to the planting of trees) had contacted us regarding a license to work with TNS in Australia. This happened early, just a couple of years after the Swedish TNS launch, and we certainly didn't have any plans for international organizational promotion at the time. Nor did we have any resources to promote or support organizations abroad. Finally, Australia seemed to be so far away from Sweden that it was a good story that they had even heard about us — a story good enough for us to just endorse their determination to work with TNS and wish them good luck. So, without any experience in international affairs at all, we signed an agreement with Leigh Crocker from Australia. He seemed to do well and sent us letters about his progress, but, burdened with all the work on our own backyard, it was all perceived as just nice anecdotes from Down Under.

One argument, however, was difficult to deal with. Mats Lederhausen claimed that a role model in Sweden, not being known by anybody outside of Sweden, was not only a bizarre thought in itself but would also mean a lost opportunity within Sweden. Being a real expert in international cooperation in one of the world's leading franchising businesses, Mats's arguments carried some weight. He claimed that if TNS were well received abroad — and indeed a number of articles in international journals spoke in favor of that — that would spill over inside Sweden. This could lead to a self-perpetuating positive spiral that it would be a crime not to attempt. Why not give it a try or at least allow me to accept a few invitations and just see what would happen? We could always change our minds later, and certainly TNS wouldn't die just because of a couple of trips abroad, would it?

So I accepted a few lecture tours in Australia, the US, and the UK. I was received in a very generous way, was invited again, and before I knew it, I was surrounded by a number of good new friends from all the countries I visited. Out of fear of not mentioning them all, I have decided to mention only the people who took part in "turning points," that is, occasions by which the course of TNS took another, often unexpected and sometimes painful, turn.

My new friends attempted to start national TNS organizations in their respective countries. However, it soon turned out that this wasn't easy. It wasn't until much later that I understood why. Nobody had, at this time, ever started a TNS organization. This included me, since TNS in Sweden grew organically as a consequence of the "Big Mailing," and from the dialog between scientists and decision makers that followed. The heart of TNS was a process, not a set of tools that could be sold right off. I wondered how much of the Swedish experience would even be relevant outside of Sweden.

The Need to "Package" Intellectual Capital

Certainly, some of the TNS concepts had international applications. If matter does not appear or disappear in chemical reactions in Sweden but has a tendency to disperse and reach vast areas of nature, the same was probably true also outside of Sweden. And if I and other Swedes seek knowledge but often end up drowning in information, this probably happens in other countries, too. And since all of us in the Swedish TNS network rather liked to be treated with a "Yes, and" attitude and to enter respectful dialogs built on a transparent and structured principle understanding, rather than to enter attack and defence arguments that were built on untested presumptions and confusing misunderstanding, well, the same was probably true also for people outside of Sweden.

However, very little of our experience was "packaged" for an international arena. The first person to say this to me was Hans Dahlberg, the first chairman of TNS in the Arlanda Group. He tried to explain it even at the start of TNS, but my limited experience in business didn't allow me to really understand what the "packaging" of knowledge meant. To me, knowledge was knowledge, and the packaging was all about writing about it and presenting it. Later on in San Francisco, Paul Hawken, the world famous US activist and author of *Ecology of Commerce* (HarperBusiness, 1993), said the same thing.

Paul and I had been invited by Peter Senge, the systems thinker and author of *The Fifth Discipline* (Doubleday/Currency, 1990) to present at MIT in Boston. I'm sure I can speak for all three of us when I say that we were struck by the similarities in our ways of thinking. However, unlike me, both Peter and Paul had long-term experience in creating organizations, and they both said the same thing as Hans Dahlberg: "TNS cannot just be transferred to other cultures; it has to be packaged."

Later on, at a restaurant in San Francisco, Paul explained this in a way that finally made me understand it: "The progress of TNS in Sweden is built on an attitude more than anything else, and on a systematic and devoted trust in this attitude. It has initiated a process of learning, which has given rise to a number of valuable assets. Some intellectual capital belongs in this category. The system conditions and backcasting from them for strategic planning are examples of this. Other examples are the pedagogy, metaphors like "trunk and branches," and "simplicity without reduction," to broadcast the typical TNS way of systems thinking.

"However to me your social tools are at least as important, such as the very concrete "Yes, and Technique" to make it easier to remember how to communicate an attitude that people have appreciated since ancient times. This was the starting point really, because without the social tools and your systematic way of applying them, the intellectual capital of TNS would never have evolved.

"However, virtually nothing of your present assets can be "sold" like stuff you can put your hands on — things like cars and carpets. What you have is virtual capital, and this capital has been gathered and packaged the way it is by Swedes in Sweden. This story certainly deserves to be told, and it is likely to trigger some interest also in other countries like the US. However, you cannot just "sell" the intellectual capital that TNS has developed in Sweden.

"There are two reasons for this. First, the soul of TNS is built on mutual respect and trust between you and your scientific peers and the business people in the Swedish TNS network. This means that there is shared responsibility for the process. You own TNS together, which is a value in itself. Second, the specific ways you have broadcast the intellectual capital — with the "Big Mailing" and all — is not necessarily relevant in other cultures. In conclusion, the way to communicate this must be developed as a process each time, and this process must be run by people belonging to the culture where TNS is later to be established. Together, we can discover all the assets that can be said to be common denominators for other cultures, package them together, and then expand the dialog faster and faster in the international arena."

Paul offered to make a try for the US and wanted to know if I had the patience to wait for a very long process, or if I wanted a quick launch with the assets we had at that point. I was immensely grateful that Paul had any interest at all and realized, of course, that he was right about the process and everything else. And I realized that I could trust his integrity. This was a man with great connections in his country, and if he was interested in repeating the process in the US — well, the TNS learning certainly had taken off. I said yes, of course.

Paul was allowed to find the US way for the US, and my peers and I in Sweden would be there if Paul needed anything. It took Paul four years of struggle — sometimes painful — until TNS was a reality in the US. (In retrospect, I can say that it took eight years in Sweden until we were established, so Paul's thoughts about speeding up by learning from earlier experience, seemed to be right).

The experience in the UK was similar. It took some years until I met with Jonathon Porritt — a foremost personality on the UK environmental barricades just as Paul is in the US. And it took Jonathon and his secretary general, David Cook, and their peers in the UK quite a few tough years until they were up and running. Those two, Paul and Jonathon, have taught me more about international work than anyone else. This is partly because they know so much about it, partly because my desire to learn was so desperate, and partly because they both embody what international work is all about. Both are brilliant; both are charismatic. But their highly different personalities would probably not have worked if they had been obliged to switch places — Paul to the UK and Jonathon to the US.

Paul is a poet on the "green" barricades, broadcasting "soul" to the wild business community in the US. A master with words, he can make people feel their own spiritual relationship to sustainable development. Paul creates a desire in people to partner up for the better goals of life, thereby stimulating action. I think this is the US way. Jonathon is a giant in a more academic arena. He is a genius at critical thinking. He has no illusions; he knows that nothing comes for free, and people fear his sharpness in debates. I think this is the UK way.

Paul and Jonathon created their respective business models. In the US, in a bold searching process where seed money was gathered from some of all the funds that exist as an inherent part of the US social culture, trial and error created pain and progress in a very turbulent way. And in the UK, a strict business plan was created and followed. Every now and then, people from the respective US and UK teams phoned me up and expressed worries about each other. In the UK, people were sometimes afraid that the US attempt was too wild and "non-critical," and in the US, people were afraid that the "stiff-upper-lips" of the UK were too academic and rigid to really make it in the real world. The fact is that they were both extremely helpful in finding different ways of transmitting the same thing and in helping us all find the common denominators. The latter was the most important, I think, just as Paul Hawken had told me.

The Need for Case Studies

When I started to collect experiences from international business corporations abroad, one thing struck me as specific to Swedish business, something that actually has made me quite proud of my native country. Swedish CEOs had been able to initiate very substantial changes in their respective organizations and had built that change on an intellectual understanding of the TNS Framework. Often very well educated, they had understood the concept of the funnel, the self-benefit in planning ahead in time to avoid its walls, and the strategic principles of launching such "low-hanging fruits that were flexible platforms" to approach the opening of the funnel. The great thing about this is that there were no cases to build on — they *were* the cases. And with few exceptions, their approach was to recruit their employees into the process through teaching and through an open communication process. This was both a way of getting intellectual input from employees and discovering "smart, low-hanging flexible platforms" and a way of building teams — an example of flat organizational thinking and leadership. I had seen this happen so many times in Swedish business corporations that it was with some surprise I was repeatedly exposed to the following question abroad: "Isn't Sweden a bit unique in their way of building consensus? Do you have any case studies outside of Sweden?"

Since I didn't have any case reports outside Sweden in the beginning, my response was that the funnel was global and so was the science that underpinned the TNS framework. These things were not influenced by attitudes or cultures, I argued, and the sole benefit from applying the TNS Framework was not just community building and shared values with customers, but also foreseeing and avoiding certain costs that were to increase in the global market. The less prone a culture normally is to consensus (and if teamwork is what you want), the more effective the tools must be. And finally, I said, this tool was developed to come to grips with the problematic signs of controversy that I had encountered in Sweden.

Often people heard what I said and probably understood it, but in their eyes I could see signs of skepticism. How were they to convince the board and the shareholders that a funnel would influence their business in a negative way if they didn't change direction? So in the beginning, it was simply harder to collect good case studies abroad. Over time, however, the international experience has sharpened the TNS strategy even more: "Go for the proactive firms first, coach them to make them even more successful, and then go for the others."

The First US Role Model for TNS:
Ray Anderson and Interface

Ray Anderson is Chairman and Chief Executive Officer of Interface, Inc., the world's largest producer of carpet tiles. Ray first encountered The Natural Step in August 1994 while reading Paul Hawken's book *The Ecology of Commerce*. But Ray says he read right past the references to TNS without them sticking in his memory. Not much else in the book eluded Ray, however, and he calls his reading an epiphany. Inspired by Hawken's treatise, Ray set out to lead his billion-dollar global manufacturing company toward sustainability. That was pretty ambitious for a manufacturer of petro-intensive carpet tiles, broadloom carpets, textiles, and architectural products. But Ray meant it, as subsequent events would prove.

A year later in 1995, Ray met Paul. By then Ray was well into his revolution within Interface, and he was looking for expert advice on how to move his company toward its new goal of sustainability. Paul became an advisor to Ray and during their first meeting, Paul took Ray more deeply into the meaning of TNS: the funnel, the system conditions at its opening, and how to strategically approach compliance with the system conditions. When Ray began to speak out publicly about his aspirations for Interface — to lead a new industrial revolution and to influence all of industry to become part of the sustainability movement — he began to mention The Natural Step as an important factor in the movement.

Still another year would pass, however, before Ray and I would meet. In June 1996, I traveled to Atlanta, Georgia, in the US at Ray's and Paul's request and made presentations about TNS to two separate audiences. The first was to some 400 people from the community at large who were interested enough in environmental issues to come to dinner at the Atlanta Botanical Gardens to hear about TNS. During that evening, Ray publicly committed Interface — as the first American corporation — to the ultimate objective of complying with the TNS system conditions. "Watch us," Ray said in his wonderful southern accent when he finished his talk. I had encountered America at its best and immediately fell in love with that particular vitality — an almost boyish one — of which Ray was such a charming example. In Sweden we have learned that even mediocre ice hockey teams are dangerous when they come from the States: the puck is supposed to end up in the goal of the competing team, the passion to make that happen is complete, and you don't get any extra points for fancy style.

The second Atlanta presentation was the next morning at the Georgia Institute of Technology (Georgia Tech), one of the leading technological universities in America. The audience, consisting of about 200 scientists and engineers, gave me the opportunity to go deeply into the underlying science of TNS without fear of losing my audience. At lunch, following the morning presentation, I met face to face with several of the academic leaders of the institution, including Dr. Jean Lou Chameau, then Provost, now Dean of Engineering and avid proponent of sustainability. Also at lunch that day were Dr. Gary Schuster, Dean of the College of Science; and Dr. John White, then Dean of Engineering at Georgia Tech, now President of the University of Arkansas, another major US institution of higher education.

The lunchtime conversation with Dr. Schuster was particularly stimulating, as he assumed the role of the devil's advocate in a very challenging way. Ray had warned me that this was Gary's way, so I came well prepared to that lunch, and I had decided to learn from Gary by applying the good ol' "Yes, and Technique." Gary's warm and humorous skepticism left no doubt that his devil's advocate's role was all a methodology of learning together with others — it was certainly not about rigidity and the defense of old assumptions.

The ultimate proof of the power and veracity of TNS came a month later when Dr. Schuster invited me to serve on the Advisory Board for the College of Science. However, of still greater importance was the fact that Georgia Tech has since designated Sustainable Technologies as one of its three major initiatives in the new century, along with Biotechnology and Telecommunications Technology. Ray Anderson and I did good work at Georgia Tech that day, if I may say so.

Because Interface has European operations for the manufacturing of it products, I found myself advising Interface's European management team about the framework and how to adopt it. Thus, I too became a member of Ray's advisory team, which he began to call his "Eco-Dream Team." Paul Hawken asked Ray to join the TNS-USA board, and Ray has been a valued advisor and mentor from the business community to us ever since.

Ray calls the Interface effort, "climbing Mount Sustainability." The TNS system conditions, expressed in the present tense — "Concentrations of substances extracted from the Earth's crust are not systematically increasing in nature" — define the top of Interface's mountain. To Ray, this doesn't only mean that Interface will ultimately comply with the TNS system conditions. Ray wants Interface to be restorative (that is, to clean up the biosphere from society's previous violations of the system conditions) and to help others (for instance, suppliers to Interface) to do the same. Ray describes TNS as the compass and the magnet, drawing Interface toward that top of Mount Sustainability.

The Interface model for transformation from a typical company of the 20th Century to the prototypical company of the 21st Century is described in detail in Ray's book *Mid-Course Correction: Toward a Sustainable Enterprise, the Interface Model* (Peregrinzilla Press, 1998). The book devotes the better part of a chapter to TNS and thus helped to spread the word about TNS throughout the environmental, business, and educational communities, not just in America but in Europe and the Asia Pacific, as well.

Ray is, like most good managers, surrounded by competent and loyal peers who have also become friends and peers of mine. Mike Bertolucci, Jim Hartzfeld, Joyce LaValle, Steve Martin, Andy Wales, and the head of the European division of Interface, John Walker, are some of his comrades-in-arms for the Earth.

Inviting Scientists into the International Process

The difficulties we had collecting good examples in non-Swedish companies was a problem that could be dealt with professionally and patiently. Our response was to go for the most proactive firms first. The learning experience and friendship I had developed with Ray Anderson certainly gave extra support to that idea. Due to its size, there were, of course, more proactive firms in the US than in Sweden. Another problem was more difficult, and it has haunted me since I started TNS.

The overriding idea of TNS was to serve as a bridge between science and decision makers by providing conceptualized knowledge that is relevant for strategic planning. To keep this idea alive, and to allow it to create more and more substantial knowledge from the dialog, scientists are as important as the decision makers. When TNS was started in Sweden, I was a well-respected scientist in medicine and cancer science. This created momentum for the initiation of a number of high-level scientific reports and doctoral dissertations that elaborated the TNS Framework. However, we had no scientific case abroad. In fact, the problem was greater with the scientific community than with the business community. It may be difficult to sell an intellectual framework to business if there are no national cases to identify with and build on, but to the scientific community it is inherently impossible.

Science is built on a systematic learning process, in which critical thinking questions and re-shapes old knowledge. This has no value in itself but is there to cut away dead flesh from old knowledge so that we can trust it as a platform for leaps into new knowledge. Where does one find scientists who, in the eyes of other scientists because of their successes within their respective fields, are prepared to take the lead in the new arena? If they were successful and clever, why would they take the time to change arenas? Also, the new arena linked to sustainable development, was inherently trans-disciplinary, involving physics, chemistry, biology, ecology, economy, psychology, and sociology, to mention some of the most important. And trans-disciplinary science has a somewhat flaky reputation.

In the beginning of a new discipline, many mistakes are inevitably made when new knowledge cannot be found by the application of existing scientific tools but must rely on the development and application of non-traditional tools. Furthermore, for very simple statistical reasons, most of the brilliant minds are still in the traditional fields of science. This goes also for the people who sit on evaluation committees for scientific funds. In the beginning, the trans-disciplinary science of sustainable development not only wrestled with a relative lack of reputation but also with a relative lack of money.

John Holmberg and I ran into difficulties, in fact, with the first major scientific experience outside of Sweden. Paul Hawken and Peter Raven — one of the world's leading scientists on biodiversity in plants and also manager of Missouri Botanical Garden — had agreed to mentor a scientific consensus process in the US. Together with Paul Hawken and the TNS-USA team, Peter Raven hosted the meeting, called the TNS "Wingspread" meeting (named after the wonderful resort where it took place). Peter Senge offered to facilitate it, and a number of very prestigious and world-famous scientists in physics, chemistry, ecology, industrial ecology, and other disciplines turned up. John and I were invited to describe the Swedish experience, and we had planned the meeting very thoroughly along with Peter Raven, Paul Hawken, and Peter Senge. Although we didn't have any experience outside of Sweden, we realized that we had to be extraordinarily careful to allow the process to flow in a constructive way. These were brilliant people and would quickly understand what we tried to say. After that, we could just hope that they would recruit themselves to the process and merge forces with us to develop the concept further.

The meeting process went beautifully, as planned. On day one of the meeting, the scientists listened to our rationale for the system conditions, heard what we said, discussed it in break-out groups, saw no weaknesses in the scientific underpinning as such, but had some difficulties in understanding the point. What was it good for?

On Day Two we talked about the application for decision making — systems thinking, backcasting, upstream thinking, shared mental models for group creativity, and the other stuff that precedes the need for basic principles. Day Two became a great temporary success, building on the more slow and considered process of the day before. The TNS Framework was now perceived in the same way as it was in Sweden — as a framework for decision making, underpinned by science in a relevant way; not a replacement for specific knowledge "among the leaves" but rather an aid for structuring it in order to ask the right questions and make strategically sound decisions. A manifesto with these contents, created by some leading scientists in the world, was signed at the end of the process.

It was not until John Holmberg discovered a couple of years later that there was something wrong that I also saw it. We had never told the scientists that there was no institution to support a follow-up. At least we didn't stress this very essential piece of information very clearly. TNS is built on personal engagement and responsibility, and we should have made it very clear from the beginning that the people at this event were there to learn about their presumptive interest not to support the process but to actually run it. Since TNS was, and still is, built on some robust ideas but with very small financial resources that, in turn, led to a need for large personal engagements, our neglecting to say so up front was a big mistake. So, the scientists must have been waiting for some spectacular TNS initiatives that never happened.

Some of the scientists are still around and act as mentors and supporters of the TNS process in the US. But although nobody has said so explicitly, I have a strong fear that many of the other participants at the "Wingspread" meeting feel like they were taken hostages in the process. They were signing some document that something was really good, and then nothing happened. This flies in the face of good science, which must build on an ongoing process of critical thinking and creativity. Because of this, we decided not to publish the manifesto or to use it in any public promotion activities. It was not to be used until the process had really started in the US.

A number of very smart young scientists have now entered the scene, and a number of the best old ones — like Peter Raven — are still around as mentors and supporters. I have good hope that the process will gain momentum again. Since that first meeting abroad, John Holmberg has run one similar consensus meeting in Australia and one in the UK, and together we ran one in South Africa in December 1999.

At the meeting in South Africa, we were extremely clear — up front even before the meeting. We explained that it was all about their personal interest in taking responsibility for a new organization in their country, in critically assessing the TNS tools and concepts that had been developed so far, and then in furthering the scientific process nationally and internationally as they would prefer it themselves. This has created a very sound dialog between South African scientists and the South African TNS office. Regardless of how it goes, no scientist in South Africa will be able to claim that TNS has given him or her false expectations.

In April 1999, in Portland, Oregon the TNS concept was handed over from Sweden to The Natural Step International (TNSI). The creators of this organization (friends from the US, the UK, Australia, New Zealand, Japan, South Africa, Canada, and Sweden) agreed on core values, a mutual logo, license agreements, checklists of requirements to start new national TNS organizations — the whole lot.[2] This event was a major success for me and my peers in Sweden. We had made it. TNS was established internationally and a bunch of very smart people felt a shared responsibility to further the TNS process in a critical and transparent and inviting way. It felt like we made it to the goal after running a 10-year marathon. I am now in the middle of a team, with people whom I admire immensely, and who have successfully done something that I have never done: they have purposely created a Natural Step organization in their countries.

Thirteen years ago, I happened to ignite a process that Sweden was ready for at that time. Through trial and error and organic growth, it led to what TNS is in Sweden today. Because of so many brilliant and wonderful people entering the process in Sweden and abroad, and since some of them were willing to take a personal risk by entering the organization, I can today say that I have a 13-year experience of a wonderful learning process that beats anything I could have dreamed of. Without these people, I would have had a 1-year experience that would have been 13 years old today.

CHAPTER 13

GROWING PAINS

THE NATURAL STEP WAS AT ITS PEAK. We were influential not only in Sweden, but had also started to gain momentum abroad:

> Dr. Karl-Henrik Robèrt has succeeded in the extraordinarily difficult task of getting scientists to agree on fundamental system conditions for a sustainable society. Now we can all benefit. The Natural Step concepts allow top management to view environmental considerations in a systematic way and to integrate them into corporate strategy for long-term prosperity.
>
> — John Naisbitt, *Megatrends*

> Systems thinking needs to be introduced not only to business but to the broader society, as well, to have the potential for a full and more powerful impact. Learning about Dr. Robèrt's work gives me a real hope that this could happen. He has applied systems thinking to our ultimate frontier — the planet Earth.
>
> — Iva M. Wilson, President, Philips Components, North America

> The Natural Step focuses on restructuring the entire industrial economy to make it fit better with the natural processes of growth, decay, and recycling. The program's virtue is both that it aims to promote change at the system level where the problems have their source and that it constructively involves people of all ages in all walks of life. One can only hope that The Natural Step spreads rapidly from Scandinavia to all the most heavily industrialized countries.

— Dr. Willis Harman, cofounder of
World Business Academy

When we were introduced to The Natural Step, we realized we had found our framework.
—Tachi Kiuchi, CEO Mitsubishi Electric America

The work of Karl-Henrik Robèrt and his colleagues through The Natural Step process in Sweden is one of the leading examples in the world today of society-wide learning. Learning based on systems thinking and continued dialog is not only transforming Sweden's approach to sustainable industrial development but holds great promise for many of the most intractable societal issues of our time.
— Dr. Peter Senge, Center for Organizational Learning,
MIT

The Natural Step is the leading international movement encouraging businesses to be sustainability- promoting.
— Philip Sutton, Director, Policy and Strategy,
Green Innovations, Inc., Australia

With the living cell as the point of departure, Karl-Henrik Robèrt brilliantly helps us understand the non-negotiable conditions for a sustainable society. He and The Natural Step offer a scientific yet very inspiring and operational model for helping us, individuals as well as corporations, in setting a new course.
— Dr. Göran Carsted, President of IKEA,
North America

As in nature, the gift of the work toward sustainability is its meaningfulness. By diligently trying to understand the boundary conditions that prescribe the fulfillment or demise of life, the Natural Step principles provide a critically important tool for action.
— Paul Hawken, author and founder of
TNS in the US

The King's Birthday Present

So, in 1996, after eight years of struggle, TNS had made it. In retrospect, I think the time peak happened on one single day — November 28, 1996. TNS had given the Swedish king (our patron) an international seminar on the environment as his 50-year anniversary present. Four hundred Swedish business people were gathered at "Cirkus," a big lecture hall in Stockholm. TNS peers from our daughter organizations and networks in other countries attended — Paul Hawken and Ray Anderson from the US, Jonathon Porritt from the UK, and scientists like Peter Raven and a physicist from Berkeley, Don Aitken, knocked the socks off the audience with their very inspired presentations. His Majesty, King Carl Gustaf, initiated the seminar by thanking us for this birthday present.

Ladies and gentlemen, friends of nature and the environment:[1]

As a child, I preferred the hard packages for my birthdays — like most children. But now, when I have matured both in age and in wisdom, I do appreciate gifts with other dimensions as well.

Earlier this year, when I celebrated my 50th anniversary, I was presented with a gift, hard to pack but easy to accept. The Natural Step promised to arrange a symposium in my honor later this year. I was not told that they expected me to open it, but I am pleased to do it as a token of my gratitude for the gift and for the important work that the organization is doing for the environment in Sweden and elsewhere.

The organization has indeed grown ever since it was founded seven years ago and I was asked to be its patron. Its projects and programs have been exported to a number of countries, and I do hope that this development will continue. Because, as all of us know, non-sustainability is a problem that does not recognize any geographic borders. Therefore, international cooperation on a practical level is essential in order for us to be successful.

To be able to act, in a community or a municipality, decisions must be made. For this you need devoted individuals but you also need leadership — people who know where to go and how. Education and knowledge are necessary prerequisites.

But the solutions are not always simple. There might be more than one answer to every question. And even if we could make perfect estimations of the effects of different measures on nature beforehand, we have to take the economy into consideration as well. In order to be able to act, we first need a definition of sustainability, then a strategy for action, including priorities from the economic perspective. It is also important that society at large, when enacting its legislation and measures to taxation, takes the ecosystems into account by supporting them rather than destroying them.

The Natural Step has created a unique model for attaining the goal of sustainability. This framework includes the overall principles for sustainability as well as a strategy by which you will be able to optimize your economy by doing the right thing at the right moment. This so-called mental model aims at helping people, organizations, business corporations, and municipalities to talk to each other from the same starting point and along the same lines. The dialog will be more efficient and the cooperation much easier.

Of course a model does not solve the actual problems. But it is a useful tool for reaching the goal of sustainability. It presents a common framework within which different individuals and organizations can develop their own specific needs.

I look forward very much to listening to the following speakers. I am convinced that this day will contribute to the development of sustainability in our own society and maybe even abroad, since we have a number of distinguished foreign guests.

Thank you very much for coming and for sharing your views with us. Welcome and good luck!

When I heard the King speak and the presentations that came after him, I felt that the situation was almost surrealistic. In a way it was. Here we were, representatives of TNS, and this organization was presented as a sort of hope for humanity. But in reality we were just a bunch of individuals who knew that we were part of a learning dialog and who had some intellectual tools that seemed to have created some change. But we had no organizational back-up to meet expectations that were now likely to build up fast. I had heard people tell me nightmarish stories about business corporations that had succumbed because of — not in spite of — very smart and clever products. Such products may impact the market too much and too fast. So they have to be taken over by others, because the first entrepreneurs who developed them cannot deliver as market expectations outgrow their ability to supply. I remember that my wife whispered to me: "Kalle, it is a bit worrying with all this success. I think that there is a risk for backlash now." And there were already some worrying rumors and signals floating around in that vein that were vaguely disturbing.

At the King's seminar, two things happened that symbolized — in retrospect — that the TNS organization was in for its first major crises. One was that Russel Johnsson and Lennart Dahlgren overheard me when I was talking in an irritated way to a couple of my colleagues in one of the breaks at the King's seminar. I had gotten the incorrect impression that they had forgotten to bring the abstract books for the symposium, which would have been a major disappointment to me. I had worked hard and the stakes with this seminar were high. So I didn't listen well enough. But it soon turned out that our lean organization had just not had the time and resources to organize for the dissemination of any handouts; instead the abstract books were put in piles by the door for the participants to pick up themselves.

It was a minor controversy, and I calmed down immediately when I saw my error, but it was too late. Lennart and Russel were deeply impressed with the devotion of my small staff to pull off this major event but not as impressed by my way of showing gratitude. Later on, they had a serious conversation with me about this and advised me never to forget the humble attitude that had made TNS such a success. They also advised me to start looking for ways of "just being there" for my colleagues and to reduce my input into the day-to-day operations. It was essential that people around me be allowed to grow, and I had a tendency to occupy a lot of space.

During the conversation with Russel and Lennart, I experienced a mixture of fear and gratitude. Fear because until now, I hadn't noticed any problems linked to me as a person — none. Seriously, it had never occurred to me that I could ever become a stumbling block for TNS, which I had started and which I loved so much. And I felt gratitude, because the whole atmosphere of the meeting was the good old one that I had begun to take for granted with Russel and Lennart by now. They invited me for dinner and were critical, not because they were irritated with me but because they felt a personal responsibility to bring TNS further. The conversation helped me a lot, and still today, not many days go by that I don't think of that particular dinner with Lennart and Russel.

In another break, Mats Lederhausen approached me and told me that a book was being written in which a professor in physics presented deep concerns about TNS and our way of dealing with scientific matters. The old professor Tor Ragnar Gerholm is a well-known "contrarian" in Sweden. He has been fighting against "greens" and for nuclear power, for as long as I can remember. However, TNS does not take a stand in matters of that kind — we just respond in a way that is traditional to us: "As long as nuclear power would systematically develop to comply with the four system conditions, it must be free to do so in competition with other energy sources that do the same." We always leave the conclusions to the individual, so as not to mix the clarity of the planning methodology with our own beliefs and values.

So, at first, I didn't take the news seriously. Whatever the professor wrote in his book, we would be able to respond in our traditional and neutral way. And if any of the science around TNS was flawed, we could just correct it, the same way TNS had developed so far. But the news about the book started to add up with other dark clouds on the horizon. And some of those were more worrying than others.

Tensions at the Office

My peers had started to talk about tensions at the TNS office. The personnel simply didn't feel good any longer. "PUA wasn't the right secretary general any more." And when I talked to my peers about it, the answers I got were so subtle that I never picked up on what they were trying to tell me. In retrospect, I know what was wrong with me. My personal strategy to start TNS was to be generally positive and supportive, because I had nothing else to offer, such as money. So people were afraid to disappoint me by delivering bad news in a clear enough way, especially since most of the staff members were younger than me. It probably took experienced business people like Lennart and Russel to reach me on those levels, and very few of the TNS networkers were as sophisticated in TNS organizational matters as they were.

I had reached my limit. I remember that PUA had made a speech several years earlier, around 1993, at a personnel seminar at Sånga Säby Conference Hotel. He had explained that his leading style was at its best in the early stages of organizational development, but later on, when the organization needed to move into a more consolidated stage, TNS would need somebody else. I had hardly paid any attention, because I thought that it was something PUA had read somewhere, perhaps in some business literature, but that it certainly didn't apply to us. Maybe PUA was even fishing? In the break I put something in his net, just to make sure that this alternative explanation was not neglected. But one of the senior staff members, Lars Bern, had heard PUA, too. Lars had had long experience in the top management level in big business corporations in Sweden. He had been cured from cancer, and I had helped him a bit with this. We had become good friends, and Lars had decided to spend some of his life on TNS. He had certainly agreed with PUA then about the need to change the secretary general. He did so even more at this stage.

Lars had the authority to tell me up front what he thought, just like Lennart and Russel did, and he asked me — no, begged me over and over again — to simply sack PUA. PUA was no longer the man to run TNS. TNS had become an established organization, the honeymoon with business was over, and from now on the expectations of us to deliver fast and professionally would grow by the hour. But PUA was still running everything *ad hoc*, because he knew no other way.

My response to all this was simply to try to keep everything together as it was and just talk to people to smooth the wrinkles out. It quickly turned out to be a doomed strategy. Tensions grew. People started to gather in groups at the office and had secret rebellion meetings against PUA. It became obvious that I had run into my first management crisis, and I soon realized that talks wouldn't do it. The same people who had admired PUA enormously for his gifted and creative way of designing unexpected projects in the early days, now felt a deep mistrust when it came to his ability to deliver trust to all stakeholders, particularly in business.

Although I simply could not fire my good friend PUA, I talked to him about the two of us starting a search for a new secretary general — one who could transform the organization into a consolidated state, whatever that was. The attempt was to have PUA stay as a sort of senior adviser to TNS and to the new secretary general. Lars Bern said acidly that it was a beautiful idea, but that it wouldn't work. In spite of his reasoning, and in spite of the authority that Lars's experience in business had given him, I decided to try to rescue PUA. I wanted to be gentle, find a new secretary general together with PUA, and then to renew my ambitions to pull it all together. I failed.

The Attack

Just a few weeks after the King's seminar, I had reason to put yet another worry on the pile of the others. Suddenly, an editorial in *Svenska Dagbladet* exposed me as a dilettante of science. The same newspaper that had attacked us a few years earlier (that time describing me as dishonest) had done it again. But since claims of dishonesty hadn't made it, maybe they thought a label of stupidity would.

The editorial was based on the book that Mats had talked to me about at the King's seminar and that was now evidently printed. The book, written by a retired nuclear physicist, Professor Tor Ragnar Gerholm, was titled *Letter to The Natural Step*. Ironically, this "letter" didn't make it to The Natural Step's mailbox. But the publisher, Timbro, gave it away free of charge to a large target group of influential people and to business corporations. Timbro wears two hats: one is their publisher hat; they have published a number of books in Sweden throughout the years, many of them by very good and respected authors. At the same time, Timbro is a lobby group for the "new liberals." They believe in the "invisible hand" of the market, which will supposedly spontaneously make people socially and economically happy as long as this hand can be left in peace from political influence. New liberals fear influence from the left wing the most.

Timbro, which was founded many years ago, had successfully raised enough funds to make it possible to survive on the interest from them. Since they didn't need to earn all their money, they could mobilize the time needed to be quite powerful in lobbying, and they could give books away for free. This part of Timbro's activities — to fight for free market forces against political influence — has played a growing role in their activities. I think that this increasing focus on lobbying and the almost religious beliefs they had in the "invisible hand" cost them some credibility and influence. But I am not objective here any longer, of course. Lars Bern has, in one of his books about TNS, pointed out that most religious systems have a dark power besides the light one, and that it is a mistake for any new religious system to neglect that. There is an "invisible foot" out there as well, ready to kick anybody's butt. I haven't had the opportunity to learn about Timbro's possible reflections on the foot issue.

Letter to The Natural Step seemed to be about flaws in the TNS philosophy as well as the science that underpinned it — at least according to the editorial in *Svenska Dagbladet*. The book supposedly proved that we had messed everything up that could possibly be messed up. And the reason was simple to understand. I, the leader of TNS, believed that I was knowledgeable in science, which I was not.

The whole attack in *Svenska Dagbladet* seemed to build on the premises that I was the guiding demon of TNS and that by knocking me down the rest of TNS would fall too. They seemed to have missed, or purposely left out, the fact that TNS was all about networking and was a social movement that built its power on cooperation between a growing number of scientists and business leaders. All the stupidity that was attributed to me was, in fact, an offense to everybody involved. I thought that whoever had merged forces behind the attack were smart enough to avoid stirring up the supporters of TNS more than necessary by simply restricting the attack to me personally. But I was still a bit puzzled.

Nobody would have paid any attention to TNS unless industry in Sweden had listened to me and the other scientists involved, or if no dialog and no change had occurred as a result. But in a free market and out of their free will, Swedish business corporations with high visibility had launched very substantial and proactive programs. And most of them had reported a very good social and economic pay-back, also. In fact, their cooperation with TNS could even be used as an argument for the "invisible hand."

Since we never got the "letter" from Professor Gerholm, we had to ask Timbro for it. They were generous and gave it free of charge to us too. Once I had read it, I had an explanation for my first puzzlement but got a couple of new ones to consider. First, Professor Gerholm expressed no criticism about the TNS framework, nor did he say anything about all the firms applying it. Instead, the philosophy of the book was all about the need for free market forces and the ability of such market forces to support individual creativity. And it was about the danger of jeopardizing such forces with too much political interference. In this case, the presumptive support provided by TNS to such politics carried no weight. The science that underpinned my thinking was completely flawed.

Of course! Gerholm, as well as the editorial page of *Svenska Dagbladet* were simply trying to protect the "invisible hand." Therefore, a number of business corporations being proactive by taking part in the TNS dialog made the whole thing even harder. The visibility of those firms and their activities would only give more ammunition to restrictive attempts from certain political camps.

In fact, there were examples of business corporations who had actively and successfully influenced politicians to implement "green" taxes and other measures in order to gain more momentum for their own new products in competition with less proactive firms. Examples were the way cadmium-free batteries were launched on the Swedish market by Electrolux, or the way OK Petroleum did the same with cleaner gasoline and renewable fuels. I remember that Jonathon Porritt and Paul Hawken, independent of each other, congratulated me about the attack. This was an initiation ritual they had told me, and TNS had been "selected" because of our indisputable influence. Maybe I'd been a bit flattered, but mostly, their friendly peer support had helped a lot.

So, what now puzzled me with Professor Gerholm's book was not the driving spirit as such, or the philosophy behind the attack. The difficult thing to understand was the chosen methodology of the attack. The scientific criticism was completely isolated to one source — the science of my first book *Det Nödvändiga Steget* (*The Necessary Step*). This book had disappeared from the shop's bookshelves several years earlier, since it was about my early thoughts at the start-up period of TNS. TNS was a learning organization that wanted to use the frontline of knowledge, so we hadn't used the book. If Professor Gerholm had been academically interested in our work, he would have gone to some of the scientific publications or doctoral dissertations or perhaps studied our actual teaching materials. He might also have gone to my new book. But for him to have studied my first book — aimed at the general public and describing my early personal motif and thoughts — was indeed puzzling.

Anyway, according to *Letter to The Natural Step*, I probably "meant well." But as *Svenska Dagbladet's* interpretation of Professor Gerholm's letter had pointed out, I certainly didn't understand the nature of science. According to the book, I used flawed arguments to regard nature as one of my patients. But nature was no patient. In fact, nature had never felt better in her life.

Here I was, attacked by a professor in physics. But science itself was not the objective here. It was only used as a tool to reach a philosophical goal. Professor Gerholm seemed to be just another actor, driven by the same interests as lay behind the editorial page of *Svenska Dagbladet*. (It was not until later that this would be revealed in public.)

So, I was puzzled that the professor had restricted his scientific attack to a book that was out of print. But when I read the contents of the criticism, I was stunned. To attack my book, if you really wanted to attack it, would have been a piece of cake for a professor in physics. Being all about my early thoughts and dreams, it was not a difficult target. So why were quotes from my book falsified? In fact all the quotes that backed Professor Gerholm's standpoint about scientific flaws — and the ones that were used by *Svenska Dagbladet* — were errors of thought that he himself had first invented and then corrected in the same blow. Examples were quotes in which I seemed to claim that chemical reactions didn't involve any change of material mass (which is wrong), whereas the original text explained that the number and type of atoms didn't change (which is right). There was a quote in which I had supposedly confused the principle of matter conservation with the first law of thermodynamics, and another in which I apparently believed that destruction of the environment can be measured in terms of entropy. But again, the original text gave no hints of those ideas. Another "quote" from my book was a completely new sentence that had been created by pasting together a half-sentence from me, with another half from a text by Karl-Erik Eriksson that I had referred to in an appendix. All done to appear silly. My greatest frustration was reached when I saw a quote — the only one that wasn't falsified — which really *was* stupid. The only problem was that I had used the quote, too, to demonstrate an erroneous way of thinking. But here I found it — with my name on it.

I showed Professor Gerholm's book to Professor Karl-Erik Eriksson and asked his advice. He had debated against Tor Ragnar Gerholm many times throughout the history of the green movement in Sweden, particularly in the public debate on nuclear power. They are both nuclear physicists, but have had radically divergent positions in the debate — Eriksson being against, and Gerholm for. Karl-Erik was as puzzled as I, and couldn't make any sense out of it. Professor Gerholm was known as a very tough and even ruthless debater, but he was certainly not known to be dishonest.

Since TNS was positioned as a bridge-building organization between science and decision makers, a blow to our scientific bridge-head was a blow intended to kill. And it was a smart move, since all the decision makers taking part in our dialog didn't need to be attacked. And this was certainly how *Svenska Dagbladet* used the opportunity. Although its editorial page didn't have much of a scientific reputation, and although the book from Professor Gerholm was built on obviously fabricated flaws, such facts didn't help us much. This was not the type of criticism that I was used to in the peer review processes of scientific journals or within the TNS public process. It was not primarily a matter of right and wrong but about trustworthiness and personal motives beyond right and wrong. Just the thought of starting a public debate about who said what and why, and how this or that was misunderstood was depressing. Particularly since the whole idea of TNS was to constantly apply the "Yes, and Techinique" to create dialog and learning. How did you apply this strategy if you were lied about and when the cause was not to study reality together? Something needed to be done, and quickly.

A number of friends from industry now swung into action, and the whole scenario became even more bizarre. Timbro claimed (and still claims) to be "The Thought-Melding-Pot for Industry." But here I was being protected against Timbro by industry — by people like Leif Johansson and Gustaf Uggla at Electrolux, Russel Johnsson at IKEA, Ola Ivarsson at Scandic, and Mats Lederhausen at McDonald's — all of whom were educated academics, mostly in natural sciences and engineering. They didn't need any help from Tor Ragnar Gerholm to understand the natural laws that underpinned the TNS framework. But the attack on TNS had created a problem for them, and they wanted me to do something about it.

Since every informed person in Sweden knew how much resources these men's respective firms had spent on moving in the direction given by the TNS framework, a number of customers and clients and business partners had started to pose questions about TNS. Certainly, it would be impossible to sit by the phone, talk to everybody in Sweden who harbored doubts about TNS, and straighten out all the question marks by going through the science that was now under debate. Although my friends in industry wanted some action from me to help the situation, they made one thing very clear: I was forbidden to accept a debate on the editorial page of *Svenska Dagbladet*. The reason was obvious. Those writers were not scientists; they were not even curious and interested in an amateurish way. Quite the contrary, they had already taken a stand without paying attention to even minor conventions on critical source evaluation, and had published claims about my supposed scientific flaws without even allowing me to respond to them before they were published. The intent was to kill, so no matter how well I argued, I would never win that battle in their backyard. Instead I was instructed to challenge Tor Ragnar Gerholm to an official debate. The challenge was delivered on the editorial page of *Svenska Dagbladet*, and the date was chosen to be after the New Year, on February 12, 1997.

In the meantime, my life was miserable. TNS employees continued to say that they weren't happy at TNS any more, and even more so now that we were under attack. At last, PUA and I found our new secretary general, just a few weeks after the King's seminar, and, of course a lot of hope was attached to him. Magnus Huss was an agronomist who had been an environmental adviser to the finance department of the Swedish government, and he had long experience at a top-management level in the waste management business. He was very pleasant and very firm. And he brought with him, from his previous job, an extraordinarily intelligent young engineer, Jonas Oldmark, with whom he had established a close partnership. I hoped that the two of them, together with PUA, would be able to create a better atmosphere in the office. That happened, but not in time to salvage the situation we were in right then. I remember that I looked out through my office window at the snowy streets of Stockholm, and reflected on the possibility that we might lose it all.

My fears deepened when Magnus told me that he and PUA didn't work well together and that PUA, too, had decided to leave the organization. I talked to them, and tried to convince them that it was very bad timing to reduce the manpower of the team even further, but nothing helped. PUA felt that his days at TNS were over and that our relationship from now on would be as friends on a personal level only.

At least PUA felt that I had done everything I could, but since it was-n't enough, he wasn't particularly happy. I felt an almost tangible sorrow. PUA had been so kind and funny and creative to work with. Without him we wouldn't have been able to pull it off, and he had always been completely loyal. Why was it impossible for me to keep him in TNS?

I remembered Lennart's and Russel's words: "Give more space to your peers so that they can grow." Was all this my fault? Anyhow, it was late now to do anything about it. And whatever I did, it didn't seem to help. So I decided to leave organizational matters behind for a while, and let Magnus Huss do his thing. I needed to focus com-pletely on the public debate with Tor Ragnar Gerholm, and decided to let this moment be the moment of truth.

On February 12, 1997, I came to the seminar room with my wife Rigmor. Gustav Uggla at Electrolux had been selected by my friends from business to coach me, and coach me he did. Together with some consultants that Electrolux used to work with, I had to train like a heavyweight boxing champion during the whole Christmas vacation. In my briefcase, I had a number of transparencies, on which I had photocopied what I actually had written in my first book, and under-neath each of these examples I had photocopied what Tor Ragnar Gerholm claimed that I had written — "quote" for "quote." The transparencies were collected in a file that my personal assistant at TNS, Kerstin Abrahamsson, had prepared for me.

The chief editor of the international environmental magazine *Tomorrow*, Claes Sjöberg, hosted the seminar and earned the money from it. *Svenska Dagbladet*, in a new editorial, decided to take a shot at the idea that it was The Natural Step and I who would earn money, even from this crucial intellectual event in our history. Claes Sjöberg corrected this, of course. Just before the seminar *Svenska Dagbladet* published yet another article in which it was claimed that TNS was at the edge of bankruptcy because we didn't make enough money. In my eyes, they seemed at least as desperate as I was.

Miljörapporten had successfully invited 250 people from the envi-ronmental scene in Sweden — "green" managers and people from academia. And in the other corner, "contrarians" without any interest in sustainability issues — friends of Tor Ragnar Gerholm and Timbro. My wife and I heard the murmurs from all the voices downstairs when we came through the entrance and hallway, where young men from some organization were handing out flyers about the need for more nuclear power and less political restrictions. When I came into the seminar room, I went over to Tor Ragnar Gerholm, wished him good luck, and hoped for an intellectually rewarding combat.

A first match, to warm the audience up, was on the agenda. Lars Bern, although he had just decided to leave TNS because of my inadequate way of dealing with PUA and my domineering way of stopping him or others from dealing with this matter in my place, was meeting the vice president of Timbro, Matthias Bengtsson. This was an uneven match. Matthias represented the "thought-melting-pot" of industry, but Lars — with a long career in top management in some of the most prestigious companies in Sweden — represented industry itself. And, further more, Lars — a doctor in chemistry — was interested in the subject, the environment. Matthias on the other hand, had no other interest in the environment but as a presumptive stumbling block to his beloved "invisible hand."

Lars was in good shape and the clear winner. This was so obvious that it carried an unforeseen risk. Mr. Bengtsson performed so badly that I think even his supporters didn't like it — in fact, there were no signs at all of support from the audience. At a certain point, Matthias claimed that the issue of extinction of species was highly overestimated and that far fewer species had actually become extinct than the public believed. When asked, he didn't know how many species the public thought had disappeared nor how many that actually had disappeared. The sounds of disbelief and mistrust from the audience were escalating. I was afraid that the debate climate would deteriorate and get out of control. If the audience started to boo, it could always be claimed later on that the conditions for the match between Timbro and TNS were not even. And to be honest, I would not have been able to deliver exact figures either.

Claes Sjöberg rescued the situation. He simply moved in and asked Mr. Bengtsson if he knew that a very high number of species were living in certain habitats only, and that they didn't exist outside of those. Mr Bengtsson said yes. And furthermore, did he realize that if such habitats were completely eradicated through the squandering of rainforests for instance, the species that lived only there would then disappear too? Mr. Bengtsson said yes again. And was he aware that very large areas of rainforests were gone? Again a yes, even weaker this time. "So, what you mean, Mr. Bengtsson, is that environmentalists exaggerate sometimes?" Mr. Bengtsson eagerly nodded his head to this indisputable truth. The issue was dropped, and the floor was ready for Professor Gerholm and me.

Needless to say, I was nervous. Attempts had been made to humiliate me and TNS in public, and in consideration of the organizational tensions we were suffering otherwise, the stakes were high enough. But one thing made me even more worried. What was it that made Professor Gerholm dare to show up at the debate? Personally, if I knew that I had built my case on falsified quotes, I would have found the situation difficult if I were in his shoes. But here he was, seemingly self-confident. What had he planned in surprise for me? I had decided that whatever new stuff he brought into the discussion, in order to hide from the real crucial issue about misquoting the scientific underpinnings of TNS, I wouldn't let him. Whatever new things he felt needed to be discussed I would offer to deal with at a later time. But the agenda for this debate was set.

Professor Gerholm didn't try to hide. Instead, he claimed the same things that were presented in his book. And each time, I hauled out the appropriate overhead from the file that Kerstin had prepared for me — on the top the original text; underneath the falsified quote from the professor. Silence — a stop-ball. Another claim, another overhead, another stop-ball. Professor Gerholm started to sweat, only a little in the beginning; then his suit became dark from being soaked. We were photographed after the debate, and the photographer told me that he had never seen anybody's suit that wet before.

Lennart Dahlgren at IKEA had told me very firmly before the seminar that if things started to go the way we expected them to, I was under no circumstances to be arrogant or display any signs of victory. Although Professor Gerholm was known in Sweden as a demonic debater, with a demagogic potential that could kill even ingenious arguments, I was a young and strong scientist leading an influential organization. Tor Ragnar Gerholm, on the other hand, had certainly falsified quotes. But he was a retired old man who could easily score on plain sympathy. Humbleness and politeness; humbleness and politeness... "Come on, Professor Gerholm, as long as we can agree on the scientific matters, and as long as it is made clear to any one in the audience that Chalmer's University and Stockholm's University (the latter was the academic home of Professor Gerholm before his retirement) have the same scientific worldview, well then, we can relax — no harm done."

As a last joker in the game, I hauled out of my sleeve a review that I had done of a book by Professor Gerholm. *Futurum Exactum* was published in the '70s and was about the promise of nuclear power. I had used this book to demonstrate how far you can go with the use of quotes, even if you don't falsify them. Just by putting the right quotes into the "right" context, I successfully showed that Professor Gerholm in fact had been thinking in terms of system conditions already in the early '70s and that he was desperately concerned about non-sustainable development.

As if this were not enough, the fascinating book of Professor Gerholm in fact demonstrated that he himself didn't believe in today's form of nuclear power as an energy source for the future. His whole focus was instead put on the promising new fusion power that was under development. (Since nothing had happened in this arena since, the conclusion could be made that there was little room for hope about nuclear power, at least if you listened to Professor Gerholm.) The strongest advocate for nuclear power had, in fact, doomed nuclear power, and nobody had thought about it. The reason was, of course, that in the '70s there was still hope about fusion power, and fission plants could be regarded as a preparatory stage. By the time of our debate, the environmentalists had forgotten about *Futurum Exactum*. I provoked some cheers when I elected Professor Gerholm an environmentalist on the barricades.

Claes Sjöberg finished the seminar by asking Professor Gerholm if he had been correctly quoted. Tor Ragnar Gerholm nodded "Yes" without any further ado. And the time had come for the question and answer session with the audience.

A journalist asked Professor Gerholm how he had ended up in this situation. Professor Eriksson's description of Professor Gerholm as an honest man came true. He hadn't acted out of his academic interest. Instead, he had been hired as a consultant by some people linked to the Swedish Employers Federation (SAF). His work had resulted in a report that was put in a drawer for later use. Since the initial intent was not to publish the report, Professor Gerholm had allowed himself to be lax in the reading and quoting. Later on, when it was felt that TNS had started to become more influential, the people behind the plot simply phoned Professor Gerholm up, told him what a great piece he had written, and suggested that it was time to go ahead and publish it. So when I challenged Professor Gerholm a couple of years later, he simply thought that he was going to talk physics with some medical doctor in public — nothing that scared him, really. The old man had forgotten how his book was fabricated, and he didn't bother to control it before the debate, either.

So all the pieces came into place afterward. The aim was to kill, not to bring the dialog on science in sustainable development further.

What We Learned

The follow-up to the debate was as interesting to me as the debate itself. The day after, in another editorial in *Svenska Dagbladet*, it was claimed that I had "hugged Professor Gerholm to death" — a notion that was impossible to understand, of course, for anyone who hadn't been at the seminar. And only 250 Swedes out of 9 million were. Not a word about how the "hugging" had been done, and not a word about the documented Gerholm falsifications that I had handed out at the seminar. A professor in human ecology, Professor Bengt Hubendick, sent an angry reply to the paper about intellectual dishonesty, asking if the people from *Svenska Dagbladet* had attended the same seminar he had. It wasn't published, of course. Other people, some of them peers of mine, claimed that part of the lack of public impact from Gerholm's defeat could be blamed on me. I had been too polite and too careful not to appear arrogant. For people who are not used to scientific arguments, my reticence may have hidden the spectacular results from the debate. According to some, I could at least have looked happy when Professor Gerholm's actions were exposed!

Only one tiny piece of media coverage outside of *Svenska Dagbladet* appeared after the seminar. It was by Helle Klein, a senior journalist at one of the two leading evening papers, and she talked about Timbro's defeat. Later on, and with no apparent connection to the debate, a report on Swedish TV displayed Professor Gerholm as a member of the Global Climate Coalition. The Coalition was a contrarian movement that dealt with the political turbulence around the greenhouse effect and that attempted to minimize any political consequences for "free market" forces. Together with some veterinarians and dentists and other people from academia, Professor Gerholm had tried to appear as a specialist in meteorology, which he and most of the other "specialists" were not, of course. It also turned out that he was a member of the "Moonies," a quite dubious organization for the financing of such activities.

Professor Gerholm hadn't quite given up yet. He wrote a very long report, in which he tried to explain why it had been important to falsify my quotes. Sometimes the motives had been "pedagogical" and sometimes it had been out of "politeness." This wasn't published as a new book, of course, because (with one exception) nobody would touch it — TNS published it in our own journal. Since the debate, people working at *Svenska Dagbladet* have been openly apologetic to us about the misconduct that occurred. For instance, some of the editors of other pages in the same paper have made comments in their own editorial page. One of them even referred to the editorial page as a case of "group psychosis."

Before the debate, Timbro had warned that the attack on TNS was only the beginning, and that from now on they would mercilessly reveal all the flaws of the whole environmental movement in Sweden. Aside from a vague and toothless attack on the Swedish Society for Nature Conservation, which didn't lead anywhere, we still haven't seen any of this. But the president of Timbro recently got himself a new job as one of the two chief editors of *Svenska Dagbladet*, and Matthias Bengtsson is a steady contributor of articles.

People from the mass media explained to me that the sudden silence after the debate was as typical of journalists as it was for "you medical doctors." We generally don't display each other's professional mistakes, at least if we are not under attack ourselves. So, the wake of the debate was not a public success for TNS but a dead end to the attacks on us and an internal celebration together with our clients in industry. Together, we had pulled it off.

TNS slowly recovered from its depression. A number of wonderful people had left the organization, among them my friends PUA and Lars Bern and an extremely competent colleague, Anders Frisk. Another close friend, Pelle Landstedt, had planned to leave. But when the attacks from Timbro and *Svenska Dagbladet* hit us, he decided to stay out of plain loyalty. Somewhat later, when the battle was over, he went to South Africa and did a masterful job in establishing TNS there.

Still others suffered through the whole process with me: Kerstin Abrahamsson, for instance. Kerstin was my secretary at the hospital where I started TNS and became the second employee of TNS. She is the most loyal and devoted person I have ever met in my professional life; without her we would never have made it. Together with Magnus and Jonas, we slowly turned everything around. The personnel that left were exchanged for new staff, and everybody was now even happier than before.

Today, from his place in the driver's seat, Magnus has successfully consolidated TNS into a very firm and self-confident team, and he has done so without selling out any of our entrepreneurial soul. Imagination and strictness, in combination with a completely honest and non-sentimental attitude toward business were the characteristics in Magnus that we needed.

We have discussed this dramatic story a lot among ourselves, of course. What had we learned? Some of our experience was just plain unpleasant, something we simply didn't need. "Bad faith" or, in Sartre's words, "*mauvaise foi*", is to invent errors, put them into the mouth of your opponent, and then correct them yourself. Sartre considered this the worst form of intellectual dishonesty. To spend time on refuting lies and arguing with people who were genuinely ignorant in our field of expertise wasn't very rewarding. But was that all? Were we the good guys, and were they the bad guys, and was everything going to be fine now?

In the end, the issue was not about winning a battle. First, the people at Timbro certainly don't think that we were right just because things didn't go their way. Second, Timbro was of little significance on the environmental scene, since they were not interested in it. What mattered was what part TNS played in the problem we had run into, and what we could do to make things easier on ourselves next time we were attacked. And that will happen, as long as we continue to be successful.

A few things came up during our self-questioning. John Holmberg, my closest colleague in science, felt that although the attack from Timbro had missed its target, there was good reason to take the whole thing seriously. Had we really been self-critical and humble enough at all times? Hadn't we ourselves appeared a bit pretentious every now and then? And didn't we have some as-yet inexperienced communicators in our network, who were not all that careful when they explained the science behind the TNS Framework? According to John, some of the false claims from Professor Gerholm might have come from such sources.

It had been claimed that I considered the system conditions to be laws of nature. A law of nature can never be violated, but a principle for something can — even if it is as incontrovertibly a condition for this "something" as any natural law. According to John, and I am certain that he is right, we will continuously have to safeguard TNS from within, being even more self-critical, so that rumors of this kind will not get the chance to weaken us the next time we are under attack. Had we been even humbler and even more successful in communicating science, maybe a public back-fire would have forced Timbro into a more radical self-questioning from their defeat than was now the case.

Another thought came from our new secretary general, Magnus Huss. He felt that TNS was occasionally perceived as being Social Democratic, in spite of the fact that our core values would forbid any political linkages or other affirmations. PUA had been an active Social Democrat in his earlier professional life, and although this could not in any way disqualify him for his top job at TNS, it could certainly have influenced Timbro to believe that we were a dangerous bunch of Social Democrats in disguise, just using scientific arguments to hurt the "invisible hand." Both these arguments were not particularly difficult to absorb. An ongoing self-critical assessment of science, and even more skilful ways of communicating a strict political neutrality, are key elements to an organization of our kind.

The TNS concept is not a set of ready-made claims. It is the opposite — a manual to discover knowledge together, and it evolves organically by the engagement from its stakeholders. It builds on the good old scientific methodology of critical thinking, improvement, more criticism, and so on, in a constructive cycle. Another asset is our focus on good examples, rather than on being adversarial. Furthermore, we present how others have applied our concept instead of boasting ourselves or being adversarial to those who don't want to work with us.

When attacked or criticized, we apply the "Yes, and Technique" for two reasons:

- to get our real message through, that is, to avoid debates that are based on misunderstandings (misunderstandings are more likely to happen when people get defensive); and

- to expand our learning by listening. The "Yes, and Technique" makes people more relaxed, and this helps them to maintain their intellectual sharpness and integrity.

No matter how innocent this may sound, no one in the TNS network that I am aware of is a saint (even if Kerstin does come close).

Sainthood wouldn't even be desirable, since the TNS concept is about involvement from everyone, based on equality. So we have to help each other and maintain an ongoing self-critical assessment of our performance. It's the only way. In the very nick of time when we think that "Now we have got it; the rest is a matter of teaching the others," we are finished.

Long before Professor Gerholm's attack, I had been asked many times if TNS was ever criticized. The debate with Professor Gerholm gave me the opportunity to really think this through. First I felt ashamed when I thought about it. I recalled how I had answered differently each time this question was given to me, depending on my mood at the moment. The first mistake in this was not reflecting on the context to the question.

Such questions may have been posed to me out of plain curiosity, of course. Other times the question may have carried some disguised criticism: "This concept sounds so damned good, and such things always make me suspicious." Anyway, when you are asked about criticism, it's a neutral question, and you have to respond. So what do you say? Talking about some silly attacks and how cleverly the attacker was knocked down is no good. Pretending that we never get attacked or that we only get silly attacks is no good, either, since it is not true. And being a saint and saying that whenever we get attacked we just improve is even worse. Rather than trying to respond to the general question of whether we ever get attacked, I have tried to make a systematic display of the different types of criticism that we have experienced in Sweden:

- **Rumors** There have been rumors that we mistrust politicians and the democratic process. And the opposite, that we are always patting politicians on the shoulders, being "good" all the time. Exactly the same rumors have been around regarding our attitude to business: we are sometimes enemies of the free market, going for "eco-fascism," at the same time that we have a naive belief in what free market forces can achieve. We are too simplistic, too scientific/academic, too rich, too poor, and so on. To judge from rumors, at least the ones I have heard, we must be quite centered and focused, since they are scattered all over the place. Consequently, the critical rumors cause no real worry, and shouldn't take too much time from us.

- **Informed criticism.** This is criticism from people who know what they are talking about. This is the main resource of TNS, our key asset — though it is emotionally difficult to enjoy it at the time. To listen to informed criticism, to learn from it, and to evolve from it is at the core of what TNS is, or at least wants to be. And so far, we have been good enough at it to develop into what we are today. And again: whenever we think that now we have got it, and now we are going to "convince" the others that we have, there is no TNS any more. The temptation to forget that will increase with each success story, of course, and it poses a threat to us that will never go away. So we will just have to work hard on it, and hope that we will get as much help as possible from critics who are there to help us improve rather than to kill us.

- **Disinformation.** Such attacks have not been common. We have only experienced the two that I have already described.

Finally, what happened to Professor Gerholm, and what are our thoughts about him? We tried to make it good — we even had an "at home with Professor Gerholm" report in our TNS journal, and we offered him our journal free of charge. We said that he should always feel free to criticize us and get his criticism published. But after the debate, he showed no further interest in us.

I had no problem with our philosophical and personal differences — Professor Gerholm and I are simply different personalities. My view is that the longer we delay measures out of our free will that are sufficient from a social and ecological sustainability perspective, the closer we get to harsh political legislation that tries to enforce it on us — exactly what Professor Gerholm wants to avoid. Professor Gerholm on the other hand, seems to think that society is already so clearly on the right track from an ecological and social standpoint that more political influence can only be negative.

Personal discrepancies between people like Professor Gerholm and me are not relevant to the bridge-building organization TNS. This organization tries to describe and disseminate a framework for planning that is neutral to the people who apply it. At TNS we believe that this framework will not be abused or misused, or at least that it will be used more often in a constructive way than in a destructive one. Professor Gerholm probably believes the opposite, and we have to live with that.

The Natural Step had become a bit smaller. We had been through an ordeal, had grown together, and we felt stronger and more self-confident than ever. I was not afraid anymore of being too public, because now we had a business plan that made explicit that we were going to concentrate on a more introverted life. The "molding of opinion" aspect had been dealt with; very few doubted that the environment was an important issue, and now it was more a matter of "how" than "why." One of the first steps was to consider how the TNS Framework related to various tools and concepts, such as Factor 4 and Factor 10 and ISO 14001 and Zero Emission and Life Cycle Assessment and Ecological Footprinting and.... There were many expressions around, and there was substantial confusion about how all these tools related to each other.

In 1998 I was invited to a UNEP workshop in Paris to meet with a number of influential organizations that were working with some of these tools. That work triggered the writing of an article, published in *International Journal of Cleaner Productions* in the year 2000 (see Appendix 3). In this article, I elaborated a five-stage model for planning in any complex system and used the model to put the TNS Framework in the context of other initiatives and concepts for sustainable development. I was then invited to lead an extensive work where pioneers of many concepts (Zero Emission, Cleaner Production, Ecological Footprinting, Factor 10, Sustainable Technology, Natural Capitalism) had their respective concepts studied in the same way. This article is to be published in the same journal in February 2002. The conclusion was that the different concepts highlight various aspects of sustainable development and that they are complementary in this respect — which suggests synergies and cooperation rather than competition between the respective NGOs supporting the concepts.

I found the work more and more rewarding, and it was with a great feeling of contentment that I started to work more intensely with scientific development and with business corporations that wanted coaching on ever deeper levels.

PART FIVE

Into the Future

CHAPTER 14

THE CRUCIAL ENERGY PROBLEM

WE HAVE 12 NUCLEAR POWER plants in Sweden. One day in 1996, I was invited to one of them (Ringhals) to make a presentation about the A, B, C, D Analysis to the whole management team. They had decided to become more proactive and introduce an environmental performance system, and I must admit that I was a bit nervous. How was I to help them insert Ringhals into the TNS Framework? The comforting thought was, of course, that they would have to do it by themselves. Regardless, it would be an ordeal, because virtually no other issue in Sweden was as controversial as nuclear power.

Fifty percent of the electricity we use comes from nuclear power, and the other 50 percent comes from hydropower — we have lots of that in the mountains up north. We use more electricity per capita than anyone else in Europe — almost twice as much as Germans, for instance. To a large extent this is because expanding the need for electricity (for instance by introducing direct electric heating in houses) was a conscious strategy by industry and the government to introduce nuclear power in Sweden. It was believed that this new energy system carried a lot of potential and hope to a nation with industrial export ambitions, so by making us all need more electricity, it would be easier to introduce nuclear power.

This strategy, together with political handling later, made nuclear power one of the hottest political topics in the political history of Sweden. Not only was it free of traditional market demands to pay its own insurance costs — profit should be shared in line with a capitalistic rationale and costs in line with a communistic rationale — but the democratic process was in itself sidestepped in a more or less scandalous way. Nuclear power was introduced above the heads of people.

People felt uncertain about the new technology, and the government eventually felt obliged to bring the issue to a public vote. The opinion was that a simple "Yes/No" choice would most likely lead to a "No" vote, which would have been the end of it. Our Social Democratic prime minister at the time, Olof Palme, was for nuclear power and didn't want to take the risk. So he invented an ingenious move. He offered us three choices: "Yes," "No," and a sort of "Perhaps" alternative. The "Perhaps" option was designed in terms of a phase-out but a phase-out in due time and not too abruptly.

One needed to know only a little of statistics about voting processes to figure out that the "Yes" and "Perhaps" alternatives would together beat the "No" alternative; thus the result of the voting was predetermined. The psychology of this was a bit too subtle and the joint lobbying power of industry and government a bit too strong for this to be a fatal political scandal. Olof Palme pulled it off.

So there I was standing in front of well over 100 managers of Ringhals, where I was expected to deliver a speech as a kick-off to their new environmental plans. I presented the TNS Framework — the funnel, system conditions at the opening of the funnel, and a program built on backcasting to take you there. And I presented the manual for the framework — the A, B, C, D Analysis. And, in line with our traditional policy, I didn't say a word about the energy or utility sectors. To keep everybody in a relaxed and learning mode while the model was displayed, and out of respect for the particpants' competence in their own field, we trained the model on furniture and agriculture. Then we had lunch.

After lunch I got the inevitable question: can you apply the framework to Ringhals? I responded that the framework should be applied by professionals, not laymen, but I offered to facilitate the discussion. Step A (discussing the framework and testing its relevance) was already done, so we went straight ahead to Step B. And instead of telling them anything, I started to pose questions with reference to the system conditions in a "today perspective."

"Is there anything at all coming from the Earth's crust in your activities, leading to increasing concentrations of compounds anywhere in the ecosphere?" After some embarrassment, I got, "The fuel, of course — uranium, but also fossil fuels (support energy) and some heavy metals in the construction of the reactors." Under System Condition 2, I got waste, the production of new isotopes and leakage of those from the plant, and the spread of very high and sudden amounts from potential accidents. Under System Condition 3, I got the stripping of land during mining.

A very interesting thing happened as we went through the first three system conditions in the Step B. Some of the managers jumped in and claimed that this and that problem didn't exist or was minor or could be solved with some ease. But their own colleagues corrected them, or made the dialog subtler. One exchange, for instance, went something like this:

"We use few materials from the Earth's crust, since uranium is such energy-intensive stuff."

"Well, I am not so certain that I agree. If you consider the full life cycle, it is actually plenty. There are, for instance, enormous amounts of sludge from the mining process, with leakage of considerable amounts of radioactive isotopes, and we use much more fossil fuels as support energy than the public generally is aware of," and so on. And as a response to claims that hardly any ecological areas were consumed at all since the reactors were so small in comparison to all the energy they supplied (System Condition 3), a manager brought the stripping of land for uranium mining into the discussion.

So what happened? The managers found themselves in a frustrating tension of polarities. On the one hand they wanted to be loyal to their company. On the other, it was clear that they didn't want to appear stupid or consciously hide smart ideas that could be helpful for the process. The latter generally wins. If a large enough number of smart people meet, it is virtually impossible to even imagine that they all would just sit there and hide intelligent thoughts in order to be loyal to their company, unless, of course, you offend people or try to appear smarter or more knowledgeable than you are. If you do that, then anybody can just grab hold of one of your flawed thoughts or erroneous pieces of information and stick to the slaughtering of that, without ever looking at the big picture. But in this case they were only to apply a neutral framework that would help to bring the big picture around for the ordering of data and information. My role was only to ask questions with reference to the framework.

The really interesting stuff happened at the end, when we started to talk about System Condition 4 under Step C — the envisioning part. "Nuclear power is really efficient in meeting human needs and has a great potential for that, particularly if you compare it with fossil fuels."

"Well, I am not so certain about that. Nuclear power, in comparison with fossil fuels, plays a minor role on the global scene. And it's a global funnel we are contemplating here. Even at today's production volume, we have come up with quite an impressive list of problems in stage B. If we in the nuclear power industry are to play any significant role when fossil fuels have been phased out, we would have to expand nuclear power greatly. And this would be needed even without considering the growing needs of the developing world. In light of the impressive list of problems we have just discovered, is Ringhals really an example of an energy source that will be efficient enough on the global scale?"

"Well, we could move to breed reactors; they are much more efficient."

"No, they produce plutonium, which is even more problematic from a global perspective. Would you really like to have thousands of producers of plutonium distributed around the world with all the terrorist groups there are? Would that be an efficient or economical way of meeting human needs?"

Right before my eyes, the group of managers slowly phased out today's forms of nuclear power. They also told me that they had known even before the seminar that today's nuclear power is but a parenthesis in industrial history. The framework merely helped them structure thoughts and conclusions that they already were aware of, so that they could look at the whole picture together. One of them, driving me to the train after the seminar, even started to talk about which reactors in Sweden we should close down first. Ringhals was not one of them, he argued, since it is quite modern in relation to some of the others. I believe he was right.

A few years later, the government decided to close down Barsebäck, a reactor located so close to Copenhagen in Denmark that it has caused political tensions between the two neighboring countries. Many people have told me that this political event — to some extent motivated by the government in terms of the TNS Framework's way of thinking — was probably the trigger behind Professor Gerholm's attack. I don't know if this was true, and I probably never will.

I learned a lot about nuclear power, and about energy in general, from listening to the experts from Ringhals. And I was impressed by their intellectual integrity and honesty. At the same time it was clear that a similar analysis of today's forms of fossil fuels would lead to the same result: they have no long-term future, either. These two energy sources, fossil fuels and nuclear power, are often confronted with each other in a sort of "pest or cholera" debate (at least in Sweden) and treated as if they were the only options. A much smarter public debate could be based on backcasting: "Tomorrow's energy systems are complying with the system conditions. Which route is the smartest way to get there?"

The meeting at Ringhals sensitized me even more for the events in the energy sector that were going to take place in Sweden and internationally in the coming years. Although I had often claimed in debate articles and such that the funnel made it inevitable to expect a lot of things to happen shortly, I couldn't imagine how fast the intellectual paradigm shift would take place. Along with my scientific peers John Holmberg and another friend at our Institution at Chalmers, the physicist and climate expert Christian Azar, we studied the change of perspectives that the energy sector had been subjected to during recent years, and we published our findings in the World Business Academy's journal *Perspectives on Business and Global Change*.[1]

Nuclear power represents a tiny sector of the global energy economy — around 2,000 TWH (terrawatt-hours) against fossil fuels' 80,000 TWH — so economic activity and investment patterns in the global energy sector are still centered around fossil fuels (global oil markets alone represent some $US400 billion per year). Fossil fuel industries or energy-intensive industries have generally been skeptical about warnings of global warming and climate change, and in particular about policies to combat it. In *The Carbon War*, Jeremy K. Leggett provides interesting case studies into how oil and coal industries have "been guilty of manipulation and distortion" on a massive scale over the past decade.[2] Still, John, Christian, and I could see many signs of growing interest and awareness in a number of business sectors. Policy statements in a proactive direction were being made, as well as investments in new, more climate-friendly technologies.

It follows from basic scientific laws that increasing amounts of carbon dioxide (CO_2) and other greenhouse gases will affect the global climate. The informed debate was not about the existence of such effects but rather about their magnitude and seriousness. In the year 2000, the concentration of CO_2 was approximately 30 percent higher than its preindustrial level, and scientists have already been able to observe that there is a discernible human influence on the global climate.[3] There is a substantial risk that the changes will be devastating in several regions of the world. Even a quite radical decrease of CO_2 emissions (on average about 50 percent lower than at present over the next century) will still lead to increased concentrations in the atmosphere. That increase could bring about a corresponding potential increase of global mean temperature that is twice as high as the natural temperature fluctuations during the past 1,000 years.[4] There are also many other environmental problems associated with the use of fossil fuels, for example, acidification, metal pollution, local air pollution, and accidents in the distribution systems. We can therefore expect increasingly stronger pressure from the market (consumers, industry, and finance institutes) and the political system (governments as well as other democratic institutions) to diminish the use of fossil fuels in favor of renewable energy and increased energy efficiency.

The rate at which change will happen is unknown, and this is sometimes seen as an argument for companies not to take action. However, in reality, the implications of this observation work the other way around. Once a transition away from fossil fuels is initiated, companies that have not taken measures to reduce their dependence on fossil fuels are vulnerable (a risk of rapid cost increases and loss of market share), whereas companies having developed and invested in the energy technologies of the future will have the flexibility to take advantage of future market conditions.

Potential changes to future markets because of environmental concerns is becoming more and more important when energy strategies are discussed. Previously, it was mainly the geopolitical features of the oil reserves that caused concern. Then increasing fossil fuel reserves were used as a major counterargument against the need of a transition toward renewable energy sources. And indeed, coal does exist in large quantities, although oil reserves are less abundant. We can foresee that an increasing share of production capacity and oil reserves will be located in the Middle East, with associated risks of price control. To have the availability of coal as the sole basis for strategic planning is not only insufficient from a socioeconomic perspective, but also from a self-beneficial point of view in the individual firm.

Currently the use of fossil fuels contributes to regionally — and sometimes even globally — increasing concentrations of compounds such as carbon dioxide, nitrogen oxides, sulfur dioxide, heavy metals that contaminate the fuels, and so on (System Conditions 1 and 2). Some of the polluting compounds have already reached concentrations that cause such effects in the ecosphere as climate change, ozone depletion, eutrophication, acidification, and other eco-toxic effects as well as human diseases such as asthma and cancer. Direct physical influence on the ecosystems from activities such as the extraction of petroleum contributes to the physical impoverishment of the ecosphere (System Condition 3). However, in comparison to the road system, petroleum extraction is a relatively minor problem (on a global scale).

We can also see many problems related to System Condition 4 when we study the use of fossil fuels — for example, the external effects from the use of fossil fuels, particularly in the developing world, are most likely not paid for. Furthermore, a phase out of fossil fuels is a long-term project to avoid ever greater problems to future generations in all parts of the world. If we don't commence the phase out now, it's just a way of pushing the problems ahead of us. Future generations will then have to do it, with even tighter time frames and from a weaker standpoint due to the expected damage and costs from the greenhouse effect.

In light of these considerations, one may foresee increasing political and social pressure regarding CO_2 emissions as well as the other environmental problems associated with the use of fossil fuels. These problems can be solved by increasing energy efficiency and increasing the use of renewables (with careful considerations of the environmental problems such an expansion could cause). The potential for doing so is large. The Earth receives more than 10,000 times more energy from the sun than all other forms combined: fossil fuels, nuclear, hydro, and bioenergy. In addition, the technology that can utilize solar energy is developing at a rapid rate. For example, using solar cells at today's efficiency, an area corresponding to about 10 percent of the Sahara desert could supply as much energy as is used today in the whole world. Solar energy can also be used to generate hydrogen, which subsequently could be fed into fuel cells for the generation of power (and heat) or used directly as a fuel in industrial processes. Thus, we may envision a future energy system that is virtually pollutant-free compared to the present fossil energy-based system. This has also been recognized by a number of leading industries, including auto manufacturers and oil producers who have made some initial steps toward abating greenhouse gas emissions.

Automotive Industries

In the automotive industry, much attention is given to fuel cells, which in combination with an electric motor would provide a new propulsion technique. DaimlerChrysler has already demonstrated several proof-of-concept cars run either on hydrogen or methanol and has stated that it will put 40,000 fuel cell cars on the road by 2004. DaimlerChrysler recently (1998) bought shares in Ballard Power Systems, a leading fuel cell manufacturer, at a cost of $US 276 million.

Other car manufacturers, such as Toyota, claim that they will beat DaimlerChrysler in commercializing fuel cells. Essentially all major car companies have fuel cell programs.[5] Cost reduction remains the main research and development objective for a successful commercialization of the technology. PEM fuel cells, the most promising fuel cell technology for cars, cost today more than a $US1,000 per kilowatt, and to be competitive with today's internal combustion engines, the target is set at $US50 per kilowatt. Detailed studies carried out by Directed Technologies, Inc., commissioned by Ford, claim that these targets can be met once mass production is established. By their nature, such studies are uncertain, but it nevertheless shows that fuel cells may turn out to be a major competitor to the internal combustion engine.

Fuel cell cars will initially run either on methanol or gasoline, which will be reformed into hydrogen before being used in the fuel cell. These fuels are based on fossil fuels (methanol is mainly produced from natural gas) but would nevertheless give rise to major environmental improvements. The technology can be expected to be twice as efficient as the internal combustion engine and therefore will produce lower CO_2 emissions. There would be virtually no other pollutants. Furthermore, such a development could serve as a platform for a complete switch toward renewable energy sources. In the longer run, fuel cells would ideally be fed by hydrogen directly. If the hydrogen were based on renewables, then we would be very close to a zero-emission transportation system. Thus, if fuel cells become the winning technology, major changes in energy supply, fuel distribution, and car manufacturing can be expected. Car manufacturers have a lot to win by being proactive in this race.

Interestingly, Paul Heston, fuels technology manager of BP Amoco, claimed that cars in the future will run on fuel cells powered by hydrogen obtained by splitting water, according to a report in *New Scientist*.[6] Clearly, these are long-term visions. But it should also be kept in mind that BP Amoco is prospecting for new oil discoveries in 24 countries, according to the same report. There are also advances in the automotive industry that are not related to fuel cells. European car manufacturers have, for instance, entered into a voluntary agreement with the European commission to reduce CO_2 emissions by 25 percent over the years.[7]

Oil industries

Interestingly, some big oil companies have also taken major steps in a promising direction. BP has set up a voluntary target to reduce greenhouse gas emissions by 10 percent by the year 2010. The head of BP, John Browne, has called for new taxation to curb energy use and guard against the threat of climate change.[8] He stated that he is aware of the future stakes of the enormous energy potential from the sun, and that this awareness will change the strategy of BP's planning ahead.

BP is also one of the world's leading solar cell manufacturers. Following the merger with Amoco, BP Amoco stated that it will buy Enron's share in Solarex (jointly owned with Amoco), and thereby create the world's largest solar cell company.[9] Its aim is to make solar cells a billion dollar business by 2010.

Encouraging developments can also be seen at Shell. The company states that it has already reduced its CO_2 emissions by 5 percent over the period 1990-1997, and that it aims at a 10 percent reduction by the year 2002.[10] The company has also stated that it will invest $US500 million in renewable energy development over the next five years.[11]

Oil giant ARCO has also voiced its concern about climate change. Its chairman and CEO Mike Bowlin even stated that "we have embarked on the beginning of the last days of the age of oil."[12]

In well-publicized moves, first Shell and then BP left the US-based Global Climate Coalition (GCC), which combines many fossil fuels companies in an attempt to lobby against international treaties aiming to reduce global carbon emissions. Several student governments at universities across the US, including Stanford and Harvard, have passed resolutions calling for their respective universities to divest or in other ways put pressure on GCC members.[13]

Interesting developments also are occurring in the Norwegian oil and gas industries. Carbon dioxide is obtained as a by-flow from gas extraction and normally released to the atmosphere, but Statoil captures the unwanted CO_2 and injects a total of 600,000 tonnes of CO_2 per year into the floor of the North Sea. Eventually 1 megaton of CO_2 will be injected annually, a figure that represents some 3 percent of Norwegian CO_2 emissions. This activity is mainly a response to the Norwegian carbon tax, and it gives Statoil important technological experience in a technology that may grow increasingly important over the following years. Equally interesting are Norsk Hydro's plans to produce hydrogen from natural gas. The hydrogen would be used to generate electricity, and the separated CO_2 would be sequestered in oil wells in the North Sea. The project has been postponed, but if successfully implemented, could compete with photovoltaics and other CO_2 free electricity sources.

Other Industries

Finally other parts of industry have also expressed concerns about climate change and have committed themselves to abatement targets. A survey by the Confederation of British Industry (CBI) has found strong support among its members to set tough targets during the Kyoto conference. Eighty-three percent of the companies that responded to a survey on this and other topics said that they believed that "the world community should agree to tough reduction targets (15 percent) for greenhouse gas reduction by the year 2010."[14] Several major international companies including metals, chemical, and semiconductor manufacturers have taken on voluntary agreements.

DuPont recently announced that it will reduce its greenhouse gas emissions by 65 percent (!) between 1990 and 2010, and it has already met its 45 percent reduction target for the year 2010, primarily by controlling non CO_2 greenhouse gases.[15] Dennis Reilly, executive vice president, stated that "the absence of incentives and the continuance of subsidies for our fossil fuel-based global economy will only serve to strengthen the status quo — a scenario that shows increasing carbon concentrations in the atmosphere with unknown but potentially significant changes in our global climate.... As a company, we believe that action is warranted, not further debate. We also believe that the best approach is for business to lead, not wait for public outcry or government mandates."

Similarly IBM has committed itself to cut its worldwide emissions of PFCs (a set of industrial greenhouse gases).[16] The European

Electronic Component Manufacturers Association, the Electronic Industries Association of Japan, the Korea Semiconductor Industry Association, and the US Semiconductor Industry Association followed suit and agreed on a 10 percent reduction.[17]

The Pew Center on Global Climate Change has organized 21 major multinational companies, including oil and car companies, into a Business Environmental Leadership Council.[18] These companies have expressed support for the Kyoto process and they claim, in a joint statement, that they "believe that one of our most serious challenges at home and abroad will be addressing global climate change." Economic rationales for "beyond compliance" behavior have been discussed in the literature by several authors.[19]

Conclusions and Strategic Planning in Practice

In our paper on corporate risk assessment for fossil fuels, Christian, John, and I reached the conclusion that backcasting needed to be stressed as an important strategy concerning investments in the energy sector because:

- The environmental and health risks from the use of fossil fuels are increasing;

- The scientific community lacks tools that can safely determine strict thresholds for various adversarial effects. This means, in practical terms, that the scientific consensus is that we are out of control concerning the risks linked to further large-scale use of fossil fuels;

- Any costly consequence of the use of fossil fuels can be attributed to flying in the face of one or more of the four system conditions. Being relatively dependent on or being a large contributor to this is not only unwise from an altruistic standpoint, but also from a self-interest point of view. The "polluter pays" principle may in practical terms be implemented not only through legislation, but from other mechanisms such as insurance costs, more costly financing, credibility in the market, business agreements, and so forth.

In conclusion, economic dependence on fossil fuels will be more and more risky in the future — ecologically as well as economically. This implies that the burden of proof for large-scale investments in a continuing dependence on fossil fuels will switch from the "green sector" of society to the investors themselves. Based on this reasoning, we suggest that any large investment decision should be accompanied by the following strategic questions:

- Does this investment decrease our economic dependence on fossil fuels?

- Is the investment a sound platform that enables further reductions ahead? (Can it be further elaborated in line with the system conditions?)

- Will it pay off soon enough to enable further investments toward even less dependence on fossil fuels?

- If the answer to the last question is that such rapid payoffs are doubtful, one must ask whether there are other alternative investments that can be elaborated in a step-by-step fashion to meet the frame given by the system conditions.

- If the answers to the questions above do not provide sufficient impetus to decide for a proactive course, the following question should be posed: if this investment increases our dependence on fossil fuels, or maintains our dependence on them, are the arguments for not changing strategy stronger than the arguments supporting proactivity? If the decision is not to be proactive, then that is also a decision. There is no rational reason to embrace a traditional decision the evidence for which is weaker than a decision to be proactive.

The 2000 Anniversary Book of Vattenfall

I had the opportunity to present my knowledge and experience in the energy sector in a chapter in the millennium book produced by the Swedish utility company Vattenfall. This story deserves to be told, because it is yet another example of intellectual honesty.

Vattenfall owns nuclear power, so I told the editor of the book that they would probably not like a contribution from me. I told her that a thorough analysis of the situation gave very little hope for nuclear power the way we know it today. She thought that I was wrong, and furthermore she said that she was in charge of the book. So I went ahead and wrote an article that was built on all the knowledge and experience I had collected during the years. (For the full article, see below.)

After I had sent it in to the editor, I didn't hear from her for a couple of months. Then she phoned me up and told me a story that may sound amusing, but which is in fact a story about decency and honesty. The editor had shown the article to the manager at Vattenfall who was primarily responsible for the book, who said he felt a clear discomfort, but couldn't really tell what it was. So he showed it to the vice president of the firm, and he too felt a discomfort, but couldn't put his finger on what was wrong. He, in turn, sent it to some environmental guru at Vattenfall, who said that there was nothing seriously wrong with the article and that it would be a demonstration of integrity for the company to dare to publish it in one of their own books. When I talked to him on the phone, he wanted to add and delete a few things that he felt were incorrect, and eventually a somewhat improved article was published in the annual book of Vattenfall, below.

Energy Yesterday, Today, and Tomorrow

The part of the world known as "the industrial world" has changed its energy systems on two previous occasions: from wood to coal, and from coal to the energy systems currently in use, such as oil and nuclear power. Each time the transition took some 40 years, and each time it was preceded by disdainful resistance from powerful vested interests in the obsolete energy systems. Once again we find ourselves in the same situation, only this time the opposition is stronger than ever before, possibly because investments in energy systems have never been larger. As one might expect, media attention is focusing on existing energy systems. The sort of scenario being presented is that society has to make a choice between fossil fuels and nuclear power. Long-term development, the future potential of various other resources, the market potential of alternative energy sources, and the need for a tie-in between the energy systems of the future and those of today are very rarely discussed. Hardly any attention is directed to those new energy systems that are being introduced and developed in markets today.

Rather, proponents of those energy sources that are growing strongly in world markets — solar and wind power — are often referred to as "regressive." Others advocating energy systems that are not growing at all in world markets, such as nuclear power, are perceived as "progressive." Lead writers and commentators are portraying a more or less fragmented picture. For the most part, these are people who respect the dictates of the market. After all, the market is always right. The same voices that ignore developments in the world's energy markets are at the same time playing down the dangers of the greenhouse effect and warning of the dire economic effects of phasing out fossil fuels. And, in the next breath, they are using the dangers of the greenhouse effect as an argument against phasing out nuclear power.

On both previous occasions when energy systems were phased out, it was not commentators or politicians who instigated the change. This is not likely to be the case this time, either. The silent majority — effectively a sort of "invisible leadership" — in companies and local authorities are instigating change on their own initiative. For instance, when wind power was introduced a few years ago, it was ridiculed as an idea that would be effective only if enormous areas of land, at huge cost, were given over to wind turbines. The environmental movement defended wind power, claiming that it could be made much more efficient than its critics were implying. Today, 20 years later, the reality has by far exceeded the most optimistic arguments used by the environmental lobby. Already, some local authorities are giving local people the opportunity of investing in wind turbines. Revenues generated are so good that it is actually profitable to put money into such ventures. The Danes, initially encountering strong skepticism, have for many years been exporting more wind-power mills than all of the rest of the world put together. Wind power has become an industry turning over billions of Danish crowns.

Industry is always capable of executing projects competently if it has a clear vision of what it is doing. Or, to use another example, Americans put an electric car on the moon in 1971. What a shame that we seem incapable of using such vehicles a little closer to home, where they would be so much more useful to us. History shows that development is driven by anxiety, by visions that bring people together, and by creativity. Once paradigms have shifted — that is, once the motorcar had replaced the horse-drawn carriage, once Germany had recovered from the wreckage of the Second World War, or once the Berlin Wall and its associated unsustainable system of values had collapsed all over the world — then suddenly all the old approximations of what was humanly possible seemed like childish underestimations.

The Rules of the Game — "Role Models" Do the Investing

Successful planning is all about linking long-term visions with present-day perspectives, so that every measure along the way can be made profitable. The starting point for all planning is to recognize that the future holds the key to the resolution of all current problems. Each organization or country should be part of the solution, not the problem. The actions are then worked out by asking the question: "What can we do today to get there?" Simple logic favors investments that fulfill the following two criteria: Are they upgradeable — as flexible as possible — from a technical, sustainable perspective? An example of a product that fulfills these criteria might be a car that consumes less fuel while also being capable of conversion to other fuels than petrol [gasoline]. It is crucial not to close off large-scale development. Doing so will result in costly "dead ends." In addition, investments should target "low-hanging fruit" — that is, they should be capable of bringing financial returns in due time. Examples might be investments in resource-saving, or initiatives targeting expansive, growing markets.

The integration of these criteria brings a real "punch" to sustainable development — using strategies that actually make development profitable. If progressive organizations (known as role models) succeed in doing this, their economic performance improves even in the short term and continues to be strengthened in the longer term as they advance their positions. Meanwhile, their competitors have "bad luck" and crash into the brick wall of increasing raw materials costs, waste handling costs, punitive insurance premiums, loans and taxes, and loss of market share to other, more proactive, companies.

The A, B, C, D Analysis Shows the Way [20]

B. TODAY'S ENERGY SYSTEMS

FOSSIL FUELS

We want to avoid globally increasing concentrations of substances such as carbon dioxide, sulfur compounds, nitric oxides, metals, and ground ozone (System Conditions 1 and 2). Further, we want to avoid the continual, gradual impoverishment of the ecosystems as a result of oil spills, coal mining, and so on (System Condition 3). What will happen if less-industrial countries such as China begin to use fossil fuels as intensively as we do? Certainly, future generations will not reap any rewards from our present use of fossil fuels. The whole question must be approached from a broader perspective than that afforded by narrow national or short-term self-interest (System Condition 4).

NUCLEAR POWER

From a global perspective, at least in comparison with fossil fuels, nuclear power is an insignificant energy system. In spite of its small-scale use — no more than a few hundred reactors exist worldwide — nuclear power has been heavily criticized because of safety concerns and other problems. The main reasons for wanting to phase it out are rising concentrations of toxic and/or radioactive isotopes as a result of uranium mining, leaking reactors, spent nuclear waste, and reactor incidents and accidents (System Conditions 1 and 2). Another reason is to put a stop to the impoverishment of ecosystems as a result of uranium mining (System Condition 3). Using nuclear power in the industrialized world will increase the risks for expansion of this technology to the developing world (System Condition 4). Nuclear power also has dangerous associations with the proliferation of nuclear weapons (System Conditions 1, 2, 3, and 4).

RENEWABLE ENERGY

That renewable energy cannot be a self-contained solution is readily understandable if one looks at it from a global perspective and analyzes it in relation to the system conditions. A large-scale transition to biofuels would very likely lead to extensive deforestation. Expanding hydroelectric power by building more dams would also damage fragile ecosystems. In both of these examples, we are actually committing system errors in relation to System Condition 3 by opting for renewable energy. In the same vein, it is conceivable that a large-scale use of solar panels would lead to higher concentrations of metals as a result of inefficient mining and recycling methods (System Condition 1). Hazardous substances might also be dispersed in the burning of biofuels (System Condition 2). Unless underlying principles are properly understood, there is a high risk of causing additional problems by opting for imperfect solutions.

THE DOUBLE CHALLENGE

The fourth system condition focuses on the satisfaction of human needs — both now and in the future. About one billion people are already short of adequate supplies of food and clean drinking water. Economic growth in developing countries is therefore a doubly challenging proposition. If one considers China's plan to drastically expand its use of coal, and if one incorporates the many other nations similarly on the verge of industrial development, it becomes plain that the current energy debate is hopelessly inadequate — too narrow and limited by short-term perspectives. Questions such as whether to use nuclear energy or coal-generated energy are simply not sufficiently cohesive or forward-looking for modern industrial nations. Our behavior today will affect the range of possibilities open to us in the future.

The aim in the industrial world should be to develop energy systems attractive enough for ourselves, while also being salable for other countries in the long term. Doing so would show far more insight than persevering with nuclear power, while at the same time dissuading developing countries (already saddled with corruption and social unrest) from taking the same nuclear option.

C. Tomorrow's Energy Systems

In trying to make a prognosis of various available energy systems, two principal issues come to the fore: the potential for technical upgrading in relation to the System Conditions, and comparative development costs.

FOSSIL FUELS

In theory, fossil fuels can be used in a sustainable way for many hundreds of years yet. It is often suggested by proponents of nuclear power that, on scientific grounds, fossil fuels must be phased out. This is not strictly true. Certainly, within a few decades — say 20 to 30 years — we must have started developing large-scale alternatives to oil-based power generation. However, there are many other carbon minerals, and hence there will be few supply problems in the foreseeable future. Habitats can be restored after mining activity, and there are certain theoretical arguments for using coal, for instance, as a fuel for extracting hydrogen (a non-polluting fuel) from water. Carbon dioxide produced by this process could be returned into deposition in suitable places, such as disused natural gas fields. At least in theory, all the system conditions can be fulfilled while still using coal or other fossil minerals. But to do this will require development and investment.

NUCLEAR POWER

Problems already in existence as a result of nuclear power will have to be assessed on a radically different scale if we choose to develop nuclear power as an energy system of global significance. Ten thousand reactors dispersed all over the world (as opposed to a few hundred at present) is a sobering thought that clarifies the importance of examining different technological solutions. Otherwise the world, with all of its social instability and terror groups, will become an unbearable place. Even if the problem of storing nuclear waste were solved, there would still be problems such as human error in enormous technical systems, as well as proliferation of nuclear weapons. To keep within the framework of the system conditions, there would have to be an entirely different development. A breakthrough in nuclear fusion, suggested by Professor Tor Ragnar Gerholm in 1972, is the only realistic alternative to solar power.

Since then, however, another alternative has appeared on the scene. In so-called thorium reactors, the fuel (even in large-scale use) would last for hundreds of years. The process would also be capable of burning dangerous nuclear waste already produced, such as spent plutonium. Both of these alternatives and other hypothetical energy systems have as yet no promise of commercially viable production. Any adequate debate would therefore have to incorporate questions such as technical requirements, investment needed to scale the development globally, and political problems that might stand in the way of success — after all, the technologies involved would have to be based on large-scale, centralized solutions. There would also have to be a comparative analysis of potential problems experienced in scaling other forms of energy for global use.

SOLAR ENERGY

The most promising of the known renewable energy systems are solar and wind power. These are currently used even less than nuclear power. Unlike nuclear power, however, they are growing; in fact, growing more quickly than any other form of energy, because, among other factors, they do not depend on centralized planning or government legislation on issues such as liability. Above all, these systems rely on known technology, usable on a global scale without risk or associated waste-handling problems. At the moment, technological excellence is evolving so rapidly that today's technology will be obsolete within a matter of a few years. One perceived problem commonly articulated is that solar power could never provide enough energy for our needs. The reality is quite the opposite. The sun provides earth with 10,000 times more energy than human civilization uses — including all energy systems in use. This means, mathematically, that by covering an area corresponding to 10 percent of the surface of the Sahara desert in state of the art solar cell panels, we would be able to satisfy the current energy use of the human species. In addition, efficiency is steadily improving with the application of research and development.

Critics usually present two views:

- New energy systems are expensive; and
- The transition to new energy systems cannot be made until they are fully developed.

These objections are like postponing jogging until one's stamina has improved. All development happens by degrees. Alternative energy is obviously more expensive because its production volumes are comparatively low. However, production volumes, especially of solar and wind power, are now increasing, with commensurate reductions in prices. Researchers at Princeton University in the US used the so-called "learning curve" to make some interesting calculations. It is a general experience in business that production costs for a product are usually reduced by some 20 percent each time production volume doubles. Looking at the development of solar cells, it was calculated that once investment of around $10 billion has gone into this sector, production costs will be level with those of fossil fuels. If this sounds expensive, one could put it like this: $10 billion would be raised in five days if all countries in the world hiked their fossil fuel taxes to the same levels as in Sweden. Or, even if the researchers have underestimated their calculations by the power of ten, in 50 days.

Both BP and Shell have advertised their intention of sinking hundreds of millions of dollars into solar power technology. The car industry has taken its own initiative, investing in advanced power systems that close the loop with solar energy. The best example of this is the so-called fuel cell — a sort of open battery that continues generating electricity while its positive terminal is fed with hydrogen gas and its negative terminal with oxygen. The current is capable of powering an electric motor in, for instance, a car. Anyone with respiratory problems might do well to breathe straight from the exhaust pipe of such a vehicle — its only waste product is water vapor. Hydrogen gas can be extracted from water using an electrical current from a solar cell. The development of this new technology is being spearheaded by manufacturers such as Volvo, Chrysler, Toyota, and Mercedes. Further impetus has been gained by the discovery that through using a "reformer" — thus extracting hydrogen from other fuels such as methane, ethanol, or even petrol [gasoline] — the market can be kick-started without waiting for new hydrogen distribution systems. Working prototypes of such vehicles are already in existence, and, in Chicago, buses fitted with fuel cell technology are already in commercial use.

Will "the invisible leadership" be too late? Whenever planning to solve complicated, serious problems, there must be broad perspectives both in terms of time and space. The assumption has to be that one day the world will be a place where people and other higher life forms will live sustainably. Having recognized this attractive vision, one has to work backward in time, and then ask oneself: "What can we do today to get there?" There can be many different visions, some of them running parallel to each other. But the important thing is that any vision of the future must fulfill the conditions for sustainability – the system conditions. Otherwise there is the constant risk of development blundering into blind alleys, with serious negative consequences both for nature and society. Using this as a springboard, we can be categorical about certain aspects of *tomorrow's* energy systems:

- **There are no limitations in terms of supply of resources.** The sun, for instance, can supply us with more energy than we will ever need;

- **There are no technical limitations.** Technology has already been developed that would fit within the framework of the system conditions on a global scale. There is a continual development of improved energy systems, as well as smarter ways of saving resources;

- **There are no financial restrictions, apart from the fact that new technology is usually more expensive.** In fact, in reality the alternatives to sustainable development will be far more expensive.

What about the resistance from vested interests in the old energy systems? It would be a mistake to view this resistance as a wholly negative factor. Some delay may even be advantageous so that unfinished technology is not launched prematurely, or perhaps so that competitors have time to evolve alternative sustainable technologies. (To put it in mythological terms: the prince is not ready for the princess until the dragon is completely dead.)

No type of energy can be ruled out as a possibility in a sustainable context. Nor can it be said that any renewable energy system has an automatic place in a sustainable society. It is rather the case that all development must be grounded in the principles that define sustainability, so that all energy systems are competing on the same terms. From a dynamic, technological, and developmental perspective, economics will determine the most appropriate energy systems. To put it more simply: Which sustainable energy system or systems would best respond to investment? Whether we choose to develop nuclear power and/or fossil fuels to be the sustainable energy systems of the future, or stay with energy systems that already fulfill the sustainable criteria, the levels of investment required will be enormous.

At this time, nuclear power has very limited global significance. Present-day technology is not suitable for development at a global level, and nuclear power is not growing in any market. There are no prospects of a technological breakthrough in the near future. Fossil fuels have total dominance in energy markets, but associated problems are building up and massive investments will be needed if we are to integrate fossil fuels into a sustainable framework.

As mentioned earlier, the sustainable energy systems growing most quickly today are solar and wind power. Steadily developed for improved versatility, prices are going down all the time. Even though sustainable energy systems are growing quickly in world markets, many scientists are concerned that the starting point is so minuscule that, unless given extra momentum, these energy systems will not have time to catch up. There are already many worrying signs that the greenhouse effect is starting to cost a great deal of money — for instance, damage caused by flooding and hurricanes. Perhaps human society will never again be as prosperous and able to invest in and speed up the development of new energy systems. Perhaps in a few years time, we will look back and regret our passivity. The question is, when (and if) it becomes expedient and politically achievable to demand that all economic activity — including that of the energy-generating sector — must satisfy the conditions for sustaining life. Furthermore, that it should pay its own development and insurance costs arising in the process. In short, when should it be a requirement that all must pay their own way? Possibly, these kinds of decisions will become easier once society's "invisible leadership" (see Chapter 16) is more prominent and the dream of the sustainable society has become the norm.

The Traffic Issue

In the industrialized world, perhaps the most crucial of all sustainability issues is today's non-sustainable traffic systems, partly because the damage from the traffic systems is so big, partly because the traditions are so deeply rooted culturally as well as in society's infrastructures, and partly because the infrastructures, together with the cars, tie up very large capital investments. This means that the time between proactive decisions and their result is long, which makes it even more urgent to start the work now.

So the problem is serious, urgent, and difficult to solve. Therefore, a success in this area would have enormous psychological significance, and positively influence our chances to come to grips with other sustainability problems as well. And *vice versa*: whatever we do with regard to sustainable development, it will be difficult to have hope unless we start to find solutions to traffic's non-sustainability problems.

The traffic system occupies larger and larger areas through its space-consuming infrastructure. And it involves enormous flows of matter, and very large amounts of that matter is not assimilated into the ecocycles but accumulate as waste molecules in our habitat. Increasing amounts of metals and other materials from the construction of the cars have started to be recycled, new and lighter and more resource efficient materials are under development, and, in our "funnel," there is no reason to believe that this development will cease. So by far the largest amounts of linear flows of matter that are "left over," are — in line with the previous part of this chapter — to be found in the fumes from the cars, not from the manufacturing of them.

In turn, the traffic system's contribution to the energy problem at large can be regarded in two ways — one proactive and one defensive. The most appealing one is the proactive perspective, of course, in which the relatively large amounts of money in the car industry, in combination with its relative vulnerability on the market and relative mobility with regard to responding to market trends, may lead to the development of new energy systems that can later be utilized in society's energy sector at large. An example of this are the hydrogen-powered fuel cells described earlier.

The Swedish Road Authority's A, B, C, D Project

The potential that lies in actually using the traffic system as a vehicle for sustainable development led the Swedish road authorities to initiate a cooperation project with The Natural Step that I find so elegant and challenging that I have decided to finish this chapter by describing it. In a way it goes against our policy to make a project public so early on, but I feel that it contains such a huge potential for major change, that it should be described right away. If we fail, somebody else must do it.

In short Jonas Oldmark and I have written a 30-page A, B, C, D Analysis of the Swedish road/sea/air/IT system — the whole communications system. We did it as well as we could, and allowed our laymen's eyes to put as many "communications leaves" as we could on the TNS Framework's branches.

We have now invited a number of important players in Sweden to become partners in the project — for instance, companies for construction, car manufacturing, purchasers of traffic services, telecom companies, and so on — all knowledgeable about various aspects of the problem, but also with economic power to do something about it. These players are now going to criticize the text produced by Jonas and me, delete errors, and add what we have forgotten. In the end this will give us a consensus document, in which the structure is given by the A, B, C, D Analysis, and where (we hope) the envisioning part of the analysis — Step C — will be so challenging, and in the same time relevant, that it will play a political role. It is the Swedish Road Authority's plan to be able to deliver this document in time for the next general election in Sweden.

CHAPTER 15

THE SECOND ARENA (FROM *AD HOC* PROJECTS TO A SYSTEMATIC APPROACH)

OR CERTAIN TNS HAD NOT evolved internally in total isolation from the society it wanted to change but had grown out of a very active and bilateral dialog with a society that had been changing quickly and abruptly on its own. The first ten years of TNS history occurred simultaneously with substantial progress by society at large in its awareness that we are on a dangerous, non-sustainable course. In fact we had seen signs of the inevitable paradigm shift since the late '60s, when Rachel Carson's book *Silent Spring* (Houghton Mifflin, 1962) woke many people up. However, the first decades of this progress were slow, since it was centered mostly on debates and talks, and not much materialized, at least with reference to business. But the '90s have seen an acceleration with a more and more professional attitude. Though still insufficient, the transition pace is no longer so slow in general.

Sweden and TNS

During my expanding international experience, it became clear to me that Sweden had a good reputation for being relatively proactive. In fact, I have often been asked whether TNS could have taken off anywhere else. (I have never heard this from a Swede.) Only recently have I had a more thorough explanation from Dr. Mark Everard in the UK.

Mark is a scientist, a limnologist by background who has been seconded to TNS in the UK from the Environment Agency, which was keen to promote the introduction of systems thinking for sustainable development in the UK. For several years, part of Mark's payback to the Agency has been to publish a regular newsletter, *Stepping Stones* to tell about his learning experience at TNS.

In a personal reflection from *Stepping Stones*, Mark wrote the following:[1]

> Up until relatively recently, Sweden's industry has been overwhelmingly forest-based. And in forestry, one plants and manages for the long term — not just the instant payback of many other industries — and so stewardship is part of the ethos. However, around the turn of the century, Sweden faced two huge blows. First, it ran out of trees and, around the same time was hit by a devastating famine that claimed many lives. And so Swedish society knows in its recent national history exactly what it means to "hit the walls of the funnel" and to reorient its policies to bring sustainability for the longer term very much to the fore. The nation has also not been at war for over 200 years, and so the common challenges that have united its people have been not conflicts but overcoming the environmental threats. Add to this the hostile climate of Scandinavia for much of the year, and the consequently greater dependence of people on one another, and you have a social cohesion and common purpose that is the envy of many other nations. I would add that this is very much a personal view.

For sure, the Swedish authorities have made a number of commitments and policy changes that deserve international attention. Long before the TNS era, the Swedish parliament reached a decision to phase out the heavy metals mercury, lead, and cadmium from Swedish use. Although we still haven't come to a decision on a deadline, this decision is built on upstream thinking and the awareness of the relatively larger risks of concentration increases of scarce elements. And they were first in deciding on the creation of national parks in the forests as a means of protecting their biodiversity. And lately, they have taken some substantial steps regarding the policy in industry.

Mark Everard again, in *Stepping Stones* October 1999:

> The Ministry of the Environment in Sweden held seminars about a full life cycle perspective of products in 1988, and studies on the subject were also published by the Ministry. Working groups were established within the Ministry in 1988 and 1989 and, as a consequence of concerns raised at the time, an inter-ministerial working group was set up in 1990 which consequently published a report in 1992. This

report has been translated into English with the title "Hazardous Goods." The Hazardous Goods report was one of the inputs to the "Bill Laying Down Guidelines for Ecocycle-Oriented Development" (more commonly known as the "Ecocycle Bill") in 1993. The "Ecocycle Commission" was set up by the Swedish Government in 1993 after Parliament had passed the Ecocycle Bill. The Bill in fact announced the setting up of the Commission.

The Ecocycle Commission worked for five years in all, between the years 1993-1998. It had two main tasks:

- to formulate strategies for an "ecocyclic society"; and
- to propose producer responsibility for different product groups.

Proposals on producer responsibility were formulated in close contact with industry itself. The proposals formulated and handed over to the government covered a range of topics: tires, cars, electrical and electronic equipment, the construction industry, and furniture. Based on these proposals, the government has, until now, decided on producer responsibility for all product groups except for furniture. The commission also proposed a general producer responsibility for all goods; the proposal has been sent out for a hearing and the government is now discussing the matter. In cooperation with this, the government has succeeded in reaching some concrete goals, for instance, implementing a green tax on fossil fuels, and some legislation regarding producer's responsibility for waste.

During the '90s, TNS played an indirect role in the latter events and a direct role in the shaping of the general Swedish attitudes regarding sustainable development in business and municipalities. We have also influenced the government and the Ecocycle Committee both directly through seminars, and indirectly through our work with municipalities and business corporations. A number of influential officers and politicians around the Ecocycle Committee — like Siv Näslund, Lennart Daleus, and Olof Johansson — have told us that their roles have been so much easier because of the support they have received from us and from the organizations we have educated. The most proactive firms in Sweden have, almost without exception, been educated by us, and they are generous when it comes to acknowledging us for their achievements.

I do believe that it is fair to say that Sweden has been a relatively proactive country for a long time, which probably helped a lot when TNS started its activities. However, it is equally important to point out that the rationale behind TNS was to avoid unnecessary resistance based on misunderstandings — and we had our share of that in Sweden, too.

It is also true that some firms and municipalities have gone beyond using the TNS Framework as a tool to increase their engagement in sustainability issues in general. Some firms have been so clever as to teach the framework to the people in their organizations, and then to support a dialog with the framework as a shared mental model to support backcasting from a sustainability perspective, and to do so systematically. However, those firms are relatively few.

The same is true if we look at municipalities. Almost all Swedish municipalities have endorsed the TNS Framework at their Agenda 21 offices. But only around 60 of the 286 municipalities have the TNS Framework implemented in the other policy documents, which means that in a clear majority of Swedish municipalities, only the green managers and interested politicians know about the TNS Framework. This means that the term "having endorsed the TNS Framework" doesn't mean much. It is a statement that means substantially different things in different organizations.

But change doesn't occur only as a result of everybody taking part in a conscious dialog. It is fine when that happens, but it would be a mistake to underestimate the importance of the small changes that occur as a consequence of much more subtle influences, a combination of direct and indirect spin-offs from the big and visible events. Billions of communications in a web of interacting questions and answers eventually lead to cultural change — like a slowly growing breeze that eventually fills a sail. I am proud to say that TNS has played a devoted and passionate role in filling that sail through the education of hundreds of thousands of decision makers about the funnel, the self-benefit in avoiding its walls, and the rationale behind our framework. Our impact is far greater than the relatively few firms and organizations that apply our framework as intended. The really systematic firms can merely be regarded as "laboratories" in which it has been demonstrated that it actually works, and as "locomotives" at the leading edge of societal change. And through their influence and guidance, the changing wind has become much stronger than it would have been without their presence, through all the indirect effects.

But I am aware that we cannot just sit and wait for a slowly growing number of firms to apply a sustainability perspective to their work, and to expect others to continue with their *ad hoc* programs, even if they get somewhat more radical. Working *ad hoc* has been the most typical way during the '90s in general. We can call that being active in "Arena 1." The few systematic "laboratories and locomotives" that apply backcasting from a sustainability perspective — firms like IKEA, Sånga Säby, Scandic, Swedish McDonald's, Interface, Collins Pine, Patagonia, Body Shop and a few more — are active in Arena 2.

From a business perspective, the two arenas can be characterized thus:

> Arena 1 = Lantern navigation
> Ethics, market, profitability
> Head of environment
> EMS
> "Eco-efficiency"
> Indicators/key figures

In Arena 1, firms have realized that it will be necessary from an ethical point of view to take sustainable development seriously. Profitability will grow from this in the long run, partly for ethical reasons, partly because of higher "eco-efficiency" — waste is lost money. To that end, firms in Arena 1 have selected a head of environment and an environmental performance system. To demonstrate the seriousness of all this, they run a number of projects *ad hoc*, and they have a number of indicators and key figures to monitor progress. Those projects and indicators are selected in terms of what the market likes or wants right now, and in terms of what legislators are likely to say soon. This is like orienting around the lanterns of other boats in an archipelago that is full of rocks, and it will not be adequate in the long run.

> Arena 2 = Lighthouse navigation
> Systems perspective
> Social, ecological, economical sustainability
> Course-corrective investments
> Head of environment has influence on all kinds of large investments
> EMS as a business-strategic tool

In Arena 2, firms have realized that it will be necessary to have a sustainability perspective in planning. These companies generally talk more about social, ecological, and economic sustainability than they do about the environment. Profitability will grow only if objectives and strategies are planned in a backcasting perspective from principles that are robust enough to cover ecological and social sustainability. In these companies, the head of the environment is part of the management team or is closely allied with it. The EMS is a business-strategic tool, not a dust collector. This is like orienting on fixed lighthouses, and the risk of hitting rocks farther ahead is greatly reduced.

At the start of the new millennium, we need a new awakening in society at large, much as when Rachel Carson wrote her book. But this time the awareness of urgency is much lower than it was then. Firms were then caught off-guard — birds were dying, and nobody knew what to do about it. Today, many firms believe that they are in control, just because they have a "green" manager and an environmental management system. However, few professional groups in society today are more frustrated than "green" managers at large companies. They are rushing around screwing on filters and asking for higher budgets, whereas the dynamic top management team is running business more or less as usual. If asked, perhaps by journalists, the CEO refers to this poor chap, who sits there in his green office with his EMS that nobody reads. I don't know what will be needed to make the majority of firms want to break out of Arena 1 and make it to Arena 2, but I hope that we won't have to wait too long for it to happen.

I think that social sustainability (System Condition 4) may hold the key to our salvation. Being a contributor to the violation of that system condition will cause very serious backlash effects just as for the first three system conditions, and it is just as bad for business as anything ecological linked to non-sustainability. However, most firms have not begun to reflect in a systematic manner on how they are an active part of that problem. This means that today's non-sustainable social make-up of modern society contains the potential for a "big bang" awakening — just as when Rachel Carson raised the first awareness of ecological non-sustainability. And not only that. Social sustainability may be the vehicle for a new dawning of urgency that may bring the whole sustainability perspective into focus. In fact, it is difficult even to perceive a successful cultural change built on visions of an ecologically attractive sustainable society, without a deeper and systematic view also on social sustainability.

The protest against the World Trade Organization (WTO) in Seattle in the fall of 1999 is an example of a dawning of a more powerful social awareness on the global scene. When I was invited to the year 2000 World Economic Forum, I saw further evidence that social responsibility is building momentum.

World Economic Forum 2000

I had never before been to the World Economic Forum at Davos. After receiving an invitation, I was contacted by so many people that I became nervous before I left Sweden. Many people believe that the annual Davos meetings are crucial and relevant, as witnessed by the invited heads of state, politicians, and CEOs. Others say that it is a colloquium for the rich and not relevant to most of the world.

Regardless of what one may think about the World Economic Forum, its organizational capabilities are impressive. That year, 2000 thousand people were invited to the Davos Central Congress Center. About 200 of them were experts of different kinds, while the rest were decision makers in business and politics. During the seminars, expert panelists were allowed only a five-minute talk. The rest of the time we interacted with the audience. The discussions in corridors and coffee shops between sessions were just as important as these interactions.

To enable further networking, the whole Congress Center, including the hotels of Davos, were equipped with numerous computers. By using your personal Congress passport, which all participants wore around their necks, you could at any time open a computer to reply to an email from delegates who would like to meet with you, check the time with the official agenda, and print it from the attached printer. All participants seemed to comply with the main purpose: to meet other decision makers in a format that did not build on previously determined agendas. This created a surprisingly open, creative, and relaxed attitude.

The seminars were about everything from the "string theory" in physics — an effort to create an overall theory that links the classical physical disciplines into a worldview of general value for explaining reality — to strategic business development. I have many impressions and thoughts from my Davos experience but will restrict myself to two that exemplify differences in awareness about ecological and social non-sustainbility.

THE GREENHOUSE EFFECT

A positive surprise was that scientific knowledge about global climate change seems to have finally reached decision makers. It was commented on over and over again, and I did not see one single example of an effort to sweep the issue under the carpet. A questionnaire among the delegates showed that a clear majority was of the opinion that the greenhouse effect deserves stronger political measures. The nebulous attitude that had characterized the mass media discussions of global warming during the last years was not present. The general message was that we must cut down on the global use of fossil fuels by much more than half in a few decades in order to avoid increasing risks. This, of course, means even greater reductions in the industrialized part of the world. This confirmed, on site, the impressions that I had collected with John Holmberg and Christian Azar during our literature studies on industry and sustainable energy described in this chapter.

During one of the seminars, the international head of Greenpeace, Tilo Bode, and the chairman of Shell, Mark Mudy Stewart, reached consensus on the need for significant reductions in fossil fuel combustion. They also reached consensus that the road to success lies in a speeded-up transition to other fuels, and that the only economically possible way is through a reduction in overall fuel use — that is, through various means of improved resource efficiency.

GLOBAL SOCIAL INEQUITY

The disappointing experience was that the word "World," in "World Economic Forum," didn't seem to apply. Very little was said about the poor parts of the world. Few people from the developing countries were even represented at the meeting. There were also protests against this. Down the road from the Congress Hall, activists were smashing windows at the local McDonald's. President Clinton exemplified a positive exception, and may reflect the early dawning I was referring to. In his address, he spent considerable time on the growing gaps in the world and warned that it would be a great mistake not to take protest activities of this kind seriously.

According to Clinton, the Davos meeting ought to sketch out attractive future scenarios in which the gaps have been bridged, and programs for the transition ought to be designed to take us there (backcasting). The trustworthiness of politicians when it comes to shaping such a vision was, according to Clinton, limited. In other words, Clinton asked for help.

Perhaps we can look forward to more politicians realizing that the growing gaps between rich and poor are untenable and a threat to all, considering today's worrying trends:

- More and more people are investing in the stock market without any clear idea how it is beneficial to society. Larger and larger sums of money are turning over faster and faster. The short-term profits are generally without any link to human services or value added;

- We are drifting further and further away from what work is all about. In short, money has taken on a life of its own;

- Business leaders, when are asked on TV about their ambitions, are eager to testify that they are "serious" and trustworthy. In the terminology of the '90s, this means that they think only about profit and shareholders. Hardly anyone today claims that he or she has any ambitions for his or her firm other than earning money — no agenda for any other purpose. Almost without our noticing, money has changed from being a means to enhance society, to becoming the goal itself — the only goal;

- Money is allocated to the sectors of society where the opportunities for growth and profit are the largest. At the same time, schools and medical care are being deprived of resources. Who expects the teaching of children and treatment of patients to grow in competition with the Internet? But isn't care for children and the infirm and the elderly the major indicator of a developed culture?

If, from time immemorial, cultures have been held together by "living stories of meaning," then what is the story of our times? That everyone should take care of himself or herself? That economic growth is the tide that sooner or later will lift all boats? We live in a world where we can phone anybody anywhere in a few seconds. Is it then reasonable to envision a rich and happy world — fenced in and surrounded by even more starving people than today's one billion, who do not even have access to safe drinking water or enough food? Is it even theoretically possible to expect this development to occur?

The question now is not only a moral one; it is also an issue of common sense. Today, the rich part of the world seems to be more focused on consumption than on worthy global visions. If that trend continues, we will fail to develop the wherewithal and institutions that are needed for the inclusion of the developing world into meaningful and secure prosperity. Is it possible that only the poor part of the world will be affected if we fail?

The TNS funnel denotes that the room for maneuvering is diminishing because of non-sustainability. Degrees of freedom are systematically diminishing due to reduced productivity in ecosystems, while demands on living systems increase. It is not difficult to imagine how the walls of this funnel will constrain those firms who are primarily responsible for creating the narrowing: green taxes, waste management costs, insurance costs, increased liabilities, and so on. But how are social matters part of the funnel, and how will social non-sustainable activities affect the individual firm? It is easy to foresee a series of events that could cascade into second- and third-order effects, creating anxiety and tension, as the rich part of the world becomes less secure.

1. **Anxiety and tension (a few examples)**: Loss of culture and alienation, as illustrated by the graffiti on subway cars: "You destroy our future, we destroy your present." Children have even started to kill each other. Money is a bad substitute for a living culture. Certainly there is a reason to start seeing a connection?

   We violate our conscience and sense of self, since we are violating the Golden Rule: "What you do not want others to do to you, you shouldn't do to them." We are, for instance, using more fossil fuels per capita than we would like the Chinese people to use, and we buy resources from poor countries at such low prices that social costs are not paid for. Many people feel an increasing uneasiness, and would probably take action if they only knew what to do.

   The costs — for instance, of the United Nations — of dealing with conflicts about water, small eruptions of violence, ecological refugee, and famine catastrophes are increasing year after year.

   Many environmental consequences of poverty are already hitting the rich world indirectly. Examples are deforestation contributing to around 20 percent of the greenhouse effect, loss of biological diversity and thereby future resources, polluted food that we import from the developing world, and so on.

Worries have already started to influence "the market": companies have been stigmatized because of their global oppressive behavior. Shell's exploitation of poor people in Nigeria for instance, is but one example that has cost that company a fortune.

2. **Market changes.** These worries, that of course have many more implications than those discussed here, are channeling more money along new pathways in the market. Some examples are:

   • Thirteen percent of funds in the US were reported ethically invested at the Davos 2000 meeting. Although there is not much discussion yet, this means money is being withdrawn from one sector, industry, or company and being placed into another. Isn't it likely that this trend will continue as long as the walls of the funnel continue to lean inward?
   • Certain private funds are allocated directly to certain projects in the developing world — for instance to vaccination programs for the poor.
   • Some firms have started to launch projects in poor regions of the developing world. Shell, for instance, has recently started installing solar photovoltaics in South African townships using so-called smart cards, costing residents no more than a month's worth of kerosene.

3. **Political measures.** The more of these good examples we get, the easier it will be for proactive politicians to start acting. This is probably what Clinton meant when he asked for help at Davos. In a democracy, politicians have difficulty taking the lead in setting goals in the beginning of a paradigm shift. For example, politicians cannot implement heavy taxes on fossil fuels until the alternative fuels are available on the market. A changing policy generally starts as a dialog between proactive people and proactive firms. New political means, laws, money for welfare projects, and institutions for social justice will be feasible to implement only when there is a growing political "market" for it. Then good cycles will drive development much faster; more good examples will appear, and then it will be even easier to speed up the political development.

For those firms and institutions that are today trying to hide behind the idea that they are far removed from the have-nots, and that there is nothing that can be done anyway, there is a growing risk that their thinking will backfire. For those who want to keep a brick wall between poor and rich, we might contemplate another brick wall in our history: the Berlin wall. The breaking down came so fast that the defenders of the wall could not catch up.

I was invited also to the next Davos meeting in 2001. It was interesting to see that though this year's event was also heavily criticized for not taking the developing world's problems seriously enough, the theme of the whole meeting was "Bridging the Divides." Clinton had opened the way with his excellent speech the year before. Most of the criticism in 2001 was focused around the powerful security routines and the forced exclusion of a number of the most active critics even to make it to Davos — they were stopped and sent back on the narrow Alp-roads. But it is perhaps inevitable that the transition of the Davos meetings must occur at a slow enough pace: otherwise the very people who need to hear the criticism will probably not turn up at all.

Cultural change may eventually occur, fostered by the only "living story of meaning" I can think of at this point — the vision of an attractive sustainable society, as in Karl-Erik Eriksson's *Taking Care of the Planet Culture*. As best I can understand, it's not even feasible for ecological sustainability to be left out. It is my hope that we have just seen its dawning, and that the relative lack of social awareness of the green movement — that goes for The Natural Step, too — is the reason why we have had to wait so long.

The Natural Step is now focusing completely on two things:

1. Developing tools for Arena 2. How can ISO 14001, Factor 4 and 10, LCA, Indicators, product design models, and purchasing manuals be selected and designed to help firms monitor their progress in line with the system conditions?

2. Coaching leaders who want to move toward ecological and social sustainability. Clinton pointed it out in Davos — it's all about leadership, and much of it relies on what happens in business. The social dimension of sustainability will have to foster this part of TNS's focus. To that end we have started to study the fourth system condition in a systematic way.

There is, after all, a larger context for leadership — the world arena.

CHAPTER 16

THE HIDDEN LEADERSHIP

T HIS BOOK IS DIRECTED TO the hidden leaders of today. Don't worry, you don't have to recognize yourself as a leader — that's one of the things I mean by "hidden" leaders. And if you are a recognized leader, you may still be "hidden." The reason is that today's recognized leaders are generally recognized for leadership in line with the old paradigm, whereas their leadership toward tomorrow goes on being unrecognized. So even some of our overt leaders are "hidden," in that respect.

Thirteen years ago, in my native Sweden, I founded The Natural Step (TNS). In this last chapter, I want to present a view of the wider political context in which TNS has developed. This context includes business and politics and the mass media in a world of great threats and challenges, and the emergence of a new, hopeful leadership.

I am presenting a personal perspective, which is therefore bound to be European, even specifically Swedish. And not only that. This perspective is from politics, an arena where I am a true amateur. However, I am aware of this and fear that my perspective may not always be relevant, particularly to other cultures of the world, such as the United States. But I believe many of the underlying hypotheses could make some sense and perhaps trigger some recognition in people who are more educated in these areas than I am. Regardless, this book is a personal testimony, and my weaknesses are part of the process too.

I believe that we are on the verge of a paradigm shift, and what the leaders in that new paradigm do and say — the ones who are invisible on the cutting edge today — will soon be seen as mainstream. The new visibility of those leaders will be the first fall of a domino that will bring the others crashing down in their turn. The attitudes of the traditional Western political parties toward sustainability will be another domino, as will those institutions that are obsolete when it comes to the protection of oceans, atmosphere, ecosystems, and social equity on the global scale.

Politics in a Changing World

During the 1990s, we entered a new political path in Europe, which continues today. The vision of the old paradigm — happiness as an automatic result of economic growth in a market economy — already seemed shaky. The costs for economic growth had not been account-ed for: an ongoing deterioration of many ecological and social values. The accounting system using GNP is, in Paul Hawken's words, like having a pocket calculator with only a plus sign. The political inabili-ty to account for the unmeasured costs and to deal with them has led to tensions that we are struggling with today. At the same time, we became more and more used to the fact that ecological issues and social issues were handled in a sort of attack and defend mode. In this battle, the left-wing parties (perhaps the liberals, in the United States) grabbed hold of social and ecological issues and patented them as their own. And so far, they seem to have been more or less successful. The right-wing parties (perhaps the conservatives, in the United States) have consequently adopted a very destructive defensive position.

But even if the relative success of the left-wing policies is evident, it is equally evident that the public has low confidence in those gov-ernments to really solve the problems. Most of us are aware of the continuation of ecological deterioration and see that social tensions and crime due to the gap between the rich and the poor continue to grow. Consequently, more and more people are losing confidence in the political process. Many have started to lose confidence also in busi-ness, and in religion, and in science.

Balance Between Left and Right

So should we stick to the right or the left in politics or are these tra-ditional political poles dead? Or should we change our strategy and find ways of supporting each individual's freedom to think and act independently of the old political ideologies? Some people believe that a tension among those three alternatives reflects a real contro-versy and that one of the alternatives will eventually take over and render the others obsolete. However, I believe this is a false contro-versy. It is the balance between left and right that is the first precondition for freedom.

Many people have noticed that it is left-leaning — "red" — politicians who keep launching programs for the support of ecological and social issues. Since these issues are so high on the public's agenda today, considering the global problems we are facing, this has led to a very clear shift from right to left in the political arena. In the year 2000, almost all of Europe was governed by what the Swedish rightist leader Carl Bildt called a "red-green mess"— coalition governments between "greens" and social democrats.

How could the right allow the left to steal the show on ecological and social survival issues? It would have been much more constructive if all parties had taken strong initiatives in these areas. The differences in values between left and right could then have concerned different methodologies and strategies to reach a socially and ecologically attractive world. Today, the debate is about whether there is a problem or not, and as long as the right claims there is not, it will continue to lose. And their competitive challenge to the left's programs to deal with the survival issues will remain weak. So we all lose.

As for social and ecological issues, the political right has taken a defensive attitude, with a very unnecessary and destructive result for democracy. People who believe that social and ecological sustainability issues are the most important issues today feel forced to drift to the left, because they find it difficult to vote any other way — regardless of where the balance of right and left is for other issues in the political field.

Ideologically there are no explanations for this phenomenon. That rightists should be ignorant about nature or indifferent to its sacrifice on the altar of Mammon is impossible to understand. There is nothing in conservative values that speaks in favor of polluting and squandering our habitat. Quite the contrary: it is often the more conservative forces that have initiated various organizations for the preservation of nature. The explanation can rather be found in a Western industrial/historical perspective.

The Prisoners' Dilemma

During a sequence of several decades (almost a century) industrialism and free enterprise have harvested great success. The subsequent deterioration of the environment represents a problem that the green movement often calls the "prisoners' dilemma" (see Chapter 1). Since ancient times, man has encountered this problem whenever the economy has expanded, for instance, when the pressure on pasture land has grown beyond its carrying capacity. The individual farmer says, "Why should I reduce the number of animals in my herd, if I cannot get guarantees from my neighbors that they will do the same?" If no public institutions existed that were strong enough to establish and enforce rules, the environment was destroyed and people had to move off the land. What is unique today is that this time the "environment" is the whole biosphere, and there is nowhere left to go.

In an attempt to get some initiative back, politicians on the right often claim that private ownership is the best guarantee for safeguarding the environment: "You protect what is yours." But who owns the ozone layer? As long as the life-supporting domains of the biosphere are at risk, and as long as only parties on the left have the problem as a top priority on the agenda, it seems inevitable that we will keep the "red-green" mess.

Historically, industrialism developed from a stage of profound poverty. It developed as a strong and dynamic power and created security for the nourishment of our lives (in Swedish, "business" is called "*näringslivet*" — meaning "nourishment for life"). But now it seems to have reached its senile stage —"consumerism" or "economism." In this stage we seem to have forgotten what it was all about. Whatever we call this senile stage, it is threatening the values it was once designed to protect.

Are the new challenges in our time of affluence and threatened biosphere so fundamentally different that we need fundamentally different visions, institutions, and traditions? We may not know the answer yet, but surely it should be possible to envision a rich world, where the whole culture is tailor-made to create the best conditions for quality of life and security, in a sufficiently large perspective, geographically and in time. Whether we can make it or not, it seems to me that there are three preconditions to find that vision and start going for it.

The first precondition is that we can successfully maintain democracy and reestablish a necessary balance between right and left. Democracy should be a verb, rather than a noun. Seeing it as a noun may lead us to think of it as something we "have," and that we can relax once we have it. The balancing act of democracy should rather be a verb — something we do and must continue to do and protect, if we are to keep it.

The first sign of deterioration of democracy is something the Swedish author Lars Gyllensten calls "manipulative" rather than "participative" democracy, when decisions are made over the heads of people. If the public, or the investigators, take a stand against the decision makers, the public "gets the chance to correct their points of view" in the next election or investigation. Most of us in Europe have experienced this sort of decision making, when large infrastructural constructions threaten natural values. In Sweden, we have recently seen even more frightening signs: a couple of national economists have, seemingly independently of each other, and with leading newspaper coverage, suggested that we should limit the rules of democracy (at a time when we need them the most). They were to be changed by various experts and certain business corporations, who could design the society for us — because otherwise the experts and the firms may leave us, and move abroad with their assets.

The second precondition is that we succeed in finding new traditions and institutions. The balance between right and left is not enough as an idea, but must be put into operation through institutions and traditions that are relevant for the problems at hand. Most proactive people, also in business, believe that we need new rules that are more suited for the new situation we are in. Our freedom to choose is, for instance, threatened by a cynicism that is not all that uncommon in certain large transnational firms and organizations, whose values are flying in the face of the moral beliefs of most people. Sometimes institutions, constituted in a vague and obscure way, are the owners. So there is no geographical and social responsibility, and no one in particular to blame when things go wrong — things like destruction of the environment, greedy squandering of nature, and social battering. The American economist and writer David Korten has described the problem for years, and is even questioning whether the public for-profit company should be allowed to have a future at all. This may seem a radical viewpoint, but the right attitude cannot be to deny the problem, or require of David Korten or anyone else to define exactly what we should have instead. If we could just agree that we have a problem, then we can explore it together.

Many transnational companies really have so much power, and use it in such a destructive way, that they can be perceived as threats to the common good. But I don't believe it would be a solution to forbid them in a democratic process. A number of big and strong transnational companies even give us some hope. They have benefited from taking a clear social and ecological stand, and the very size of these companies has contributed to spreading that good example on the global scale. However, again my point is that firms are not people that you can say hello to and love or hate. They are constituted by people, and some of the employees at companies such as Interface, Electrolux, IKEA, and Shell are launching projects every day that are driven by attractive visions and that use the power of their organization while doing so.

Likewise, most of us have also seen that being a large corporation does not guarantee success. Swedish businessman Lars Bern, in his book *Sustainable Leadership* has elaborated on the vulnerability of the transnational companies. They too have an Achilles heel. During the last decades, we have entered a trademark economy, where almost all of a firm's assets are in its trademark, and relatively much smaller parts are in real estate. This makes them vulnerable, since the trademark can easily be linked to images of bad morals. When people in the market exercise the power they get from this, firms can suffer considerable financial losses. We have seen a number of examples of such stigmatization on the market that have cost business corporations billions in bad will. And we have seen other examples of companies that change the situation to play a more constructive role. Some large oil companies' reputations have suffered, with consequent stock price losses, as a result of events such as huge oil spills, paying money to lobby against effective political actions for sustainability, violations of environmental and ethical standards in developing countries, and so on. But today some of these same large companies are investing billions in photovoltaics, are withdrawing from anti-climate change groups, and making positive statements about green taxes on fossil fuels.

Our hope is, of course, that such anecdotes will become the common cultural norm. There are many powers that try to channel the good work in various networks and institutions to make that happen faster and more powerfully. Consumers' associations of various kinds, green and social NGOs, ethical funds, international business charters and agreements, banks and insurance companies with ethical core values — there are many examples, and they seem to grow in numbers and influence by the hour. If the right takes on the challenge to support such institutions in competition with the left, it may reestablish a meaningful balance act between left and right and may empower the transnational companies to be a means for people, not the opposite way around.

The third precondition, and the most difficult, is to find a "story of meaning" in exchange for the feeling of emptiness that so many people harbor today. Without it, it is difficult to imagine a revitalization of democracy or the growth of effective institutions. If, on the other hand, we find such a vision, the other two preconditions are likely to evolve by themselves.

My friend, the Swedish theoretical physicist Karl-Erik Eriksson, used to talk about the necessity of a global "taking-care-of-the-planet culture." It would be the basis of new cultures anywhere we need them, and it would build on some common characteristics from all vital and long-lasting cultures from history. For it to be successful, it must at the same time allow room for our true modern values and be open to local, regional, and national differences.

But finding a meaningful myth, a "story of what it is all about," that would fit a modern society, is not easy. It is probably not even possible, since cultures cannot be engineered. Cultures must grow organically — when the time is right for it to happen, and when people want it. But how can the evolution of such stories be promoted? How can a story like that be authentic enough to win the hearts of modern people in the age of information technology and big cities? This is when we need leaders. Where are they?

The Big Challenges of Our Time

The Western industrial world must provide the leadership to develop sustainable techniques and lifestyles that can be applied anywhere and show that it pays off even in the short term. If not, how can we help the developing countries? Do we really want them to repeat our mistakes? Or would we rather develop the new paradigm together with them, learning from each other, and heading toward visions that are so attractive that we all would long for them? For many hundreds of years, European/American economic development has undermined and sometimes even destroyed many cultures around the world. Today it is time to do our best to pay back some of the debt. Poor countries in the South cannot enter a path of sustainable development by themselves. Their acute problems (lack of sustainable sources of fresh water, food, and energy) rest in the lap of the rich world. If we cannot do this together, we will go under together — the biosphere sees no boundaries.

In spite of all the easily grasped underlying evidence of today's problems, debate about sustainability and what it means is still unclear. Bickering about details and misleading questions — such as, for instance, whether sustainable development is preferable to economic growth — throws us off course and makes us forget what sustainable development is really all about. And particularly what it will mean if we fail. The problem is partly caused by confusion. The minute we begin to draw logical conclusions about the need for a human evolution that does not depend on atomic energy or increasing amounts of concrete, a host of uninformed naysayers suddenly appears to deny the problems. At least in Sweden.

Most government authorities and all professional institutions working with sustainability issues are at last agreed on the nature of the problem. Those who provide flawed arguments and flawed information have been marginalized in their own fields. Their negative influence can be attributed to society's extreme reluctance to change itself. Society is receptive to even the most amateurish resistance. As long as the resistance is only strong enough to slightly hamper the pace of change, it may even be constructive and help us avoid mistakes. In other words, problems are not enough in themselves to create a momentum for change. We need expertise and vision.

The continuous gradual deterioration of civilization's conditions for survival can be laid at the door of our decision makers, who still have a poor understanding of fundamental principles and therefore lack strategic competence in four fields that encompass the great tasks of our time. Those four fields can easily be detected just by screening today's society through a lens of the system conditions:

- To change energy systems (System Conditions 1 and 2);

- To phase out the use of certain chemicals and metals that nature cannot assimilate (System Conditions 1 and 2);

- To manage the life-supportive ecosystems in a sustainable way — fresh water flows, forests, fields, and fishing waters (System Condition 3); and

- To heal the battered and broken cultures around the world (System Condition 4).

I believe that the positive aspect here is that the fourth area — the problem of broken cultures — can be merged with the other three areas into one overall task. Experience shows that when people who are faced with great challenges move together with shared vision, the other problems virtually solve themselves, and *vice versa*. If everyone is aware of great systemic problems in society, then without any call for fundamental industrial or economic reforms, social and political instability will tend to increase. The general feeling of emptiness and apathy in the face of mounting global problems may well prove to be one of the most significant concerns of our time.

Just "getting rid of our problems" cannot serve as a sufficient vision. Meaningful development, as pointed out by the American TNS board member and systems thinker Peter Senge, is like a rubber band stretched between present-day reality on the one hand and attractive, utopian dreams on the other. The tension cannot be maintained forever, and there are only two options: either give up the dreams and go back to the old weary plod, or stubbornly stick to our visions long enough for the other end of the rubber band to start moving. This is when the leaders must enter the scene, because it is their job to see and interpret and communicate visions, and to be stubbornly persistent in doing so.

Where Are the Leaders?

So, where are the leaders? It seems to me that good leaders are everywhere, and they are growing in numbers! The problem is not that they don't exist but that their good examples are not yet allowed to become the norm. If they are seen at all, they are perceived as unrealistic dreamers, whom we may or may not admire. In spite of all the rhetoric backed up by exhaustive facts, our present culture still evaluates everything according to the rules of the old order. It is true that encouraging words are heard every now and then. But when most decisions in society are made, and when we see the daily news on TV, it's still "more of the same." The other stuff is not "realistic." Will it ever be?

In this early stage of transition, the true leadership is visible largely on the local level. It is in certain business corporations or municipalities that people are optimistic and committed. In their case, neither "getting rid of problems" nor "increased GNP" form the story. These people are envisioning something new, and their vision is the engine of change. They are longing for it — it's that simple. And the leaders, as well as the visions, are so trustworthy that the rubber band can lose its tension only by everybody moving in the direction of the vision. People are united through a common cultural identity that provides a sense of meaning.

As the invisible leadership grows stronger, the old establishment's response becomes increasingly irritable. But suddenly, a few leaders from the old paradigm's defense lines start changing sides. They realize that it is time to listen and that it is time not only to let go but to help discharge the old paradigm. There are many examples of such "heroes of retreat." Gorbachev is one. The German author Hans Magnus Enzensbergers has written a thoughtful thesis on the phenomenon. In Sweden, the prime minister Göran Persson began his term by talking about an attractive, ecologically sustainable society as a new vision for Sweden. And former US Vice President Al Gore took a clear stand for similar visions — a bold move in the early days of change, because there is no guarantee that the pendulum will not swing back again (as he found out). And indeed, the Swedish prime minister, too, has been the object of a fair amount of ridicule from various people defending their entrenched positions in the old order, on the left as well as on the right. I believe that the change of paradigm will not be complete until it is acknowledged by the mass media as the new norm.

The Role of the Mass Media

In our industrial society, the distance between people is paradoxically wider than ever. We may not think so, as we sit in front of the TV and learn about President Clinton's private life. But we generally know much less about our neighbors. We hardly meet with people, at least not when it is about sharing our thoughts on values and longings or about the shaping of a new and better world. These things are taken care of by soap operas and political leaders once we have made it home to the TV after another hard day's work. Because of this, a lot of intuitive feelings that we may all share never become generally accepted. So we won't have a new culture until it is seen by the mass media, because only then can we trust that others see it, too.

I think that I can speak for most of us when I say that we don't really trust either of these substitutes — soap operas and politics mirrored on TV — for an active participation in the creation of our culture. The reason is simple: we may be amused, but we don't really feel that we are represented. It's as if everything we see on TV is rhetoric, while most of us feel that there are fundamental errors in the societal system that need attention but don't get addressed. The problem is that we sit there and think this, but we don't say it often. We don't sit with the others in the tribe around the fire anymore. We fall asleep in front of the TV.

In spite of what many people believe, the mass media are in fact part and parcel of the Establishment, representing an "insider" view, usually with a condescending and sometimes even derisive stance toward new ideas. Let's take the energy transition as an example. As could be expected, the daily news media are viewing the early stages of change through their old glasses and perceive the supporters and actors of the new energy systems — windmills, bioenergy, and photovoltaics — as a new breed of eccentrics. At least this is true in Sweden.

Through those old glasses, it appears that a stark choice must be made between fossil fuels and nuclear power. However, certain other areas never seem to come under scrutiny: issues such as time scales, the future availability and potential of various alternative energy sources, and how we should be linking tomorrow's energy systems with energy systems being put into place today (see Chapter 14). In fact, the mainstream news media don't even report on the development of new energy systems that are on the market right now.

And yet it is clear that things are starting to change, if only at the edges. Journalists with courage, ability, and insight are appearing in the Sunday supplements, the cultural pages, some scientific journals, and the local press. Unlike many people, I don't believe that there is a conspiracy between the news media and those in power. The inertia of television and the large newspapers has another explanation.

The acclaimed French sociologist Pierre Bourdieu has posited that an increasing commercialization of the media with ever greater numbers of newspapers and competing TV channels has paradoxically resulted in a "dumbing down" of coverage. All that frantic jostling about to bring out news before anyone else creates high insecurity. Journalists are anxiously watching to see what others publish or broadcast and match what they see, thus creating uniformity. That's why we see the same material and the same people on the sofas commenting on it, regardless of what channel we watch or which newspaper we read. News coverage is adapted to what the media believe the public will take. Wearing their "journalist spectacles," media professionals are free to go for the quick and easily digested stories while often remaining myopic to the things that require more time and reflection. The discussion of the emerging new worldview obviously belongs in this latter category.

President Clinton's private life, a Swedish minister buying a piece of chocolate on her official business card, or a world-famous singer saying something bad about her boyfriend, are examples of events that are easier to understand than the fact that photovoltaics on ten percent of the Sahara desert would produce as much electricity as the whole world's expenditure of energy, including all energy sources. Likewise, they are easier to digest than the fact that big petroleum companies are investing in photovoltaics, are buying up cheap desert land to put these photovoltaics on, and are making positive statements about green taxes on petroleum. But what is most sensational?.

The Role of Business

From whence will the new culture come? If we won't endorse the new culture until the mass media does, then who will present it to the media? This is where I think that business can find its challenge for our times: they provide the new community. The world has become so globalized that it has lost all human dimensions. And we don't sit with the tribe any more around the fire. But we do sit at the coffee table with our mates at work, so that place is our chance for cultural change, at least in the industrialized world.

For the long term, we must find ways of getting the time needed to consider and debate more subtle issues, like our future and what we really want to get out of our lives at our workplaces. And workplaces can be wonderful! That's why we need to make our hidden leaders visible, to speed up the process of making the new paradigm— the "taking-care-of-the-planet culture" — the norm.

Will the mass media resist this? I don't think so. First, there is nothing wrong with the sensational in itself. I believe that our fascination for sensations even has a value for survival. If we hear an enormous and alarming sound, we immediately look in that direction — even if there is a beautiful violin being played in the other direction. It doesn't mean that we like alarming sounds more, only that we need to pay attention to the alarming stuff first. That we don't necessarily like sensations more than the long-term stories of meaning, is an appealing challenge to journalists, of course.

So, the good news is that we do not need to stop being interested in sensations or scandals. The growth of the new paradigm and the fact that we already have some leaders who are putting it into operation can be sensational enough. We just need to start regarding the growth of the new vision as the new normality. And when reality is mirrored through journalist glasses that regard the new vision as normal, we can trust that it is not only at our working place that the shift of paradigm has taken place. Then the old paradigm is finished.

In conclusion, people in the mass media have their own rubber band. Their vision could be, of course, to play their role as observers and reporters on the Establishment and to play it to its full extent. To that end, one task would be to reveal that the old emperor is standing nude before the new paradigm. Certainly, that should be a more attractive and perhaps even a more sensational task than reporting on the cut of his clothes.

Appendixes

AGRICULTURE FROM A SCIENTIFIC PERSPECTIVE: A CONSENSUS DOCUMENT FROM THE NATURAL STEP, THE SWEDISH FARMERS' FEDERATION (LRF), AND THE SWEDISH ECOLOGICAL FARMERS' FEDERATION (ARF) (EXCERPT)[1]

Introduction and Definition of Aims

The initiative for this document was taken by The Natural Step as a way of producing consensus documents based on the ecocyclic principle. (This principle is described extensively in the document.) Other documents have already been assembled on energy, metals, traffic, political measures, and the corporate sector.

Within the environmental debate, disagreement is often emphasized in such a way that areas in which there could be collective agreement become invisible. The whole aim of this document, then, is to shape a common platform agreeable to representatives from all backgrounds on environmental questions in agriculture. Using the ecocyclic principle (TNS System Conditions 1 to 3) as our starting point, we have found a collective analytical model that emphasizes the long-term perspective over the short-term one.

This document presents a core of knowledge and insight about survival and agriculture on which all contributors are in full agreement. The document will be a starting point in our continued work to change our society into a more sustainable one and an aid to "lifting our eyes" while we work in various ways to change methods in agriculture.

BOUNDARIES

We have opted to use the ecocyclic principle as a starting point to describe the long-term role of agriculture in the sustainable society. Many related questions, though important in themselves, are not looked at in the document. These include animal ethics, health, quality of food products, working conditions and quality of life for farmers, landscape ethics, care and maintenance of national monuments, genetic engineering, etc. We also do not look at the admittedly serious disruptions to agriculture caused by industrial society through air pollution and impending climate change. Finally, we do not address political deliberation on (amongst other things) the pace of the transition to the ecocyclic principle and the question of who will bear the short-term costs.

Focusing our document on concerns that relate to the ecocyclic principle is analogous to focusing on the leaking hull of a boat: we know that unless the leaks are plugged, time will run out and related problems will not be remedied in any case. Our intention is to point out the repercussions of doing nothing, and the direction in which we must go.

The longer we delay the transition to a sustainable society, the more expensive and painful the process will become. For example, the longer agricultural land and forests continue to be physically depleted and acidified, the more difficult it will be to convert to a society that runs on renewable energy sources. The ecocyclic principle helps us describe, on a scientific basis, three ecological conditions for a sustainable society. We try to draw from the latter some general conclusions on agriculture.

Much work remains on the question of finding specific measures for individual farms: an overview of the entire chain between producer and consumer, processing of sewage, etc. This document should be viewed as a first step in that process — namely the staking out of directions for sustainable development and the deepening of our understanding of the ecocyclic principle as applied to agriculture. Our hope is that the document will provide the overriding perspective required for continued work on finding specific solutions. Unless otherwise specified, we refer in this document to Swedish agriculture and Swedish society.

TODAY'S SOCIETY IS NOT SUSTAINABLE

Environmental damage is now threatening to snatch away the very conditions necessary for continued human prosperity and health. In the slightly longer term, all higher life on Earth is threatened. We consume finite resources such as oil, coal, uranium, phosphates, metals, and gravel at a rate that significantly limits the choices available for coming generations. Byproducts and waste from manufacturing and consumption are taken to the dump or pass through the sewage treatment works. We fool ourselves if we think that it has "gone," for nothing can truly disappear. Even when we incinerate our household waste it turns into various gases, filtrates, and ashes. Whatever is not reconstituted by society or nature into new resources results in increased volumes of visible pollution and dispersed "molecular pollution" in nature.

A continued linear handling of resources will have devastating consequences: global climate change; a thinning ozone layer; rising levels of heavy metals in soils; acidic pollution of land and water; and toxins in seas, lakes, and groundwater, etc. Global environmental catastrophes will affect everyone on Earth, not just those of us who inhabit the richer parts of the world (although we are largely responsible for them and, in the short term, are the ones who benefited most from the linear consumption of resources).

To create a functioning sustainable society will require a speedy integration of all human activities into the cycles of the ecosystem. We have to direct ourselves toward a sustainable society where resources — with the exception of plentiful solar energy — can continually be reused, either within natural or man-made recycling. Overseeing such a change, of course, will demand an understanding of the non-negotiable conditions for life on Earth and especially of the conditions that nature specifies if humanity is to survive in the long term.

Furthermore, we have to enhance significantly our knowledge of the relationship between small decisions and the overall direction of social development. If we permit peripheral questions and a one-track mentality to obscure these relationships, then at best, we will only achieve marginal improvements. One characteristic feature of current environmental problems is that extended time scales and distances often separate cause and effect. For example, a person walks into a shop in 1967 and buys an aerosol spray can. Thirty years later another person in Australia is diagnosed with skin cancer as a result of the thinning of the ozone layer. We must acquire the necessary foresight to be able to prevent the kind of unpleasant surprises that have continually afflicted us during these past few decades.

THE HUMAN RESOURCE BASE

Humanity is a part of nature. It has evolved in relation to nature and is entirely dependent on it. In the language of economics, humanity needs nature for the goods and services it provides. By "goods" we mean renewable and nonrenewable resources. By "services" we mean such things as natural processes for climate regulation, water purification, or soil creation.

We must understand the conditions by which nature operates if we are to ensure a continued delivery of its goods and services. If we consume a resource faster than nature can restructure it, two problems arise: scarcity of the resource and dispersal into the biosphere of waste products from its consumption. And byproducts that cannot be taken up by ecosystems cause an accumulation of waste and molecular pollution.

THE DIFFICULTY OF ESTABLISHING AN ORDER OF PRECEDENCE

There are several difficulties in establishing an order of precedence for the many violations against the ecocyclic principle. First, we will need to make some tough political decisions so that we can classify problems and draw up a time frame to pace the transition to a sustainable society. (Of course, a politically attractive strategy would be to allow everything that falls within the tolerance limits for "what nature can withstand," thereby maximizing both consumption levels *and* political maneuvering room!)

Second, it is impossible to establish irrefutably what nature can withstand. Medical science, with the help of statistics on deceased patients, has been able to arrive at approximate tolerance limits for pollutants and byproducts in the human body. But for obvious reasons, we cannot calculate tolerance limits for the survival of the biosphere in the same way.

Third, time lags, spatial displacement, and complexity aggravate the process.

Time lags between cause and measurable effects mean that we can disperse pollutants continually over a long period of time without noticing any problems. When problems do materialize, often very suddenly, stabilizing mechanisms have already been exceeded. For instance, in many acid soils, chemical buffering (a natural stabilizer) has already been exhausted by the time we see visible effects on fauna and flora. Similarly, by the time the effects of long-term damage to global systems of climate regulation become obvious, things may have gone too far for appropriate countermeasures to be effective.

Spatial displacement means that large distances often separate cause and effect, making it difficult to predict and control damage. The diffuse spread of pollution over large areas, for example, means that damage is not easily connected to its source.

The complexity of ecosystems makes it impossible to oversee interaction among all factors or to foresee every causal chain set in motion by a change. Complex systems are always to some degree unforeseeable no matter how much knowledge we have amassed about the properties of the system. Every consequence of events still cannot be foreseen. This can be demonstrated by computer simulation, and is in every sense applicable to the complex systems for interaction within and among the lithosphere, hydrosphere, biosphere, and atmosphere — the systems that support life on Earth.

In order to create functioning sustainable societies, human activity must be linked with the natural cycles of the ecosystems. We cannot say with the same degree of certainty which measures must come first. But we must at least not invest in structures that directly contravene necessary development toward a sustainable society.

THE ECOCYCLIC PRINCIPLE

The ecocyclic principle signifies a balance between the processes of rebuilding and the processes of breaking down. Three System Conditions can be derived from this principle. In the sustainable society, nature is not subject to systematically increasing:

System Condition 1: concentrations of matter extracted from the Earth's crust;

System Condition 2: concentrations of compounds produced by society; and

System Condition 3: degradation by physical means.

Besides these three system conditions for maintaining the ecocycles, there is also a social principle for the sustainable society, and in that society:

System Condition 4: human needs are met worldwide.

The four System Conditions are all equally important. If even one of them remains unfulfilled, society cannot be sustainable. Irrespective of which of the four conditions are not fulfilled, the symptoms will be the same, resulting in a systematic accumulation of "leftover" waste and molecular pollution. Finite resources that are systematically turned into dispersed waste products accumulate as leftovers. Unnatural substances that are dispersed at a more rapid rate than they are broken down accumulate as leftovers. And when ecosystems are physically depleted, their capacity to convert waste products into resources is diminished, leading to more leftovers. There will also be leftover substances if the turnover of materials exceeds the capacity of ecosystems to process waste products locally and/or globally.

AGRICULTURE FROM AN ECOCYCLIC PERSPECTIVE

The Role of Agriculture in Society

Agriculture, gardening, forestry, and aquaculture are all directly connected to the productive capacity of the green cell. Green cells are uniquely responsible for the large-scale and systematic reconstruction of ordered structures from dispersed and worthless matter for the use of other organisms, and they function without degrading any resources or spreading any pollutants. Indeed, life-enhancing oxygen is the byproduct of photosynthesis.

When, within a few decades, we have to get by without finite energy sources, our dependence on the green cell will be very much clearer than it is today. There will be competition for "solar catchment areas" that will have to be equal to the task of supporting an expanding world population with food, energy raw materials, and industrial raw materials such as fibers, oils, and starch. Exacting demands will be placed on land to provide society with materials and energy to a much greater extent than they are today.

In Sweden the division between land in forestry and land in agricultural use is not self-evident. Forestry or agricultural activity can equally well produce raw materials for energy, fibers, and other products. But once agriculture fulfills the four System Conditions (i.e. stops mortgaging the resource base of future generations), it will become obvious that today's much-debated "overcapacity" in agricultural land can only ever be seen as a historical anomaly. Sustainable food production demands larger land surfaces to bind energy and nitrogen (among other things). When the time comes for strictly prioritizing the use of green solar catchment areas, food production will take the highest priority.

The conversion to a sustainable society will lead to agriculture and other soil-based activities regaining their role as the center of the nervous system of society. As a part of this conversion, agriculture has to be reformed so that it fulfills the four necessary conditions for a sustainable society.

Conditions for Agriculture from an Ecocyclic Perspective

System Condition 1: Finite Resources. In a sustainable society, finite resources are not systematically converted into dispersed pollution. Thus extraction of finite resources can only proceed at a pace equivalent to the very slow re-sedimentation processes that over millions of years have created existing deposits of raw materials. Currently and in contrast to this ecocyclic condition, every year as much oil is consumed as it takes nature one million years to create.

Today, as in many other sectors in our non-sustainable society, finite resources such as fossil fuels and electricity from nuclear power help to power agriculture to a very high degree (see The Natural Step consensus document on *Energy*). These finite energy sources are used both directly as fuels and indirectly for the manufacturing of chemical fertilizers and other "input merchandise," as well as for the transportation of the latter and of produce.

Finite supplies of oil are also used for the manufacture of plastics and lubricants. As in other sectors, metals used for machinery and tools are taken from finite supplies of ores. Society's present-day recycling of plastics and metals is still wholly unsatisfactory (see The Natural Step consensus document on *Metals*).

Today's agricultural production has to a great extent become dependent on a continual supply of phosphate from finite supplies of crude mineral phosphate. Of all the phosphate extracted from mines around the world, about 80 percent is used in agriculture. About 60 percent of this raw phosphate is used in the industrialized world with its 35 percent of the planet's agricultural land and 25 percent of its population.

Phosphate is a mineral essential to life, which cannot be replaced by anything else. Within a matter of a few decades, a great part of the stocks will have been used up. This does not mean that the phosphate disappears. It is dispersed into places where it is less accessible and therefore less valuable. In excessive quantities, phosphate is environmentally damaging: when it leaks into lakes, rivers, and seas, it causes eutrification.

Rationalization of phosphate use is not now a feature of either agriculture or society as a whole. On average, three times more phosphates are added — in the form of fertilizers, animal feed, and other phosphate products for agriculture — than eventually leave agriculture in the form of produce (both vegetable and animal products). Of the phosphate that leaves agriculture in the form of produce, only a small part is plowed back (20 percent). The remaining 80 percent ends up in sewage sludge

at purification plants and in household waste. Because it has been polluted, the sludge is largely deposited in dumps, and the household waste
is incinerated or dumped.

The use of raw phosphates in the form of chemical fertilisers
increased in Sweden from the mid-1940s to the mid-1970s. During the
1980s, phosphate use declined. But the average balance of phosphate
use in Swedish agriculture is nevertheless unsatisfactory. There is, however, a great difference in the phosphate balance between farms that
practice cultivation and farms that rear livestock.

A division occurred between arable farming and livestock farming
through agrarian specialization in the period 1950-1980. Now a shrink-
ing proportion of plant nutrients circulate back, via farm manure, to the
soil where animal feed is cultivated, even though most of our country's
agricultural land is used for the cultivation of animal feed! As a result, in
arable farming there is a shortage of phosphate, which is alleviated by
bought fertilizers. At the same time, there is an accumulation of phosphate in farms that specialize in intensive livestock rearing. The excess
of phosphate that cannot be made good by plants is fixed, to a large
extent, in the ground. (This phosphate could be referred to as a future
resource, but it is fixed in a form that cannot be utilized by plants.) A
smaller amount is lost due to erosion or dissolved in water.

With the usage of unrefined phosphates from mines, cadmium and
arsenic that have lain embedded in phosphate deposits for millions of
years are now being dispersed in the biosphere along with chemical
phosphate fertilizers. Already, cadmium levels in food produce can
exceed tolerance limits. Cadmium in these concentrations can lead to
malfunctions in the kidneys. Meanwhile cadmium levels continue to
increase in agricultural soils by 0.3 percent per year. If the accumulation
of heavy metals is allowed to continue, then agricultural land will eventually become unsuitable for food production.

Agriculture also uses potassium, lime, and trace elements from
deposits of finite resources. It is estimated that stocks of potassium and
lime will last much longer than phosphate deposits. For some of the
trace elements, though, it is estimated that existing levels will not last
very long at the present rate of use. These problems excepted, environmental disruption caused by the actual mining for nutrients must
also be considered.

In the sustainable society, organic waste from plants and animals
must be put back into the soil. In this way, agricultural production
does not have to rely on nonrenewable supplies of phosphate and

potassium. The extraction of minerals from geological deposits must be analogous to their very slow reestablishment in the Earth's crust. As a consequence of this, agricultural machinery, tools, plastics, etc. must be recyclable. At the same time, production must come out of renewable energy sources. All this demands radical changes to our present practices.

System Condition 2: Persistent Unnatural Substances. In a sustainable society, agriculture must refrain from handling unnatural substances that ecosystems cannot or do not have the capacity to break down into substances usable as building blocks in biological production.

Our present-day agriculture contributes to the dispersal of unnatural substances. As far as we now know, many of these are broken down into harmless constituents in nature. But other substances are more long lived, and according to this ecocyclic condition, many of these cannot be used at all (for example, pesticides such as DDT). These products are prohibited nowadays in Sweden, but they remain in use in many parts of the world.

The fact that a substance is biodegradable does not necessarily mean that it becomes harmless. Certain pesticides break down relatively quickly but their constituents are long-lived and unnatural. Other pesticides accumulate in the environment even though they are biodegradable (this may happen when enormous quantities are used seasonally or under particular soil conditions). Some of the latest pesticides — "low-dose" products — do not degrade quickly enough, which means that they find their way into rivers and groundwater.

Currently we are allowing pesticides to disperse in ecosystems in an uncontrolled way. The long-lived substance toxafen, for example, is prohibited in Sweden but imported as airborne pollution across the Atlantic from North America. Our knowledge of the effects of pesticides on ecosystems is insignificant. This is also true of our knowledge of the pesticides themselves, even though they are some of our most researched and tested chemicals. We have no knowledge of either the combined effects of different products or their side effects. In practice, these are impossible to control.

To handle long-lived unnatural substances is to risk long-term environmental disruption. What we can confidently say is that ecosystems cannot withstand a continual accumulation of any single substance. In practice it is impossible to predict how fast substances will break down in various conditions or what byproducts will be created during the process of breaking down. It is also impossible to be aware of all the effects of the byproducts. All this demands that agriculture develop toward non-reliance on unnatural substances.

System Condition 3: The Physical Management of Ecosystems. In a sustainable society, agricultural practice facilitates the long-term productive capacity of ecosystems. This capacity is dependent upon complicated chemical, physical, and biological connections.

. From a global perspective, humanity today has a thoroughgoing effect upon the structure and function of ecosystems, yet our knowledge about them and their adaptive capabilities is deficient and hence our behavior dangerous. Long-term consequences are, to a great extent, unforeseeable. But we can now begin to observe that when we wipe out or fundamentally alter a particular type of habitat, change biogeochemical cycles, or destabilize climatic cycles, biological diversity is depleted and ecosystems become more vulnerable. Taken together, all these changes result in reduced long-term productive capacity in ecosystems, both in quality and quantity.

To preserve the productive capacity of ecosystems means to facilitate their transformation of solar energy and waste products and also to encourage the development of biological diversity. To do that, the degradation of ecosystems that is currently underway must be brought to a halt.

System Condition 3 can be divided into three sub-levels:

1. **Biologically productive surfaces.** Globally, the loss of productive solar catchment areas is extensive and serious. Some of the major causes are desertification, salinization, soil erosion, and the extending technosphere. The loss of productive surfaces in places such as Central Europe, amongst others, comes about through construction and asphalting. In Sweden this problem of the extending technosphere is as yet insubstantial because population density is quite low: less than 4 percent of the land is asphalted, covered by buildings, or "hardened" in other ways.

   Historically, road networks and settlements were generally consigned to poor quality land. Since the middle of the 20th century, however, settlements, motorways, and airports, etc., have increasingly been located on fertile agricultural land, rendering it unavailable for primary production. The whole process runs counter to the increasing demands that society will place on agricultural production for food, fibers, oils, energy raw materials, etc. created without the assistance of finite resources — all of which will require more arable acreage than we have today.

2. **Habitat for biological diversity.** When sweeping changes affect the ecosystem in the short term, they generally lead to depletion. An important example from our country is the drainage of wetlands. Large tracts of land were drained at the end of the 1800s and beginning of the 1900s to ease the famine by creating more agricultural land. In certain parts of southern Sweden (Gotland, for example), 80 to 90 percent of the wetlands were drained in this period. This has led to a reduced water storage capacity in the landscape, a degradation of quality in drinking water, a reduced self-purification of surface water, and the loss of habitat and thereby also the loss of species.

    During a few thousand years, agriculture in Sweden gave rise to new habitats, often rich in species — a trend that has turned in the last half century. The cause of the ongoing reduction in biological diversity within agricultural ecosystems is that much agricultural activity is being phased out, and certain habitats (meadows and open grazing areas, for example) are disappearing. At the same time, the productivity of remaining land degenerates as a result of, for instance, reduced pressure from grazing and haymaking. Chemical pesticides (both their incidental and intended effects), other pollution from agriculture, and airborne pollutants also threaten the flora and fauna of the farmed landscape.

    Preserving and stimulating biological diversity is like taking out an insurance policy that defends the ecosystems and humanity's ability to support itself even in the midst of instability.

3. **The long-term productivity of agricultural land.** Today the continual reduction in humus levels in many soils contributes to the impoverishment of the long-term productivity of agricultural land. As humus disappears, essential amounts of nutrients are lost, the soil loses its ability to retain humidity and nutrients, there is a lesser presence of microorganisms, and the soil becomes heavy.

Insufficient recycling of harvest residuals, the addition of manure, or fallow growth cause humus reduction. So does our ever more intense soil management. This has to do with the postwar reduction in open grazing land and the increasing acreage of open cultivation, as well as with the division caused by specialization between cultivation and livestock rearing.

In arable farms, humus is lost because there is neither open grazing nor farm manure to compensate for organic matter continually being lost with harvests. Nutrients in food produce eventually end up as organic waste, sewage, etc. and are not returned to agriculture, thus depleting the nutrient store of agricultural soils, especially trace elements. And when the organic content of soil breaks down, it releases carbon dioxide. A continuous reduction of humus in the ground thus also contributes to the greenhouse effect.

In peat-based soils made viable by the drainage of wetlands, the topsoil of peat disappears in less than a century of open cultivation: we very quickly consume a resource that nature has taken many thousands of years to build.

One of the most serious threats to the long-term productivity of agricultural land is the compression of soil by heavy machinery. Compression adversely affects the transportation of air and water in the soil. Soil compression that reaches deeper than winter frost may be irretrievable. On farms with heavy machinery, soil compression is already leading to relative reductions in harvests. About 30 percent of the total agricultural acreage has compression damage, which corresponds to a 10 to 20 percent reduction in productive capacity. Measures such as extra-wide tractor tires only alleviate the compression effect in the upper soil layers. If we persist in using heavy agricultural machinery at present levels, then we can expect continued downturns in productive capacity over wide areas.

Globally wind and water erosion, as well as a sinking water table and salinization, are major causes of physical depletion in agricultural ecosystems. In Sweden, wind erosion and a sinking water table occur locally, for example at Österlen in Skåne.

Protecting green solar catchment areas, both qualitatively and in terms of acreage, is to defend the potential of life for coming generations. This demands that natural ecosystems are given enough space and are spared from stress factors such as pollution and climate change. It also demands that biological diversity (including diversity of microorganisms in the soil) is fostered in the agricultural landscape.

The long-term productive capacity of agricultural land can be maintained only if farming methods do not cause physical impoverishment through decreased humus levels, depletion of soil nutrients, soil compression, decreasing humus levels, depletion of soil nutrients, changes in the water table, and erosion.

The intensity of turnover of materials. The previous section has mainly been about substituting certain elements and compounds and management routines for others in order to comply with the first three system conditions. This will most certainly not be enough — we also need to reduce the overall turnover of materials. This applies even to the use of renewable resources or substances that are included in natural production In Swedish agriculture, nitrogen has a turnover higher than what is consistent with the ecocyclic principle: the total quantity supplied is so great that leakage (both locally and regionally) causes environmental disruption.

Surging increases in transportation of contributory materials, agricultural produce, and processed food both nationally and globally have brought with them an increased materials turnover in the form of fuel, vehicles, infrastructure, packaging, and marketing. In all countries, plant fertilizers and humus raw materials are transported from the countryside to the cities and in many cases right across the world. Pronounced urbanization and long distance trade would make it costly to close the cycles by transporting waste products back to the same ecosystem that delivered the resource. Accordingly, impoverishment occurs in one place and accumulation in another.

To stay within the limits imposed by System Conditions 1 to 3, it is necessary to create sufficiently small, energy-efficient sealed cycles, an insight for which ecocyclic solutions are currently lacking. For instance, it is a resource-hungry process to invest materials and energy to bind atmospheric nitrogen for plants at one end while investing energy to put nitrogen back into the atmosphere at the other. Yet that is what we do. We use nitrogen fixed in clover hay or from chemical fertilizers for agriculture because nitrates and ammonium are the forms accessible to plants. At the same time, nitrogen-trapping wetlands or de-nitrification equipment at water purification plants return nitrogen to the atmosphere. A cycle is created, but it leaks and also requires a large input of energy. Farming methods that keep the ground in constant cultivation, however, promote cycles between soils and plants, and both losses and energy consumption are kept to a minimum.

Small cycles are not necessarily better sealed and more energy efficient than large cycles — many of nature's own cycles are large, perfectly sealed, and energy efficient. But it is easier to devise small sealed cycles than large ones, partly because small cycles do not require such large resources to be directed and controlled.

There is little prudence, either in agriculture or society, in the use of plant-accessible nitrogen. Of all plant-accessible nitrogen, an average of less than 20 percent ends up in the actual agricultural produce; the rest leaks into air and water, and a small part is temporarily bound up in organic matter in the ground. And less than 5 percent of nitrogen in agricultural produce (all plant and meat products) exported into society are returned to agriculture.

The supply of nitrogen for agriculture comes from fertilizers, atmospheric deposition from industry and cars, imported feed, and biological fixation in the ground — about 100 pounds per acre (110 kilograms per hectare) per year. Not all supplied nitrogen gets used, either — there is a difference of about 70 pounds per acre (80 kilograms per hectare) per year between supplied and used nitrogen in agriculture.

Nitrogen causes more serious environmental problems than does phosphorus. Nitrogen is not immobilized but in fact readily disperses into air and water. Nitrate leakage and gaseous ammonia bring about the pollution of drinking water and coastal seas, nitrogen saturation and acidification in forest soils, and reduced biological diversity, etc. The seriousness of these environmental disruptions varies from region to region, depending on climate, soil, and the scale and type of agriculture.

During the period of specialization in agriculture that occurred between 1950 and 1980, the amount of purchased nitrogen for cultivation (more and more in the form of chemical fertilizers) increased markedly while livestock farms produced an excess of nutrients. The nitrogen balance today, therefore, varies widely depending on the type of farming. The greatest loss of plant nutrients is associated with livestock rearing, in which the defective handling of farm manure is an important contributing factor.

Whether it occurs in the fields or in factories, loss of nitrogen is a waste of the energy used in once again binding atmospheric nitrogen. We must take measures to minimize leakage from agricultural land, household waste, sewage, and waste products from the food processing sector — especially in areas where it is most damaging to the environment. Reduced losses will bring about a corresponding reduction in the levels of nitrogen that have to be supplied to the agricultural sector. And an increased transfer of plant-accessible nitrogen from urban areas to agriculture will reduce the need for nitrogen supplied to agriculture from other sources.

The return of material to agriculture must be of the same magnitude as flows of produce out of agriculture. Added nutrients or nutrients produced on the spot must not exceed what the crop and surrounding ecosystem are capable of assimilating and turning into new biomass.

HOW DID ALL THIS COME ABOUT?

History

For several hundred thousand years, the world's population was more or less equal to present demographic levels in Sweden. Early man lived by gathering roots, berries, and fruit, as well as by hunting and fishing. Population growth and climate change forced, and new technology made possible, new ways of living. About 6000 years ago, people in this country began to supplement their living with agriculture. Agriculture became a way of supporting more people on a smaller amount of land, but it also demanded a larger expenditure of labor than did hunting and gathering — agriculture, after all, was the maintenance of an entire ecosystem in a form far from its natural one.

During the Bronze Age agriculture was still nomadic. During the transition to the Iron Age (about 3000 years ago), the poorer climate meant that animals had to be kept in barns. This was really the beginning of field cultivation, because the domestic animals provided manure for the fields. Winter fodder was provided by open grazing meadows. Field cultivation depended on meadows providing the required nutrients via the livestock. This system was sustainable for as long as there was a high enough acreage of meadows in relation to fields. Because of the increasing population, more and more land had to be used for cultivation. During the 1700s, a reduced acreage of meadows was noticeable in terms of impoverishment in many areas. A contributory factor to the scarcity of nutrients was that farm manure was used in the manufacturing of gunpowder.

During the 1800s the population continued to grow, resulting in increasing famine. In many places, agricultural land was by now impoverished. This led to measures such as digging up and using calcium-rich soil from layers beneath the topsoil, fertilizing with kelp and bonemeal, and eventually with guano and Chilean saltpeter. The iron plow, increasingly common toward the middle of the 1800s, made possible the cultivation of heavy clays and newly drained wetlands. The cultivation of virgin tracts of Norrland began. The emergency solution for the rising demand for agricultural land was that about one million people emigrated to North America.

The 1800s bore witness to the most extensive changes that there had ever been in the Swedish landscape. Legislative changes meant that in southern and central Sweden villages were broken up, peasants evicted, and new leaseholds drawn up to facilitate mechanization. At the same time, forestry declined, the meadow began to disappear, and reforestation began. In Dalarna, rotation farming was developed as an alternative to the use of nitrogen fertilizers in agriculture. In the beginning of the 1900s, this practice spread to other parts of the country, and open grazing or leguminous cultivation became an important part of the crop rotation. By the middle of the 1940s, 45 percent of the field acreage was pasture. Furthermore, all farms still kept animals and therefore had manure. Most of the domestic refuse was returned to the fields. The system meant that there was a good balance of nutrients, improved soil structure, and less erosion.

For the most part, climate and necessity have forced change within agriculture over the last few thousand years. But the impetus for change since the 1500s has also had much to do with political ambitions and reforms. Royal decrees about new cultivation of forest areas since the 1500s and the reforms of the 1700s and 1800s are examples of political initiatives to achieve higher agricultural productivity. The political dimension played a major part in the next major change.

A growing industrial sector needed manpower. This could be released from agriculture through mechanization. There was also a need for cheap food for the expanding urban population. Techniques introduced to meet these needs were based on the use of nonrenewable resources and technical know-how brought forward by industrialization. Chemical fertilizers, the tractor, and pesticides gained entry into agriculture during the '40s, '50s and '60s. During these three decades, the number of people employed within the agricultural sector went down by one million, and urbanization gained momentum.

During the 1960s there was added pressure on agriculture to industrialize. The predominant attitude was that agricultural activity should be comparable to any other industrial sector. The fact that this was biological production involving the manipulation of entire ecosystems and livestock was not seen as reason enough to make agricultural production a special case.

Characteristics of Present-Day Agriculture

Farming methods have changed substantially throughout history, but our present-day agriculture differs from its earlier incarnations by its substantial energy usage and high degree of linear resource handling. All earlier methods have been solar powered, with varying proportions of direct solar or human labor and draft animals fed on bio-energy. The prime energy source of our present-day agriculture is fossil fuel.

Farm livestock in earlier systems were fed on household waste and grazed on land which at the time could not be utilized in any other way. In present-day agriculture, grain and cereal-eating pigs and chickens have largely replaced livestock grazing. Therefore animals now compete with humans for food. About 80 percent of the agricultural acreage in Sweden is used today to provide animal feed.

In the earlier systems, natural solar-driven processes provided agriculture with nutrients. The cultivation patterns were either regularly changed, or surrounding land (meadows) kept the agricultural fields supplied with nutrients. Neither shifting cultivation (clearing and burning of woodland) nor open meadow grazing were, however, sustainable once population levels increased above levels prevalent at the time of their introduction.

More and more people can be supported from decreasing acreages. In this sense, present-day agriculture can be seen as an extension of a consistent trend in agricultural development since the time of hunter-gatherers. But our present agricultural system also brings a sharp break with many thousands of years of tradition. The supply of plant nutrients is now taken from nonrenewable depots (phosphate), and chemical fertilizers are manufactured to a great extent with the help of nonrenewable energy sources (fossil fuels and nuclear power). And field cultivation without livestock has become possible for the first time. In the old systems, plant nutrients were a scarce resource with which one had to economize.

Older cultivation methods were fragile in the sense that there was a substantial risk of crop failure due to pests. While chemical pesticides later reduced this type of risk in the short term, over a longer period of time they created new and more insidious risks, namely the accumulation of unnatural substances in the biosphere, along with associated health risks. The practice of monoculture and increased nitrogen inputs have also resulted in increased pressure from pests and disease, thus making agriculture more and more dependent on pesticides.

Finally, a major difference between present-day and older systems of agriculture is that with few exceptions cycles used to be concentrated within a single farm or village. Nowadays, the resource base of agriculture extends right across the globe. Increased distances have contributed to the formation of larger cycles, imperfectly sealed, with higher consumption of energy, and, for certain substances, a purely linear handling of resources.

SYSTEM CONDITION 4: THE DOUBLE CHALLENGE

In earlier sections we have described how present-day society and agriculture in many ways violate the ecocyclic principle — that is, they are not ecologically sustainable. If human health, quality of life, and living environments were also taken into account, the ecocyclic principle would then be seen as a bare minimum. Today, the direction of change is not even pointing toward fulfilment of this minimum condition. This means that in our present situation we are chipping away at the possibilities for the long-term survival of humanity.

We live in a world where less than one-third of the total population is responsible for more than 80 percent of our resource consumption. Within a decade there will be an estimated one billion more people in the world and a reduction in the arable farming area of some 30 million hectares. Even if the political will existed, it would not be feasible to export the consumption patterns of the industrialized world to other parts of the world: even now when this consumption only relates to a small part of the global population, we are seriously contravening the framework for long-term sustainability.

The double challenge, therefore, is on the one hand to achieve a global adoption of ecological sustainability, and on the other to ensure that the needs of all people can be satisfied. In this context, we should set ourselves the following goal: to bring down consumption per head to a level where it can be sustained long-term across the whole planet. Until we get to this point, our whole lifestyle constitutes both a detriment to other people seeking to satisfy their basic needs, and a countdown to the end of human continuance on Earth.

When we violate the fourth system condition, we postpone our problems and curtail our future freedom of choice. Reducing freedom of choice heightens the risk of war over resources, unscrupulous scrambling for power, injustice, human rights excesses, with further violations of the ecocyclic conditions as a result — in other words, a vicious circle.

In view of the fact that Sweden, in an international sense, still has a low population in relation to the amount of available fertile land, Swedish agriculture must become self-sufficient in all basic produce. This also means that agriculture cannot be propped up by supplies brought in from "ghost acreages" in other parts of the world where the land in question is needed to satisfy other people's basic needs and/or by production that brings further violations of ecocyclic conditions in other places.

National boundaries may be arbitrary in an altruistic sense, but they do delineate an area where political decisions can more easily be made. Sweden has an excellent resource base and cultural climate to become an example to others of a sustainable society. To meet this double challenge will require both a rationalization of resource use and a change in our lifestyles.

Rationalization

The development of technology and methods in agriculture have as yet been aimed not at developing diverse and robust systems maximizing the take-up of solar energy but rather at the input of nonrenewable resources. The measure of efficiency has been maximum yield per hectare, per hour of work, per Swedish crown (SEK) of invested capital. "Rationalization," according to this narrow perspective, is nothing but a substitution of green solar catchment areas (fields, meadows, grazing land) for the utilization of nonrenewable energy sources. Only in this way have we managed to create so-called excess capacity.

To rationalize within the framework of the four conditions requires development of knowledge technology and cultivation methods. The overriding principle will be to "let nature do its work," while finding key "solution multipliers." This means that attempts will be made to improve the effectiveness of nature's self-regulating system (for instance in relation to plant nutrients). Our system of cultivation must diversify into both perennials and annuals, and nitrogen fixation driven by solar energy utilized to the full. Other examples of "letting nature do its work" are reliance on natural behavior of livestock in finding its own foodstuff (grazing), or making use of plants/weeds that are known hosts to natural enemies of particular pests. To make optimum use of nature's work is also to encourage microorganisms in the ground. It means refraining from using pesticides that may have a negative impact on mycorrhiza and earthworms, and not fertilizing in a way that creates a need for pesticides. Furthermore, it will become vital to make optimum use of plant nutrients and keep down the pressure from pests by such practices as crop rotation or various forms of crop combination, as well as by minimizing soil exposure.

Rationalization also implies that the human resource base must be as local as possible. There are several reasons that illustrate this:

1. the use of energy and associated flows of materials have to be weighed up against other alternative uses for these resources;

2. small cycles are easier to seal;

3. present long-distance trade means that agricultural land in countries suffering from chronic soil impoverishment produces animal feed for export to rich industrialized nations;

4. long-distance trade in essentials is, in many ways, an insecure supply; and

5. local cycles stimulate our understanding of cause and effect in production and consumption.

Changes in Our Lifestyle

We clearly have to find alternatives to the established order of things in industrialized society, although the latter, worryingly, is being marketed as a prototype for the developing world. But a change of lifestyle has to occur according to acceptable social norms. It cannot be dictated but must emanate from the concern people feel for each other, for coming generations, and the rest of nature.

People's physiological, social, intellectual, psychological and spiritual needs are all equally important. They cannot be substituted for one another. For instance, a lack of community spirit, creativity, and sense of identity cannot be compensated for by increased material consumption. Herein lies great potential for the rationalization of our economy in a way that cuts down on the squandering of resources and pollution while at the same time raising the quality of life. In other words, a change of lifestyle does not necessarily mean making sacrifices in terms of satisfying fewer needs. Rather, reversing the trend of deterioration in living conditions will be experienced as a positive rather than sacrificial development. Within the framework determined by the conditions for a sustainable society, human creativity must be given room to manouver and seek out a multitude of solutions for what we perceive to be a better life.

WHAT NEEDS TO BE DONE?

Structural Change of Society

Everything speaks for the need of a radical change in our mode of living if the ecocyclic conditions are to be fulfilled. In the industrialized world, excessive consumption and the "throwaway" philosophy must be discarded as soon as possible. In developing countries, amongst other things, conditions have to be created for sustainable land use. A more equitable distribution of the world's collective resources and production would contribute to this.

For a more effective use of natural resources, distances between producers and consumers need to be shorter than they are today. Long-distance trade must be significantly reduced; beyond a maximum size it is impossible to keep cities sustainably supplied anyway. Agriculture can and, in a sense, should adapt to the ecocyclic principle before society does so. But measures are also needed within the economy, legislative programs, and social planning, in order to bring about necessary structural changes within society as a whole. By "structural change," we refer to the following problems: long distances between production and consumption, an extensive chain of refining and processing, transportation, packaging, the growth of cities, sewage handling, long-distance trade etc. These areas are determined by economic and administrative rules drawn up by political decision making. These rules must be changed so that individuals and corporations gain the opportunity of making decisions in accordance with the ecocyclic principle.

Structural reform is needed, with the following implications:

1. that cities and the countryside become more integrated, with higher levels of nutrients returned to agriculture, a larger proportion of food produced nearby, and less transportation;

2. that long-distance traffic is limited mainly to goods and services that cannot be produced locally or regionally;

3. that extremely limited use, and in the longer term none at all, is made of nonrenewable energy sources such as oil, coal, natural gas or nuclear power;

4. that there be maximum recirculation of already recycled materials (minerals and plastics), with the aim of keeping annual extraction from geological deposits to levels not greater than amounts produced in processes like bio-mineralization and fossilization (with

the exception of especially dangerous substances like lead, cadmium, mercury, etc., which will be put into final storage).

Today, development is heading in exactly the opposite direction — namely an extensive trade in staple products and growing cities all over the world. To break these trends, direction-changing decisions have to be taken both on a national and international level. On an international level, a relevant decision would be, for instance, the introduction of compulsory emission quotas for greenhouse gases, determined for each country on the basis of size of population. But Sweden cannot wait any longer for these kinds of agreements. National direction-changing decisions must be reached without waiting for the outcome of slow international negotiations. A few areas of special importance are:

1. A forceful but gradual tax reform, putting progressively greater emphasis on taxing resource use, primarily nonrenewable raw materials, fossil fuels, and electricity generated by nuclear power; and a gradually lowered tax on human labor. These changes must be carefully orchestrated (not sudden or unforeseen) so that the corporate sector has time to adapt by making the right investments at the right time.

2. A legislative agenda which gives the sustainable perspective a more pronounced place in social planning. "Environmental factors" should not signify cosmetic appendixes to decisions that have already been made on short-term criteria.

3. For all large projects (private or public) and in all political policy areas, environmental impact assessments need to be made on the basis of the four ecocyclic conditions.

Changes in Agriculture

Even now, operative changes can be made in agriculture. The rapid establishment of this kind of work is important, as it will expedite the political climate of change in a positive spiral. Some measures have already been introduced and need to spread to other farms. Others require a certain level of technical development. Much can be achieved with education and information, but many reforms will still be hypothetical as long as they have no corporate or economic basis. For this reason economic and administrative measures are needed to stimulate more sustainable movement. It must become economically possible for those farmers who want to pioneer this evolution to develop and practice a more sustainable agriculture.

Economic and administrative measures have to be applied that encourage:

1. a lower use of assist-energy and conversion to renewable fuels;

2. integration of livestock and plant production for the best possible balance within each individual entity, as well as on a regional and national scale. This means, amongst other things, that rules on maximum density of farm animals must be tightened;

3. a higher proportion of winter cultivation (autumn sowing, or grazing and perennials) counteracting the leakage of nutrients;

4. appropriate crop rotations, counteracting the propagation of weeds and pests, with the ultimate aim of substantially reducing the application of pesticides;

5. the fixation of nitrogen by solar energy;

6. defence and re-creation of important habitat for the fauna and flora of the agricultural landscape;

7. preventing accumulation of heavy metals in agricultural soil; and

8. an improved utilization of plant nutrients in farm manure.

THE NEED FOR DEVELOPMENT OF METHODS AND TECHNOLOGY

It is vital now to put effort into the development of new methods and technology to make progress within the framework of the ecocyclic principle. Some of the important fields are:

1. to develop cultivation systems that require less energy input in the form of chemical fertilizers and chemical pesticides, that do not need fossil fuel or electricity generated by nuclear power, and that are feasibly labor intensive.

2. to develop new crops, both annual and perennial, which can contribute to improved soil quality; economizing on plant nutrients and thus reducing the burden of damage, while at the same time meeting the demand for biofuels, vegetable lubrication oils, fibers, biodegradable packaging, etc.;

3. to examine ways in which the landscape can be structured to minimize the pressure of pests on harvests, by creating habitats that

encourage the natural enemies of those pests, for instance; and to look at other ways of coordinating the interaction between wild and domesticated flora and fauna, as well as the formation of a variable and productive agricultural landscape (strip cultivation, permaculture, woodland, gardens, and agro-forestry are all examples of this);

4. to develop new cultivation systems where a balance exists between the breaking down and taking up of humus;

5. to develop lighter machines which minimize soil compression, even in deeper soil layers;

6. to continue developing techniques to minimise the loss of plant nutrients during the handling of farm manure; and

7. to continue developing methods of using waste water and household waste for

8. biological production, without an accumulation of toxic substances.

Environmental problems are often caused by interactions that we do not know enough about. To a large extent, environmental problems are even caused by interactions that we do not even know we are ignorant about. If research is going to be able to play a part in finding solutions for agricultural environmental problems, and thereby the long-term upkeep of humanity, there needs to be an acknowledgment of the unspoken knowledge possessed by farmers. Terms like "green thumbs" are used to describe skilful practitioners. It should be of great interest to agricultural research to understand what this knowledge consists of and how it is best preserved. For this, farmers would have to take part and be co-responsible for research and development processes, so that their experience, creativity, and motivation can be put to use.

In seeking out solutions, there must be an openness to research that falls outside the realm of the analytical tradition. A high degree of new thinking is needed, with development of methods and a cross-disciplinary approach to look at multi-layered interrelationships in the agricultural system. It is important to be open to bold research efforts (although occasionally large-scale perspectives may be hard to handle) in order to achieve scientific renewal and to gain knowledge that will enable the transition to a sustainable society.

RETAINING CHOICE

Sooner or later we have to change course and adapt to the ecocyclic principle. If we continue to build ourselves into an unfeasible framework, then the costs of restructuring will become prohibitive. If we ruin fertile land, it will become more difficult to meet future increased demand for production from the land.

Today, agriculture is being forced to close down; recruiting within the agricultural sector is low and rural depopulation in entire areas seems imminent. Tree plantations and the development of scrub on arable land are the visible results of this trend. This goes straight against what we actually should be doing — preparing to meet demands that will come to bear on agriculture during the transitional phase to a sustainable society. It also limits our future room for maneuver.

In order to retain the freedom of choice for the future, society must immediately:

1. preserve arable land as a resource. This means both to maintain the fertility of land (for instance by not poisoning it with industrial and traffic pollution) and also to be restrictive with construction and the use of asphalt on agricultural land; and

2. protect the agricultural workforce and promote a robust agricultural system in the whole country.

How Do We Get There?

Directional change in political decisions is needed if individual farmers, consumers, business, and the food retail industry are to begin adapting to the ecocyclic principle. Political decisions should make it economically possible for individuals to adapt to the ecocyclic principle, something that will benefit the whole of society in the long run. To get there, the political debate on agriculture must move on from food prices and specific pollution sources, to global questions of householding and quality of life. A broad groundswell of opinion must also exert strong pressure on those in political power.

The following are vital steps in the creation of this necessary opinion:

1. Far-reaching educational programs in ecocyclic thinking are needed at all levels in society. Knowledge of the conditions for life on Earth and the subsistence of humanity have to be integrated into all other educational disciplines;

2. It is important that the farmers' own organizations, both by word and action, support the transition to sustainable agriculture and a more sustainable society;

3. Good examples have to be created and emphasized so that people can envisage alternatives to present ways of producing and consuming. Ecological agriculture has an important role to play in this;

4. Eco-labeling and other consumer information plays a significant part in informing people about the effects of our consumption on nature. At the same time, such measures provide stimulation for farmers and other entrepreneurs to dare to try more sustainable methods;

5. Local retailing and farm shops can be influential in strengthening the confidence people have in their farmers, while also giving farmers the opportunity to find out more about consumer preference and further direct the awareness of the general public to the biological cycles.

Glossary

agricultural ecosystem

An ecosystem which, although strongly influenced by humans, is driven by solar energy with the following exceptions: it requires assist-energy, either in the form of draft animals, human labor, or fossil fuels. It generally has a lower level of biological diversity, both in terms of species and genetic variety of strains within species. The system is characterized by human long-term selective pressure on species and breeds. The control of agricultural ecosystems is external (or controlled by man) and focuses on aims, rather than internal and based on cyclic mechanisms, as is the case in a natural ecosystem. It is also a more open system than the natural ecosystem: the movement of energy and materials into and out of the ecosystem is significant. The agricultural ecosystem is unstable and requires constant maintenance from its cultivator.

annual

A plant which completes its life cycle in a year.

biogeochemical cycle

A collective term for all natural cycles. It is commonly used, primarily because most functions in nature are dependent on a combination of several cycles. For instance, the formation of soil depends on biological, geological, chemical, and hydrological cycles.

biosphere

That part of land, water, or atmosphere that contains or is strongly influenced by living organisms.

climatic change

Regular change in climate cycles which can extend for decades, centuries, or millennia.

consensus

A decision on which all have agreed.

crop rotation

The sequence in which plants should be sown in one particular area.

depletion of organic material

Intense cultivation of the soil and the practice of open farming methods increase levels of oxygen in the soil and thereby hasten the turnover of organic material. When farming methods are practiced that break down organic matter faster than it can be rebuilt, we refer to it as depletion.

diversity

The presence of a great diversity of species or sub-species. "Diversity" is the drawing up of sub-divisions between groups within the total biomass in an ecosystem. Low diversity therefore implies that a few species dominate the system.

ecosystem

A system in which living organisms affect each other and their surroundings. What we define as an ecosystem can vary in size from a micro-habitat to all the organisms in an ocean. What defines it as an ecosystem is the interrelationship (functional and structural) among all the components in the system. By "components" we mean producers, consumers, recycling agents, as well as chemical and physio-chemical conditions.

geological cycles

Processes which construct, break down, and reconstruct rock and soil types, including their composition, structure, and form in the landscape.

ghost acreage

Land in one country that is used for the enrichment of other countries. The term was coined by Georg Borgström [see *The Hungry Planet* (Macmillan, 1972)] and is used to describe exploitation of resources in the developing world by industrialized countries.

humus

Organic material that consists of dead plant and animal residues in the process of being broken down, which have lost their original external structure.

hydrological cycles

The water cycle.

hydrosphere

All water on Earth and in the atmosphere.

lithosphere

The Earth's crust. Land that contains or is strongly affected by living organisms is defined by the term "biosphere." All other ground is referred to as "lithosphere" in this document.

märgling

The use of calcium-rich soil (soil beneath the layer of topsoil) as a way of improving soil quality. "Märgling" was a common method of soil improvement, (primarily in Skåne) before the time of chemical fertilizers. "Märgling" was primarily a calcium effect, but it also added plant nutrients to the field as well as making plant nutrients in organic material within the soil accessible by stimulating micro-fauna with increased pH values.

molecular pollution

Waste products in the form of molecules, ions, or other particles that are not tied into any cycle.

mycorrhizec

The symbiosis between fungi and plant roots. The fungi obtain carbohydrates from the roots, and the hyphae of the fungi help the plant maximise its intake of water and nutrients, such as phosphate.

open grazing

Grazing by livestock on leguminous plants and/or grass.

perennial

A plant growing for more than two years.

technosphere

All human constructions, machines, tools, etc.

THE NATURAL STEP PHILOSOPHY AND CORE VALUES OF THE ORGANIZATION (EXCERPT)

CONTENTS

September 1998 (revised at TNSI meeting in Stockholm, August 1998)

1. PURPOSE AND VISION

1.1 The purpose of this document is to set out the values, aims, objectives, and processes of The Natural Step. It is intended to be reviewed regularly.

1.2 The purpose of TNS is to promote a genuine commitment to sustainable development by all organizations and individuals. TNS will act to support, encourage, and oversee the promotion and application of The Natural Step Framework.

1.3 Our vision is that all actors in society come to understand the benefits — egocentric as well as altruistic — of applying the first order principles of ecological and social sustainability as a shared framework for dialog, problem-solving, and wealth creation.

2. BACKGROUND

2.1 Over the past 100 years, humans have been disrupting the cyclical processes of nature at an accelerating pace. Human societies are now, to varying degrees, processing natural resources in a linear direction. The complexity of ecosystems is such that scientists cannot foresee their tolerance limits to pollution and other negative influences. In addition, it often takes a long time for the consequences to appear; the effects of today's actions may not be seen until years from now.

2.2 Although many environmental and sustainable development initiatives are underway worldwide, there has been confusion about the meaning of a sustainable society. Fundamental, systemic change has yet to occur. People need knowledge to see restrictions and possibilities for the future, tools to develop relevant and attractive visions, and tools that can guide us toward those visions.

2.3 In 1989, Dr. Karl-Henrik Robèrt, a Swedish cancer research scientist, began to develop The Natural Step framework and process. After circulating 21 drafts, a group of leading Swedish scientists endorsed a consensus paper outlining a fundamental overview of ecological issues and principles that underlie sustainability. From the scientific consensus, and the ongoing dialog which arose, first order principles for social and ecological sustainability — the four "System Conditions" — were later on identified and elaborated in cooperation between Karl-Henrik Robèrt and John Holmberg. The System Conditions are an essential element in the TNS Framework for scientific work, and for decision making by businesses, governments, professions, and individuals.

2.4 The original group of 60 scientists has since grown into international networks of organizations such as NGOs, universities, business corporations, municipalities, and professionals like scientists and policymakers, who have endorsed the TNS Framework. These networks volunteered their time in organizing new consensus papers, educational programs and exemplary demonstrations of what can be achieved within their own ranks.

2.5 *Det Naturliga Steget* (The Natural Step) operated in Sweden through widespread educational activities with companies, local municipalities, and the general public. The Natural Step model was adopted into strategic planning and training operations of numerous companies — including IKEA, Electrolux, and McDonald's Sweden — and a large number of municipalities.

2.6 TNS organizations were established, under license from the Swedish originators, in other countries. In 1996, representatives from TNS organizations in Australia, The Netherlands, the United

States of America, the United Kingdom, and Canada comprised an informal Board for the promotion of further international dissemination and quality control of the TNS concept. In 2001 the Board was constituted by representatives from nine countries — Australia, Canada, Israel, Japan, New Zealand, South Africa, Sweden, the United Kingdom, and the United States of America. TNS has established work with all sectors: universities, schools, community groups, business corporations, entrepreneurs, consultants, politicians, municipalities, trade unions, and the general public.

3. AIMS AND OBJECTIVES

3.1 The aims of TNS are:

- to deepen the commitment to sustainable development globally through the use of TNS educational and decision-making materials as applied and promoted by national organizations;
- to maintain the quality and integrity of TNS materials;
- to strengthen the work of TNS offices by acting as an information exchange for materials and the dissemination of best practice;
- to encourage cooperation and debate among the network of organizations in the interests of enhancing and developing the TNS methodology, consensus documents and materials;
- to coordinate communications and to assist the process of sharing and cooperation between organizations.

3.2 In order to achieve the above aims, the following objectives must be secured:

- ongoing development of processes and materials which facilitate continuous learning about sustainable development within the context of the TNS Framework;
- a fair, open, and rigorous process for communication that both encourages a desire to participate and ensures the maintenance of the core values of TNS;
- ongoing dialog within the global science community to broaden the scientific consensus of the TNS Framework and deepen understanding of its application;
- an effective means of quality assurance and auditing of TNS materials and programs, compatible with the need to maintain the integrity and distinctiveness of TNS, as well as recognizing the cultural diversity of the membership;
- an effective, stable, respected and financially robust organization.

4. CORE VALUES

4.1 TNS is non-adversarial in its approach and always respectful of other people's views.

4.2 TNS is non-party political and non-religious.

4.3 TNS is a science-based organization, and ensures that all its work is firmly based on sound science.

4.4 The TNS task is to seek and teach scientifically based principles that can serve as common denominators for different cultures. At the same time, TNS acknowledges that for many people sustainability is as much about deep feelings and connections with the human spirit and with indigenous cultures as it is about logic and reason.

4.5 TNS wants to be an open, inclusive, sharing organization, which believes in transparency between TNS offices and with its many stakeholders.

4.6 TNS strives to be a learning organization, with considerable freedom for both individuals and different approaches and initiatives within the overall TNS Framework.

4.7 TNS aspires to achieve the highest environmental standards in its own performance, ensuring that it can "walk the talk" in all its operations.

4.8 TNS sets a very high value on the diversity of species, people, and cultures and wishes to see such diversity thrive within the "shared mental model" that it is promoting.

4.9 TNS is committed to the encouragement of continuous learning, as an organization and in its work with others.

5. TNS PROCESS

Emerging from the core values of TNS, there are certain approaches, techniques, and practices that characterize the work it does:

5.1 Defining Sustainability

Sustainability can only be defined on the principle level. The dialog in the TNS networks has elaborated first order principles for sustainability, the so-called System Conditions. Those are fundamental for the scientific dialog within TNS.

5.2 Shared Mental Models

TNS encourages the emergence of "shared mental models," based on the use of a few central features, including the four System Conditions and techniques that are built on the Four System Conditions, such as backcasting and upstream thinking.

5.3 TNS Framework

The TNS Framework is a science-based methodology for strategic planning toward social and ecological sustainability. It applies back-casting from basic principles for sustainability in a methodology referred to as "A, B, C, D Analysis."

5.4 Simplicity without Reduction

TNS strives to understand and explain systems in the simplest way. This requires the understanding of the first order principles of any system, so that "upstream causes" of any problem can be properly understood and addressed. Measures to deal with "detailed down-stream problems" then flow more logically from this upstream analysis. This approach makes it simpler to deal with complexity, yet doesn't "simplify" in the sense of disregarding any of the complexity. We describe this approach as "simplicity without reduction."

5.5 Consensus

Consensus building lies at the heart of the way in which TNS seeks to increase its influence in society. When the key task is to identify the first order principles of any system, many brains working together function better than one brain on its own.

5.6 Best Practice

TNS develops its case by supporting examples of good practice to encourage others to learn from them and to take them forward in their own way. TNS materials are specifically designed to be supportive rather than adversarial.

5.7 Autonomous Learning

As far as possible, TNS encourages people to internalize the TNS Framework at the level of general principle, and to think through for themselves the detailed implications and applications as they relate directly to their own work and expertise. This helps to create shared ownership of the solutions.

5.8 Partnerships and Cooperation

TNS believes that it can achieve more by building bridges and developing partnerships between people and organizations than by pursuing things in isolation or through confrontation.

5.9 Continuous Learning

The development of TNS relies on the performance of its employees, clients, and other stakeholders and on the willingness of those involved to always seek improvement and refinement of practice, and to share their experience with others. That requires:

- Updating — a responsibility systematically to update TNS teaching materials;
- Development — a responsibility to seek for new tools that are needed for specific purposes where the general tools are not sufficient;
- Sharing — sharing new tools and experiences, as well as failures and problems;
- Listening — always to be open to criticism.

5.10 "Yes, and…"

The conventional way of expressing disagreement is epitomized in the "Yes, but …" approach. TNS prefers the "Yes, and …" approach, acknowledging the validity and relevance of dissenting opinions and then building on them by setting them within the TNS Framework. In this way, an "opponent" (who may often be playing the role of devil's advocate) is invited into a dialog rather than an attack-and-defend debate. This is reinforced by asking for advice and help on any contested point.

5.11 "For or Against"

Rather than leaping into instant judgments for or against certain practices, products, or technologies, TNS prefers to assist people in making that judgment for themselves in relation to the TNS Framework.

6. PRACTICE AND PRODUCTS

Each TNS office uses a variety of different approaches (education, training, work-based learning, consulting, researching, advising, etc.), for which a variety of different products has been developed. Many more are now in development. Existing products include:

6.1 Consensus Documents

A number of problem areas within the field of social/ecological sustainability have been systematically elaborated by groups of experts utilizing the Framework as a shared mental model for dialog and problem solving.

6.2 Scientific Publications

A number of scientific papers and doctoral dissertations dealing directly with The Natural Step have been published.

6.3 Training/Teaching Tools

A number of videos, books, overheads, training manuals, and case studies have been developed for a variety of different audiences.

6.4 "Train the Trainers"

Some of these materials are used by TNS offices to "train the trainers" in companies, municipalities, and so on. Those trainers then become the principal deliverers of TNS materials to their colleagues.

6.5 Projects

Special projects to help raise awareness amongst the general public, involving games, exhibitions, prizes, etc.

6.6 Consultancy

TNS is developing applied tools for use in its ongoing consultancy work, covering areas like leadership and management, ISO 14001, life cycle assessment, green accounting, product development, supply chain initiatives, sustainability assessments, and so on.

THE TNS FRAMEWORK AND TOOLS FOR SUSTAINABLE DEVELOPMENT

Tools and Concepts for Sustainable Development: How Do They Relate to a General Framework for Sustainable Development and to Each Other? (Published in The Journal of Cleaner Production *Vol. 8 (3), 2000, pp. 243-254*

Karl-Henrik Robèrt [1]

ABSTRACT

We present a general framework to plan for sustainability and then relate it to some well-known tools for sustainable development. This framework follows from principles for how a system is constituted (ecological and social principles) and contains principles for a favorable outcome for the system (sustainability), as well as principles for the process to reach this outcome (sustainable development). The principles for sustainability define the favorable outcome and direct problem solving upstream toward problem sources. A program of activities is then constructed by backcasting from defined outcomes to the current problems. This is followed by "metrics" — various concepts for measuring and monitoring the activities. Most concepts and tools for sustainable development function as metrics, for instance Life Cycle Assessment (LCA), Ecological Footprinting (EF), and Factor X. An Environmental Management System (EMS), such as ISO 14001 or EMAS, is an administrative vehicle that should systematically align a firm's specific outcomes, activities, and metrics with a general framework for sustainability. From a strategic point of view, metrics should measure alignment of activities with the principles contained in a framework for sustainability. A framework is not an alternative to concepts and tools for metrics. We need them all, because they represent different interrelated levels of strategic planning.

Key Words: Sustainable development, sustainability, systems thinking, backcasting, strategies, strategic planning, Factor X, Factor 4, Factor 10, Ecological Footprinting, ISO 14001, EMAS, EMS, System Conditions, The Natural Step (TNS).

Introduction

Few trends have been growing more steadily over the latest decades than concerns about current non-sustainable development and society's increasing willingness to deal with this situation. It has led to an increased interest in the subject of ecology in general. We have also seen the development of various concepts for systematic management and monitoring of sustainable development that have gained worldwide acceptance. Examples of these are a number of Ecological Management Systems (EMS) applied for better ecological performance in firms, the most widely accepted being ISO 14001 and the corresponding system launched by the European Union, EMAS. And we have seen the development of many other tools with more specific objectives, such as life cycle assessment (LCA)[2, 3], Ecological Footprinting[4], and Factor 10, for instance Factor 4[5, 6] and 10 [7, 8].

Some of the leading edge research institutes in this area were invited to a UNEP workshop in, October 1998, to present their programs, learn from each other, discover relatedness among various concepts for sustainable development in firms, and focus on questions still needing attention[9]. This paper is a direct offspring from this meeting. How do concepts and tools for sustainable development relate to each other? A way of answering this question would be to define the end stage of all this planning and monitoring, the principles of sustainability, and then apply such principles as a reference point to determine the interrelationships of the various tools and concepts.

Together with The Natural Step (TNS, a Non-Governmental Organization [NGO] for Sustainable Development), we have previously elaborated and described a framework for systematic and strategic sustainable development, based on a set of basic principles[10, 11, 12]. Applying this framework as a reference point, we have studied concepts like Ecological Footprinting[13], Factor 10[14], LCA[15] and a model for product planning[16].

The purpose of this paper is to develop a general model for the relationship between frameworks on the one hand, and various concepts and tools on the other. Further, the purpose is to apply this model to study how some well-known concepts relate, not only to sustainability, but also to each other. In Section 1, we give an outline of the previously described framework. In Section 2, we launch a simple model that describes the general hierarchical relationship among principles for planning in any system, and various measures and tools for managing the system on the other. In Section 3, we analyze the components of the TNS Framework in relation to this model. In Section 4, we describe what a framework for sustainable development, such as the TNS Framework, *is not*. The relatively fast dissemination of the TNS Framework in policymaking and in the environmental debate has led to a number of misunderstandings. In Section 5, and based on the analysis in Sections 2 and 3, we discuss how ISO 14001, Ecological Footprinting, Factor X, and LCA relate to each other. Section 6 contains a summary and conclusions.

Section 1. Basic principles to deal with complexity.

The ecosphere's ability to sustain productivity and biodiversity of ecosystems, and thereby to sustain society with its demands for services and resources from the ecosphere, is dependent on very complex interactions among the various species within the ecosystems and between the ecosystems and the surrounding geophysical world[17]. Non-sustainability means a systematic degradation of this ability. For obvious reasons — the ecosphere is a complex system — this degradation is perceived as a very diverse range of symptoms (climate change, ecotoxic effects, disease, loss of biodiversity, loss of productivity in crop land and fisheries, social and political tensions, etc.). The delay between the cause or "upstream" activity (for instance, manufacture and use of CFCs within society) and the observed effect in carefully investigated and defined symptoms "downstream" (for instance, various symptoms resulting from increased ultraviolet radiation) may sometimes be several decades. For the same reasons, the effects of various efforts to deal with the symptoms — one by one — are also very diverse and complicated to analyze and describe. Sometimes it is even a matter of tradeoffs, that is, a favorable outcome in one respect (for instance, less toxic exhausts from cars fitted with catalytic converters) leads to an unfavorable outcome in another (for instance, consumption of precious metals). It becomes even more complicated when the economic perspective is considered. If expensive investments lead into dead ends (for instance, large investments in traditional car engines to make them a little more efficient), this may be even more of a problem than doing nothing, since it ties up resources that could be more effectively used for measures that are more essential from a sustainability perspective (for instance, developing engines that can connect today's Otto- and Diesel- technologies with tomorrow's technologies, such as fuel cells).

To be able to select relevant measures and deal with all this complexity in a comprehensive and systematic way, we need to think "upstream" in cause-effect chains, and we need to apply "backcasting" in the planning procedure. What does that mean?

- **Upstream thinking.** Problems are attacked by focusing upstream in cause-effect chains, that is, measures are taken to remove the underlying sources of problems rather than to "fixing" problems once they have occurred. The complex symptoms in nature arising from non-sustainable development must be studied, and so must the upstream societal causes of these symptoms.

- **Backcasting.** One envisions oneself acting in a desirable future when the principles for success have been met, and then plans what one must do now to move toward that point.[12, 18, 19, 20] In complex systems like the ecosphere, and with complicated projects like sustainable development, this is an effective methodology to align various measures with each other, so that each activity can be a logical platform for the next. Backcasting is different from the more commonly applied strategy of "forecasting," — that is, starting the planning procedure from today's situation, and projecting today's problems and trends and what are considered "realistic" solutions today, onto the future. If forecasting is allowed to be the only planning strategy, the risk of carrying the underlying causes of problems on into the future is substantial, particularly when today's trends are the major drivers of the problems we encounter (today's fuels, today's infrastructure, today's way of keeping account of society's economic performance in terms of GNP, today's relatively high costs of "green" alternatives in the market, etc.). What is considered "realistic" today should be allowed to influence only the pace of the transition, not its direction. That is the essence of backcasting.

Upstream thinking and backcasting require basic principles. To understand the upstream causes of today's symptoms in the ecosphere, as well as to plan systematically toward a favorable outcome when those causes of symptoms are no longer present, we need a set of robust principles that define the outcome of planning (sustainability). Such principles should, of course, cover the outcome and still not overlap — that is, each principle should cover its distinct functional aspect of sustainability. We need such principles to ensure we do not miss relevant aspects of sustainability and to monitor the transition in a comprehensive way. If our efforts to reach sustainability are not based on overall principles for that stage, there is a great risk that we solve today's problems by creating new problems. For instance, phasing out persistent unnatural compounds only when the negative effects have occurred and are known, by exchanging them with new persistent unnatural compounds, the effects — and "safe" concentrations — of which are not known will result in more negative effects further ahead. Unfortunately, a serious shortcoming of many inventory programs is that they lack such principles of sustainability.[21]

THE TNS FRAMEWORK

We cannot describe a sustainable future in detail. But we can define its basic principles. Based on this reasoning, the TNS Framework has been elaborated to provide the general public, the scientific community, and decision makers in business and politics with a mental model that makes it possible to plan and evaluate activities from a future sustainability perspective. The TNS Framework is used for dialog, problem solving, strategic planning, and as guiding principles for the merging of ISO 14001 with strategic investment programs for business.[12, 20, 22, 23] It consists of the following three components:

(i) **The funnel.** A metaphor for the awareness of the overall problem of non-sustainability — the decline of the ecosphere's capacity to support our present-day economies and life itself. Overharvesting, displacement, and other damaging forms of physical manipulation cause loss of productivity of forests, cropland, and fisheries (even if the harvests and catches may increase for a while). The consequence is that these vital resource bases require more and more resource throughput (fertilizers, pesticides, etc.) for the same harvest or catch. At the same time, the ecosystems are subject to increasing concentrations of substances that cause climate change and pollute them. Finally, more and more people on Earth contribute to the funnel effect; per capita the walls of the funnel lean inward even more. This metaphor is also used to explain the self-benefit that lies in avoiding the walls of the funnel and directing activities toward its opening. To business and policymakers, who are contributing to the funnel's narrowing in relation to our conditions for health and prosperity, the walls of the funnel will appear as higher and higher costs for waste management, taxes, insurance, resources, loans, loss of credibility in the market, and market shares lost to those who are planning ahead by skilfully taking those aspects into account.[12, 22]

(ii) **The Four System Conditions.** The basic conditions for sustainability in the "ecosphere/society" system — that is, principles that define the opening of the funnel. The first three conditions are elaborated as functionally different mechanisms for ecological non-sustainability — that is, the different mechanisms by which we can destroy the ability of the ecosphere to sustain us. Then we have put a "not" in each of these mechanisms. A fourth condition is the basic condition as regards our internal use of resources within society, to make it possible to meet the other three conditions.

In the sustainable society, nature is not subject to systematically increasing:

1. concentrations of substances extracted from the Earth's crust

2. concentrations of substances produced by society;

3. degradation by physical means; and in that society

4. human needs are met worldwide.

It is by violating the system conditions that society causes the narrowing of the walls of the funnel. In line with the general discussion above, it is very complicated to make a detailed description of all the symptoms arising in nature from our violation of those principles. Because of complexity, and the fact that "safe" concentrations for accumulating substances are extremely difficult to foresee, and because of the long delay between the "upstream" causal mechanisms in society (for instance, production of CFCs) and the appearance "downstream" of well-defined symptoms in nature (for instance, negative effects from increased ultraviolet radiation), it is essential that the System Conditions are applied to guide our decisions by focusing attention upstream on the cause-effect chains. Do we contribute upstream to the problem of increased problems downstream? In practice, this means we must put at least as high a priority on questions like, "Do we introduce persistent substances foreign to nature in the course of the economic activities of our firm?" as we should put on questions like, "Do we emit substances that are bio-accumulative and/or ecotoxic?"

(iii) **A strategy to avoid the walls of the funnel, and reach its opening.**

1. A step-by-step approach. This means asking relevant questions upstream with regard to the System Conditions. "Do these activities

decrease our dependence on contributing to society's current violation of the system conditions?" "Do we systematically decrease (a)
our demand for fossil fuels and dissipative use of metals (System
Conditions 1 and 4); (b) our use of persistent unnatural compounds
(System Condition 2); (c) any activities that physically encroach on
the vitality of ecosystems (System Condition 3); and (d) the wasting
of resources by utilizing more sophisticated methods to meet human
needs (System Condition 4)?"

2. Flexible platforms. To technically link short term with long term,
   we need a planning strategy that simultaneously ensures that each
   step is a flexible platform for future activities in line with the System
   Conditions. This is to avoid blind alleys — to avoid activities that
   may violate the System Conditions to a lesser degree, but are difficult to be further elaborated in the same direction. This is particularly important when investments are large and thereby tie up
   resources for relatively longer times. An example of a blind alley
   would be to invest heavily in the development of more energy efficient engines (System Condition 4), while neglecting the opportunity to prepare new technology for energy carriers other than fossil
   fuels (System Condition 1).

3. Low-hanging fruit. To economically link short term with long
   term, we need to put a priority on such "flexible platforms" that
   are, at the same time, likely to give a fast enough return on investment — for instance by finding activities that can save resources,
   identify a growing need in the market, or utilize a structure that
   already exists. An example is the introduction of photovoltaic cells
   for purposes where those are the cheapest, or even the only, alternative today — such as photovoltaics for satellites, watches, calcula-
   tors, or for lawn mowers that can run by themselves.[12]

Together, these three components provide a framework that makes it
possible to link small scale with large scale, upstream with downstream,
economy with ecology, and short term with long term. In an increasing
number of firms and municipalities around the world, the framework is
used not only for dialog, problem solving, and planning for sustainable
development but also to describe the need for, and interdependence of,
various tools and concepts for sustainable development. The best guide
for its application is a four-step strategy.[12, 20]

A. Shared mental model. The framework is explained and discussed
   among the participants in a planning process.

B. Looking at today's situation. Today's critical flows and problems with reference to the System Conditions are listed. "In what ways, and to what extent, are we contributing to the violation of the System Conditions today?" At this point, relevant indicators, concepts, and tools to monitor the phase-out of these contributions are also identified.

C. Thinking about tomorrow. Envisioning a future, in which the actual firm or activity is no longer part of the problem. "How can the services we provide to humanity, and in which we are specialists, be provided in a way that does not contribute to the violation of the System Conditions?" Possible solutions are listed, disregarding whether they are economically "realistic" or not, in the short term.

D. Design of a strategic program. Short term is now linked with long term by designing a program for change. In this, such solutions from Step C that are flexible platforms, as well as low-hanging fruit, are selected as the first measures. As they are undertaken, more solutions from the list will appear financially realistic, become tomorrow's "low-hanging fruit" and can be implemented.

Section 2. A model that outlines how principles, activities, and metrics relate to each other.

Before we can describe the relationship among various tools and concepts for sustainable development, we need to present a general outline of how principles, activities, and ways to monitor a process are interrelated in any system. There are constitutional principles, that is, principles that (1) describe the system — for instance, principles that define chess (the make-up of the game with its rules for how to move and take the pieces) or society's infrastructure for an air transport system (principles that describe the interrelated functions of airlines, airplanes, airports, authorities, etc.).

Then there are principles that (2) determine favorable outcomes in a system. In chess, there are the principles for checkmate. In the case of an air transport system, the principles determining favorable outcomes would be that (a) frequent enough airplane flights (b) arrive at the right destination, (c) safely, (d) comfortably, and (e) on time.

Then there are principles that (3) describe how to reach a favorable outcome in a system — in these cases strategic principles in chess or for the supervising, operating, and navigating of airplanes.

Then, there are (4) various activities that must be aligned with those principles — that is, the series of concrete activities that make all the technical facilities and logistics of a system work in line with the principles for a favorable outcome.

Finally, there are (5) numerous ways of measuring and monitoring those activities ("metrics"), so that they are really aligned with the principles necessary to reach the favorable outcome. For instance documentation and studies of smart strategic moves in chess or measures to determine that speed, direction, and altitude are in line with the planning of a flight, that the remaining fuel in the tanks is sufficient, and so on.

Sometimes, things go wrong in spite of thorough planning. It is therefore important to develop measuring systems for the negative effects also — for instance statistics on complaints from angry and scared passengers, metrics to determine material weaknesses in the production of the airplanes, analysis of "black boxes" after flight accidents and so on. The two aspects of metrics — metrics on activities for operation and improvement on the one hand and metrics on mistakes on the other — are interrelated. Thoroughly performed metrics on previous mistakes will help design more efficient principles for safe and comfortable flying, as well as suggesting improved metrics to monitor such progress. Smart strategies, activities, and metrics for improvement of the air transport system, should first be focusing on principles that deal with the underlying causes of previous mistakes, so that the need for metrics on unfavorable outcomes and accidents in the future will be reduced as much as possible.

We could apply this simple way of describing the hierarchical relationships between principles, activities, and metrics within a system to the sustainable development "journey" within the "ecosphere/society" system in the following way:

1. Principles describing how the biosphere/society system is constituted, for example ecological principles and social principles;

2. Principles for sustainability, that define a stage, a certain favorable outcome, in the systems mentioned above. Principles for sustainability should not be confused with ecological principles;

3. Principles for sustainable development are principles for a process to meet principles for sustainability (the transition toward sustainability, and then the safe development thereafter). Principles for sustainable development should not be confused with principles for sustainability;

4. Activities in this context are activities that are aligned with the principles for sustainable development — for instance, to change from nonrenewable energy to renewable energy, or to start recycling of material in the society. Other examples are changes to more appropriate tax systems or other economic measures to foster activities aligned with principles for sustainable development. Activities for sustainable development should not be confused with principles for sustainable development. For instance, it is possible to violate all principles for sustainability and sustainable development with renewable energy or recycling. Thus, the action that creates a change from using "nonrenewable" to "renewable" energy could lead to the impoverishment of forests and other parts of the ecosystems, or to increased concentrations of scarce metals in the ecosystems from poorly recycled photovoltaics. In the same way "recycling" of, for instance, cadmium batteries from households can lead to increased concentrations of cadmium in nature. This metal is normally very scarce in the ecosystems and should be used only in tightly controlled technical systems. This tight control is lost in flows between households and industry. Consequently, it is essential that we relate various activities to the underlying principles and avoid confusing these levels with each other.

5. Metrics for sustainable development are different concepts and tools for measuring and monitoring the transition. There are two levels of these. First, metrics can be used to (i) test the relevance, quality, and quantity of various activities to ensure they are really aligned with the principles for sustainable development. Examples are measurements to determine that material flows are really decreased to levels that are sustainable. Other examples are the rate of recycling and the purity of the recycled fractions, or the use of renewable compared to nonrenewable energy. Second, one can (ii) perform metrics on specific impacts in nature (when principles for sustainability are violated). Examples are various indexes on "global warming potential of gases" or "H+ equivalents of acidifying substances." As with metrics for the air transport system, metrics focusing on upstream solutions of the underlying causes of symptoms have a higher strategic value than metrics on the downstream effects — the symptoms. This will be further discussed in Section 6.

Section 3. Analyzing the TNS Framework in relation to the general model (see Fig. 1, p. 253)

PRINCIPLES OF THE ECOSPHERE

Level 1 in the model described in the previous section represents a description of the ecosphere. This system is so complex that it may seem difficult to get a comprehensive overview of its principles and consequently to proceed to Level 2. However, our main objective for sustainable development is not to study the ecosphere *per se*, but to discover the principal different mechanisms by which it can be destroyed and then to phase out all activities that are part of such destructive mechanisms. To that end, it is possible to restrict the description of the ecosphere to a limited set of principles that are relevant for this purpose, such as (a) the principle of matter conservation; (b) the laws of thermodynamics; (c) the principles of the sun-driven biogeochemical cycles; (d) the fact that the biosphere cannot sustain systematic shifts of its physical parameters (lower and lower pH, higher and higher concentrations of NOx, smaller and smaller areas for renewable resources, etc.); and (e) society's dependence on sustainable resource flows and services from the ecosphere. It is possible to describe the flows between the ecosphere and society in such a way that the principal different ways of destroying the ecosphere as a system can be determined.[10, 12]

THE FOUR SYSTEM CONDITIONS

These are principles for sustainability, that is, principles that define a stage, a favorable outcome, in the ecosphere. This is identical to Level 2 in the model presented in Section 2, to be compared with the example of air transport: (a) Frequent enough airplane flights (b) arrive at the right destination, (c) safely, (d) comfortably, and (e) on time. As in the metaphor of the air transport system, principles for a favorable outcome in the ecosphere/society system are much easier to describe than principles for the constitution of the system itself. Although the ecosphere/society system is much more complex than its subsystem, the air transport system, the principles for a favorable outcome in the ecosphere/society system are not particularly complicated to describe. The reason is that in this case the goal of the journey is that we are to stop destroying the system, and there are only four different mechanisms by which we can destroy it (see Section 2 and [10, 12]).

THE STRATEGY TO COMPLY WITH THE SYSTEM CONDITIONS

This level of the TNS Framework represents Level 3 of the model, that is, principles for sustainable development. These are principles for a process to meet the principles for sustainability (the transition toward sustainability and then the safe development thereafter). Using the structure of Section 1, iii:

1. A step-by-step approach to systematically replace activities that are not compatible with the system conditions with activities that are or that can be developed in that direction. This is often called the principle of substitution, particularly when it is about changing chemical substances. In the TNS Framework, the principles of upstream thinking and backcasting are applied in the process of seeking an appropriate substitute;

2. Flexible platforms; and

3. Low-hanging fruit in combination are strategic principles that can allow substitutions to link short-term steps with long-term technical and economic solutions; and

4. Another principle, which should be applied at this stage, is the precautionary principle, particularly when there is doubt about whether contemplated activities comply with the System Conditions or not, and when such activities would tie up large amounts of resources.

There are other principles for sustainable development — the "strategic level" —that need to be considered. It is necessary to ensure that people are both engaged with and happy about the process. Transparency belongs in this category. The TNS Framework's metaphor of the funnel and the self-benefit in avoiding its walls are also is in this category, as are others for implementing the framework. For example, the management team needs to understand and then endorse the framework and communicate its relevance to other staff.[22] Other tools will facilitate its application, such as the four-step strategy described at the end of Section 1: (A) sharing the framework; (B) looking at today's situation; (C) thinking of tomorrow; and (D) design of a strategic program.

The TNS Framework is applied to guide activities and metrics — that is, activities and metrics (Levels 4 and 5 of the systems model in Section 2) are not part of the TNS Framework as such. Being developed from a description of Level 1 (relevant aspects of the principles of the ecosphere), its focus is on Levels 2 and 3. By these means, the framework

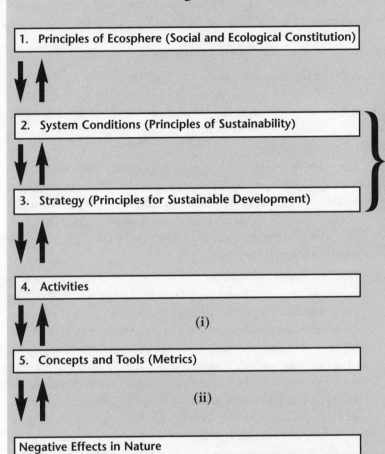

Figure 1.

1. **Principles of Ecosphere (Social and Ecological Constitution)**

2. **System Conditions (Principles of Sustainability)**

3. **Strategy (Principles for Sustainable Development)**

TNS FRAMEWORK

4. **Activities**

(i)

5. **Concepts and Tools (Metrics)**

(ii)

Negative Effects in Nature

The five levels — (1) Principles of Ecosphere, (2) Principles of Sustainability, (3) Principles for Sustainable Development, (4) Activities and (5) Metrics — are hierarchically dependent on each other. When principles of sustainability are violated, we can measure negative effects in nature (ii). What is most relevant to measure from a strategic point of view follows from what is relevant to do (i). What is relevant to do follows from the relevant path toward the goal (3). A relevant goal follows from the principles that define it (2). And the principles that define a desirable goal can be elaborated from relevant principles of the system (social and ecological) (1).

provides overall guidelines for any activity and on any scale. Activities and metrics are to be individually chosen and designed for particular situations or projects in line with the framework.

Section 4. What the TNS Framework Is Not

Because of the fast dissemination of the TNS Framework, and because of its unique positioning in the model presented in Section 2, it is often cited, and often in ways that can be misunderstood. In the following, some of the most common misconceptions are presented as quotes followed by an explanation.

- "The TNS Framework is the most important of all concepts for sustainable development." This is like saying that the principles to reach a safe air transport system are more important than the activities to do so, or the metrics to measure that it really happens. The answer is that all levels are hierarchically interrelated — one cannot do without the other.

- "The TNS System Conditions are oversimplified." This is based on the same misconception as exemplified by the previous bullet. The TNS System Conditions would be oversimplified, to say the least, if they were claimed to cover all levels in the systems model described in Section 2 (they cover only Level 2). Alone, basic principles for sustainability are neither particularly difficult to communicate nor very helpful. It is in the context of the other levels of the system, elaborated as a framework and a method to apply this framework, together with activities and metrics, that they not only make sense but become as essential as any other level in systems planning. As with the air transport system, it is sometimes difficult to assess whether in reality, the principles are met or not. This may require more research but in no way influences the relevance of the principles as such.

- "The TNS System Conditions are laws of nature." This is not true. Laws of nature are studied in Level 1 in the model elaborated in Section 2. The TNS System Conditions are constituted as logical principles for sustainability that follow from a scientifically adequate description of the ecosphere.[10, 12]

- "The TNS Framework is good for raising awareness and conveying a relevant understanding of what must be done on a principle level, but cannot be applied 'hands on,' for instance as metrics."

This is true. However, basic principles for sustainability and for sustainable development are essential as guidelines when metrics are to be determined and/or elaborated for a given activity, or process, or firm.

A number of effective concepts for metrics, and their relationship to the TNS Framework, are described in the following section.

Section 5. Some important concepts and how they relate to sustainable development, and to each other

Most concepts for sustainable development consist of various means for measuring the relevance of different activities in relation to the concept of sustainable development, that is, to monitor and manage the journey to sustainability. They belong to the Level 5, "metrics," described in Section 2.

ECOLOGICAL MANAGEMENT SYSTEMS (EMS) SUCH AS ISO 14001 AND EMAS

These tools are administrative tools for environmental work within firms. Returning to the metaphor of the air transport system, systems of administration for sustainable development are comparable with the checklists that pilots use to ensure that all activities they undertake are really in line with the principles to be followed to reach a favorable outcome. The principles and planned activities and metrics in line with those principles are the contents, while the EMS is the vehicle — that is, the administrative tool.

The principles and activities must be put into a relevant administrative context so that the principles are implemented through the planned activities that are monitored, audited, and — finally — evaluated in order to manage the next cycle of activities within the EMS. This means that, for an EMS to be really useful for sustainable development, the objectives for the planning (complying with the System Conditions) and individually elaborated activities and metrics to meet these objectives should be incorporated into the EMS.[23, 29]

As with the pilot's checklist, administrative tools for sustainable development within firms should be standardized. ISO 14001 and EMAS are the most commonly described EMS. A framework based on basic principles for sustainability and sustainable development (like the TNS Framework) provides the EMS with direction and helps firms to align business with the larger context of sustainable development and foreseeable changes in the market. The guide for application of the TNS Framework, the four-step strategy described at the end of Section 1, is a natural ingredient in any EMS. Conversely, without an administrative tool, it is difficult and probably impossible to undertake the strategy to implement a framework like TNS in an effective operational way for transition to occur.

THE FACTOR 10 CONCEPT

The Factor 4 and Factor 10 concepts, both originating from the Wupperthal Institute, have gained widespread acceptance as creative concepts for the reduction of resource throughput in the economy. They are based on a sustainability perspective and conclude that the turnover of resources must be reduced on a global scale to reach sustainability.

The Factor 4 concept was spread by the Club of Rome report "Factor Four — Doubling Wealth, Halving Resource Use",[5, 6] in which a large number of examples illustrate that at least four times as much wealth can be extracted from the energy and material resources we use. The Factor 10 concept[7, 8] focuses on materials and assumes that sustainable material turnovers will not be reached unless and until the material intensity of the OECD countries is reduced by a factor of ten.

The Factor 10 concept is a very direct way of doing metrics on various activities that can reduce the throughput of resources and energy in relation to the utility: "By what factor can — or should — this flow be reduced?" This makes the Factor 10 concept a very attractive and flexible way of monitoring activities that are to meet the fourth system condition.

The following aspects should be considered when the Factor 10 concept is applied with reference to the TNS Framework — as a tool to monitor some of the principles for sustainable development:[14]

The perspective should remain sufficiently large. The Factor 10 concept should encourage engineers, managers, politicians, and NGOs to think big in terms of resource productivity gains. At the same time, it should avoid the "technological fix" trap, by continuously relating various flows to social as well as ecological aspects of sustainability in the ecosphere (System Conditions 1 to 4). If backcasting from such a framework is the starting point, the technological aspects of the transition follow naturally and become more meaningful. By what factors must our flows be reduced to stay within the capacity of the ecocycles, and what are the technological and social objectives and possibilities for achieving such flows?

This perspective must also take the social side of System Condition 4 into account. By what factor must these flows be decreased in the affluent parts of society to allow decent living conditions in the poor part of the world?

Qualitative aspects. The factors by which certain flows need to be reduced to stay within the assimilation capacity of the ecosystems differ widely, depending on what flows we study. Differences in qualities of material flows include differences in persistence, abundance, and eco-toxicity of metals and compounds (System Conditions 1 and 2). Still other aspects of sustainability are not quantitative at all. For instance, in line with the discussion in Section 2, there is a need to phase out certain flows completely or to introduce more balanced management routines in forestry, agriculture, or fisheries (System Condition 3).

Dynamic aspects. Various flows influence each other. In order to reduce certain flows, other flows may need to be increased. Maybe the mining of certain metals will need to increase to build up a pool of photovoltaic cells. Rebound effects create a similar problem. A certain flow within a system may increase as a rebound effect to reduced flows within a subsystem. Our relatively more efficient car engines, for instance, have contributed to a higher use of petroleum, not the other way around.[24]

ECOLOGICAL FOOTPRINTING

Like the Factor 10 concept, Ecological Footprinting (EF)[4] is a way of doing metrics on various activities to meet System Condition 4. EF also takes some aspects of System Conditions 1 to 3 into account.[13] One of the major differences from Factor 10 is that with Ecological Footprinting, the outcomes of various activities in society are not determined by factors. They are measured and aggregated into units of area — that is, as a reduction or an increase in the ecological area needed to support the activities. Another difference is that the starting point is an estimate of the total life-sustaining area of the biosphere — that is all the accumulated "footprints" from various activities are related to the total carrying capacity of the ecosphere.

Psychologically, Ecological Footprinting provides a tangible way of describing the relevance of smarter technologies and more subtle lifestyles, sensitive to the demands on the environment, as a means to reduce the "footprints" of affluent societies in line with System Condition 4. Furthermore, it provides direct ways to monitor some aspects of System Conditions 1 to 3, since qualitative differences in various materials, and management routines of ecosystems, influence the size of the footprint. An example is the area needed to assimilate our CO_2 emissions from fossil fuels.

As with the Factor 10 concept, there are many qualitative aspects of the System Conditions that cannot be described in terms of footprints. For instance, contamination of nature from the use of scarce elements or persistent compounds foreign to nature (System Conditions 1 and 2) cannot be related to an ecological area in a meaningful way. The same goes for the necessary change of certain management routines in, for instance, agriculture or forestry (System Condition 3).[14]

Ecological Footprinting is an overall measuring tool to get a tangible overview of our performance with regard to sustainability and is unique in its capacity to communicate very directly how lifestyle and technical competence relate to such a perspective. It follows from the above that the footprinting concept inherently contains aggregated data concerning System Condition 4 and certain aspects of System Conditions 1 to 3. Consequently, it has certain limitations when we are studying isolated flows of society, for instance when various sub-systems are going to be evaluated and compared to each other in a planning procedure. Here, the more flexible Factor 10 concept can be used. Both concepts are relevant for their purposes, and can well be used together.

LIFE CYCLE ASSESSMENT

LCA[2, 3] is a way of evaluating all processes involved with a certain product or service, "from the cradle to the grave" — that is from resources through transport to use and disposal of the product. It is often used to compare products with the same function or to determine "hot spots" — that is parts of the life cycle that are critical to the total environmental impact. Since it doesn't focus on just one single effect from one single part of a product, the process of doing an LCA is a way of creating an overview of the total complexity of interactions between different processes in industrial society and the ecosystems. And it can be helpful in the selection of products that have an as-low-as-possible negative influence in nature today. Finally, it allows us to plan ahead, because we can simulate new conditions for the future, when various things like transport systems have changed.

The term "LCA" refers to the evaluation of the total life cycle of a product *per se*, but the perspective of this evaluation can differ with regard to the objective of the LCA. This means, that the term "LCA" just refers to the sound objective of evaluating all aspects of a product, whereas it doesn't say how this is done or for what purpose. It can, for instance, be based on strategically important aspects of various options in a production process. Alternatively, it can be based on estimates of different effects in nature (from violation of the System Conditions). This can be a valuable tool for determining the relative severity of impacts in nature among various products and processes. However, it is quite complicated to evaluate negative effects in nature, and it is a complicated matter to draw relevant strategic conclusions from data of this kind. LCAs of that kind are not optimal for strategic planning in business.

The picture becomes more difficult to evaluate when the different impacts (for instance evaluation of the emissions contributing to the greenhouse effect, and acid rain, respectively) are sometimes aggregated into one single figure. This may be relevant when the objectives and restrictions of the LCA are well known and when the categories of input data are so similar that comparisons can be made in a valid way. However, used in that way, LCA is of limited interest for decision making on investment strategies or for the "marketing of green products." This is due not only to complexity and uncertainty of the negative effects. The aggregation of data may "hide" relevant aspects from a planning perspective.[15] What happens if the same product is evaluated in a future situation (backcasting), when the conditions are different? If, for instance, a certain product is linked to relatively long transportation of raw materials, and if over time, the transport system develops in a sustainable way (or logistics are improved), the product with the "highest" impact in nature today, may suddenly turn out to be the most favorable one — and consequently may be the best to invest in.

Efforts are now made to streamline the calculations of LCA to increase their applicability.[25, 26, 27] LCA can also be performed in a backcasting perspective and in looking upstream in cause-effect chains.[15] Applied in this way, it leads to a qualitative evaluation, where the product's influences on all System Conditions, and upstream in cause-effect chains, are evaluated and displayed in a transparent way.

Section 6. Summary and Conclusion

A framework for planning should be based on relevant constitutional principles — that is, basic principles for how the system is constituted (laws of thermodynamics, ecological principles, and social principles, for example), and contain basic principles for a favorable outcome of the planning (principles for sustainability), as well as basic principles for the process to reach this outcome (principles for sustainable development). The framework's basic principles for sustainability are essential to guide problem solving at the source — upstream — and to launch goal-oriented planning programs by applying the principles of the goal as the starting point of planning — backcasting. The Natural Step (TNS) Framework is a framework of that kind. In the presented model for planning within any system (Section 2), the principles for planning toward a goal are followed by activities to comply with those principles and then metrics to monitor and evaluate the activities in that respect. Most concepts and tools for sustainable development are metrics that can be used in this way.

This means that a framework (Levels 1 to 3 in Section 2) is not an alternative to activities, concepts, and tools (Levels 4 and 5) for sustainable development. We need them all, because they represent different interrelated levels of strategic planning. A framework can be used only for overall planning, but since it contains basic principles, it can do so for any activity at any scale. To align the concrete activities with such principles — turning to renewable energy (System Conditions 1 and 2), substituting certain metals and chemicals (System Conditions 1 and 2), turning to ecologically sound management routines for vital ecosystems (System Condition 3), and relating all those activities to an as-efficient-as-possible turnover of resources to meet human needs worldwide (System Condition 4) — we still need detailed information. Often we don't have all the information we need. But the framework can be helpful for organizing such information that is relevant to problems and solutions, and for discovering which information is missing — that is to give a comprehensive overview. It is also valuable for giving a sense of direction to the planning procedure. The framework can also be used to select or develop relevant metrics for the monitoring of the process, once the planning has reached its operational stage.

Sometimes metrics are used to (i) determine whether specific activities are in line with the framework — Levels 1, 2, and 3 of the model in Section 2. First the overall objectives of a firm or an activity are determined by its relationships to the system conditions (Step B in the planning model, Section 1, iii). The qualitative aspects that follow from such an analysis make it possible to perform metrics on the relevant things and at the appropriate levels during the transition. For instance, metrics that are performed on measures such as the rate of recycling should be based on relevant questions of principle, such as: "Is the recycling performed in a way that maintains a pure and high-performing pool of the material in society, or is it a case of down-cycling (loss of purity and resource quality, System Condition 4)?" "Are the recycled materials very scarce in nature, so that even very small losses from the recycling process will increase their concentrations in nature as long as they are not phased out (heavy metals, System Condition 1; or persistent unnatural compounds, System Condition 2)?"

If in doubt, perhaps because of lack of information, a material should be regarded as persistent and foreign to nature until proven otherwise (precautionary principle). If aspects of these kinds are neglected when metrics are developed, then the use of these metrics may lead decision makers into dead ends, with harmful consequences not only for nature but also for the economic outcome for their firms. To succeed with planning based on the proposed framework — that is, to determine the overall critical flows and objectives before activities and metrics are chosen and designed, is still, in most cases, the simplest way for planning ahead.

At other times, metrics are performed to (ii) give information on the relative impacts in nature (from activities that contribute to the violation of the System Conditions): for instance, to evaluate the relative impact on the ozone layer from various CFCs, and then to use that information for the substitution of chemicals used by a firm. Such studies are essential for scientific and public reasons. However, because of complexity in the ecosphere as a system (multiple effects, threshold effects, delay mechanisms, rebound effects, uncertainty of data, etc.), metrics of the first kind (i) are generally more relevant from a strategic point of view. If this is neglected, then we are consistently — metaphorically speaking — "risking exchanging the toxic substance ammonia for 'non-toxic' and 'non-bioaccumulative' CFCs," without learning anything in the process about how to change the kind of thinking that created the problem in the first place. For firms not contributing to high and/or increasing, levels of any compounds in nature, the relative harmful effects of pollutants are of but limited strategic interest. However, contributing to increasing concentrations of compounds in the ecosphere — for instance, by using persistent substances foreign to nature — is a risky thing, even if no negative effects are known as yet.

The consequence of this reasoning is that the first priority should be to align activities as well as metrics with the principles for sustainable development given in the framework. For obvious reasons, this strategy should be complemented also with solid information on well-known negative effects in nature from certain activities (that could then be phased out at a relatively higher rate). For example, Electrolux put a very high priority on the phaseout of CFCs — based on the information on their effects on the ozone layer. However, while doing so, they simultaneously abandoned plans to change to other relatively persistent compounds foreign to nature, like HCFCs. These compounds did not fit Electrolux's backcasting perspective with regard to System Condition 2.[12, 28]

LCA, Factor 10, and Ecological Footprinting are all examples of tools that can monitor various aspects of this reasoning — that is, once the framework has been applied to determine relevant objectives and select relevant activities, these activities must be monitored so that the objectives of the planning are really met. An Environmental Management System (EMS) like ISO 14001 or EMAS is the administrative vehicle that should contain the framework, plus information on the specific objectives, activities, and metrics in each firm and their relevance with regard to the framework as well as the specific objectives of the firm.

- The firm is the airplane;
- the framework is the guidelines for planning this particular journey (to sustainability), including the map with the goal, plus a description of the principles for reaching that goal;
- the EMS is the manual and checklists needed to handle that specific airplane in line with the framework;
- the activities are everything that takes place on board; and
- the metrics are performed with the instruments needed for that airplane on this route, so that the activities comply with the plan for the flight.

During the flight, the first priority is to undertake all the activities required by the plan to ensure the airplane reaches its destination and to monitor that this is the case. Only in special unforeseen circumstances are deviations from the plan advisable.

Acknowledgment

Financial support by the Swedish National Board for Industrial and Technical Development (NUTEK) is gratefully acknowledged.

Notes

Chapter 2: Systems Thinking and Consensus

1. See, for instance, Peter Senge's "Shared Mental Models," *The Fifth Discipline: The Art and Practice of the Learning Organization* (Doubleday/Currency, 1990). In this excellent book, a very similar reasoning has been applied to business organizations.

Chapter 4: The Scientific Experience

1. The law of matter. During atomic fission, matter is exchanged for energy, but this exception does not affect the rest of the argument. (Together, the first law of thermodynamics and the law of matter are often referred to as the "conservation laws." Only the first law of thermodynamics, however, rightfully applies to thermodynamics.)

2. "Concentration" may be expressed as "energy" and "structure" as "information content." There are two main ways of expressing the information that makes up structure: genetically in cells and by human formulas or drawings.

Chapter 5: The Social Experience

1. The Social Invention of the Year award is sponsored by The Body Shop and the Institute for Social Inventions.

Chapter 6: The System Conditions for Sustainability

1. K-E. Eriksson and K-H Robèrt, "From the Big Bang to Sustainable Societies," *Reviews in Oncology*. Vol. 4, No. 2 (1991), pp. 5-14.

2. How high would the concentrations of metals rise in surrounding ecosystems if all of society's metals were dispersed? See C. Azar, "Long-term Environmental Problems, Economic Measures, and Physical Indicators," Institutionen för Fysisk Resursteori (Chalmers, 1995) [Doctoral thesis]; and C. Azar, J. Holmberg, and K. Lindgren, "Socio-ecological Indicators for Sustainability," *Ecological Economics* 18 (1995), pp. 89-112.

Chapter 8: Scandic and Sånga Säby: Test Pilots for Sustainability

1. Forest Stewardship Council, a voluntary international certification and labeling system for sustainable forest management, with its head office in Oaxaca, Mexico.

Chapter 10: The TNS Framework (A, B, C, D, Analysis)

1. K.H. Dreborg, "Essence of Backcasting," *Futures* 28 (1996), pp. 813-828.

Chapter 12: Going International

1. See, for example, Robert Gilman, "Educating a Nation: The Natural Step," in *Context* (1991).

2. Appendix 2 for The International Charter for TNS.

Chapter 13: Growing Pains

1. Abstracts, King Carl Gustaf's environmental symposium, November 28, 1996.

Chapter 14: The Crucial Energy Problem

1. C. Azar, J. Holmberg, and K-H. Robèrt. "Fossil Fuels and Corporate Economic Risk Assessment." *Perspectives on Business and Global Change*. Vol. 14, No. 1 (March 2000), pp. 63-72.

2. Jeremy K. Leggett. *The Carbon War: Dispatches from the End of the Carbon Century*. Penguin Books, 1999.

3. Intergovernmental Panel on Climate Change (IPCC). *"Climate Change 1995: The Science of Climate Change."* J.T. Houghton et al, eds. Cambridge University Press, 1996 [IPCC Working Group II].

4. C. Azar and H. Rodhe. "Targets for Stabilization of Atmospheric CO_2." *Science* 276 (1997), pp. 1818-1819.

5. For a summary of recent activities and California Fuel Cell Partnership, see J. Ogden et al., *Journal of Power Sources* 79 (1999), pp. 143-168; and <http://www.drivingthefuture.org/>.

6. F. Pearce. "Running on Empty." *New Scientist*. 9 Oct 1999.

7. *Global Environmental Change Report (GECR)* 19 Sept 1998.

8. *GECR* 26 Sept 1997.

9. *GECR* 23 April 1999.

10. *GECR* 23 Oct 1998.

11. *GECR* 24 Oct 1997.

12. *GECR* 26 Feb 1999.

13. *GECR* 23 April 1999.

14. *Environmental Watch: Western Europe* 21 Nov 1997.

15. *GECR* 24 Sept 1999.

16. *GECR* 17 Nov 1998.

17. *GECR* 14 May 1999.

18. The Pew Center on Global Climate Change [online, 1999] <http://www.pewclimate.org/>.

19. F. Reinhardt. "Market Failure and the Environmental Policies of Firms." *Journal of Industrial Ecology*. Vol.3 No. 1 (1999), pp. 9-21.

20. I have deleted Step A, of course, which was presented in the original article.

Chapter 15: The Second Arena (From *Ad Hoc* Projects to a Systematic Approach

1. *Stepping Stones.* No.33 (October 1999).

Appendix 1: Agriculture from a Scientific Perspective

1. ©The Natural Step, 1995. Translation by Henning Koch.

Appendix 3: The TNS Framework and Tools for Sustainable Development

1. Physical Resource Theory, Chalmers University of Technology and Göteborg University, S-41296, Göteborg, Sweden; The Natural Step Foundation, Wallingatan 22, S-111 24 Stockholm, Sweden.

2. R. Heijungs, J.B. Guinée, G. Huppes, R.M. Lankreijer, H.A. Udo De Haes, A. Wegener Sleeswijk, A.A.M. Ansems, P.G. Eggels, R. van Duin, and H.P. de Goede. *Environmental Life Cycle Analysis of Products: Backgrounds.* Centre for Environmental Science, Leiden University, 1992 [130 pp. and Guide, 96 pp.].

3. L-G. Lindfors, K. Christiansen, L. Hoffman, Y. Virtanen, V. Juntilla, O-J. Hanssen, A. Ronning, T. Ekvall, and G. Finnveden. "The Nordic Guidelines on Life-Cycle Assessment." *Nord* 20 (Nordic Council of Ministers, 1995).

4. W.E. Rees, and M. Wackernagel. "Ecological Footprints and Appropriated Carrying Capacity: Measuring the Natural Capital Requirement of the Human Economy." In A-M. Jansson, M. Hammer, C. Folke, and R. Costanza, eds. *Investing in Natural Capital: The Ecological Economics Approach to Sustainability.* Island Press, 1994.

5. E.U. Von Weizsäcker, A.B. Lovins, and L.H.Lovins. *Factor Vier: Doppelter Wohlstand — halbierter Naturverbrauch.* Droemer Knaur, 1995.

6. E.U. Von Weizsäcker, A.B. Lovins, and L.H.Lovins. *Factor Four Doubling Wealth — Halving Resource Use.* Earthscan, 1997.

7. F. Scmidt-Bleek. "Revolution in resource productivity for a sustainable economy — a new research agenda." *Fresenius Environmental Bulletin* 2 (1994), pp. 245-490.

8. F. Scmidt-Bleek. *MIPS and Factor 10 for a Sustainable and Profitable Economy.* Wupperthal Institute, 1997.

9. Aloisi de Larderel. "What is a sustainable enterprise?" (UNEP, 1998) [workshop, October 14, 1998].

10. J. Holmberg, K-H. Robèrt, and K-E. Eriksson, "Socio-ecological principles for sustainability." In R. Costanza, S. Olmlan, and J. Martinez-Alier, eds. *Getting Down to Earth — Practical applications of Ecological Economics.* International Society of Ecological Economics (Island Press, 1996).

11. K-H. Robèrt, H. Daly, P. Hawken, and J. Holmberg. "A compass for Sustainable Development." *International Journal of Sustainable Development and World Ecology* 4 (1997), pp. 79-92.

12. J. Holmberg, K-H. Robèrt, "Backcasting — a framework for strategic planning." *International Journal of Sustainable Development and World Ecology.* Vol. 7 (4) (2000), pp. 291-308.

13. J. Holmberg, U. Lundqvist, K-H. Robèrt, and M. Wackernagel. "The Ecological Footprint from a Systems Perspective of Sustainability." *International Journal of Sustainable Development and World Ecology* 6 (1999), pp. 17-33.

14. K-H. Robèrt, J. Holmberg, and E.U. von Weizsäcker. "Factor 10 for subtle policy making — Objectives, potentials, and obstacles." *Greener Management International.* Issue 31 (Greenleaf Publishing, 2001) [ISSN 0966-9671].

15. K. Andersson, E.M. Hogaas, U. Lundqvist, and B. Mattson. "The feasibility of including sustainability in LCA for product development." *Journal of Cleaner Production.* 6 (1998), pp. 289-298.

16. S.H. Byggeth, Karlskrona University, and Chalmers University, Göteborg, *Integration of Sustainability Aspects in Product Development.* (Chalmers University of Technology, Göteborg University, 2001) [thesis for the degree of Licentiate of Engineering, ISSN 0280-2872].

17. The ecosphere consists of the biosphere plus the whole atmosphere with its ozone layer. See also Notes 10 and 12.

18. J.B. Robinson. "Future under glass — A recipe for people who hate to predict." *Futures.* October 1990.

19. K.H. Dreborg. "Essence of Backcasting." *Futures.* 28 (1996), pp. 813-828.

20. J. Holmberg. "Backcasting: a Natural Step when making sustainable development operational for companies." 1998 [to appear in *Greener Management International* 23].

21. G. Mitchell. "Problems and fundamentals of sustainable development indicators." *Sustainable Development* 4 (1996), pp. 1-11.

22. B. Nattrass, and M. Altomare. *The Natural Step for Business: Wealth, Ecology and the Evolutionary Corporation.* New Society Publishers, 1999.

23. S. Burns, and D. Katz."ISO 14001 and The Natural Step Framework." *Perspectives* 11 (World Business Academy, 1997), pp. 7-20.

24. L. Schipper, and F. Johnson. *Energy use in Sweden: An International Perspective.* International Energy Studies Group, Lawrence Berkeley Laboratory, 1993.

25. T.E. Graedel. *Streamlined Life-Cycle Assessment.* Prentice Hall, 1998.

26. SETAC. *Simplifying LCA: Just a Cut?.* Society of Environmental Toxicology and Chemistry — Europe, 1997.

27. J.A. Todd. *Streamlining. Environmental Life-Cycle Assessment.* McGraw-Hill, 1996, pp. 4.1-4.17.

28. K-H. Robèrt. "ICA/Electrolux – a case report from 1992." [presented at 40th CIES annual executive congress, Boston, June 5-7, 1997].

29. E. Rowland, and C.H. Sheldon. *The Natural Step and ISO 14001.* British Standards Institution, 1999.

Index

About the Author

P ROFESSOR KARL-HENRIK ROBÈRT, M.D., PH.D., is one of Sweden's foremost cancer scientists and the initiator, in 1989, of the sustainability movement called The Natural Step.

While head of the leading cancer research facility in Sweden, Dr. Robèrt's research on damaged human cells provided a platform for his interest in environmental questions. Later, with others, he developed first order principles — the "system conditions" — for sustainability. Together with a growing network of scientists and decision makers in business and politics, the system conditions have been elaborated into a concrete framework for strategic planning towards sustainability. The framework is described in a number of scientific publications and doctoral dissertations around the world.

Since the launch of The Natural Step, Dr. Robèrt has initiated a number of independent professional networks to support this work. Many businesses and municipalities (including Stockholm) have begun to incorporate The Natural Step framework into their business practices, and the organization has since spread around the world, with offices in nine countries.

In 1995, Dr. Robèrt was appointed Adjunct Professor of Physical Resource Theory at the Chalmers University of Technology, Gothenburg, Sweden. His many books, articles and scientific publications on the environment and sustainability encourage an understanding of the linkage between ecology, economy and technology. In 1999 he was awarded the Green Cross Award for International Leadership, and in 2000 he won the Blue Planet Prize: the so-called 'Environment Nobel.'

If you have enjoyed *The Natural Step Story*, you might enjoy other

BOOKS TO BUILD A NEW SOCIETY

Our books provide positive solutions for people who want
to make a difference. We specialize in:

- **Conscientious Commerce** • **Progressive Leadership**
- **Sustainable Living** • **Ecological Design and Planning**
- **Natural Building & Appropriate Technology** • **New Forestry**
- **Educational and Parenting Resources** • **Environment and Justice**
- **Resistance and Community** • **Nonviolence**

New Society Publishers

ENVIRONMENTAL BENEFITS STATEMENT

New Society Publishers has chosen to produce this book on New Leaf EcoBook 100,
recycled paper made with 100% post consumer waste, processed chlorine free, and
old growth free.

For every 5,000 books printed, New Society saves the following resources:[1]

34	Trees
3,098	Pounds of Solid Waste
3,409	Gallons of Water
4,446	Kilowatt Hours of Electricity
5,632	Pounds of Greenhouse Gases
24	Pounds of HAPs, VOCs, and AOX Combined
9	Cubic Yards of Landfill Space

[1]Environmental benefits are calculated based on research done by the Environmental Defense Fund and
other members of the Paper Task Force who study the environmental impacts of the paper industry.

For more information on this environmental benefits statement, or to inquire about environmentally
friendly papers, please contact New Leaf Paper – info@newleafpaper.com Tel: 888 • 989 • 5323.

For a full list of NSP's titles, please call **1-800-567-6772** *or check out our web site at:*

www.newsociety.com

NEW SOCIETY PUBLISHERS